Lehman Brothers

A Crisis of Value

MANCHESTER
1824

Manchester University Press

Lehman Brothers

A Crisis of Value

Oonagh McDonald

Manchester University Press

Published by Manchester University Press
Altrincham Street, Manchester M1 7JA

www.manchesteruniversitypress.co.uk

British Library Cataloguing-in-Publication Data
A catalogue record for this book is available from the British Library

Library of Congress Cataloging-in-Publication Data applied for

ISBN   978 1 7849 93405 hardback
ISBN   978 1 5261 00580 open access

First published 2016

Typeset by
RefineCatch Limited, Bungay, Suffolk
Printed in Great Britain by
TJ International Ltd, Padstow

Contents

Preface

The purpose of this book is to explain the fundamental causes of the bank's failure, including the inadequacy of the regulatory and supervisory framework. For some, it was the repeal of the Glass-Steagall Act that was the overriding cause, not just of the collapse of Lehman Brothers, but of the financial crisis as a whole. The argument of this book is that the cause is partly to be found both in weak and ineffective regulation and also in a programme of regulation and supervision that was simply not fit for the purpose. Lehman Brothers certainly contributed to its own demise. When the company pursued its more aggressive policies to increase its profits and its market share, it moved away from purchasing residential real estate loans, even when these were subprime, and packaging them into mortgage backed securities, which were then sold on. From 2006 onwards, its more aggressive strategy focused on commercial real estate, leveraged loans and private equity. Its move into commercial real estate increased the levels of risk for the company, with increasingly illiquid assets. Dick Fuld, the chairman and CEO, and his senior management, ignored the increased risks, choosing to rely on over-valuations of the firm's assets.

One of the continuing puzzles is why Lehman Brothers was allowed to fail. The main players in that decision, Henry Paulson, Timothy Geithner and Chairman Bernanke, have generally claimed that the Federal Reserve did not have the legal powers to rescue Lehman Brothers in the absence of a buyer for the company. This explanation was always difficult to reconcile with the decision to bail out AIG two days later.

That is not the only issue to be considered. The failure of Lehman Brothers has many facets, and each of those is examined in the second part of the book. Much has been said about the 'destruction of value' in the financial press and academic analyses. Trillions of dollars 'disappeared' through plummeting asset prices and, as some would argue, the crisis entailed not the destruction of 'real' value but the exposure of fictitious or virtual capital and artificial value. The appointed examiner for the bankruptcy proceedings stated that 'valuation is central to the question of Lehman's solvency'. That was the conclusion of his Report, which is over 2,200 pages, based on collecting over five million documents. An analysis of some of the key elements in the Report, as well as other documents and reports, leads to the conclusion that this is indeed the case.

However, this opens up the questions about what is meant by value when it comes to valuing assets and how that value is to be measured and explained. In Chapter 7 it is argued that the valuation of Lehman's real estate assets was problematic to say the least, as the regulators did not require the investment banks to adopt a recognized methodology of valuation, and that Lehman's own methods were flawed. Chapter 8 spells out the recognized methodologies and procedures for valuation that were available at the time and which, in effect, Lehman chose to either ignore or not apply in any rigorous way. Fuld and his team ignored the risks involved; his board was not in a position to monitor the risks involved in his aggressive 'real estate' programme and did not do so.

The underlying question is: what is meant by value in the context of a market? A brief look at contemporary theories of value suggests that they provide an inadequate explanation of the way in which assets are priced by the market, and especially the role of trust. The collapse of Lehman Brothers destroyed confidence, which is why the markets froze. There is no intrinsic or enduring value in any asset. Its value, and hence its price, is simply what the market will pay at any one time.

This is the second in my series of books on the financial crisis. The first was *Fannie Mae and Freddie Mac: Turning the American Dream into a Nightmare.* The distinctiveness of my approach is to describe the role of the major institutions in the events leading up to the crisis. Lehman Brothers has a specific role in that. It was the collapse of Lehman Brothers which, though not the sole cause of the crisis, was the trigger for it. The next book will examine the role of leading financial institutions and the regulators in the financial crisis and its aftermath.

Acknowledgements

I have benefitted from discussions with Professor Kevin Keasey, Director of the International Institute of Banking and Financial Services, University of Leeds, and Professor Robert Hudson, Professor of Finance at Hull University School of Business. I would especially like to thank Robert Stowe England, financial journalist and author of 'Black Box Casino: How Wall Street's Risky Shadow Banking Crashed Global Finance' for his assistance and Lord Desai, Emeritus Professor of Economics at London School of Economics, for reading the manuscript in draft and for all his constructive comments. Any errors and misconceptions are mine.

Dr Oonagh McDonald CBE

Abbreviations

AIG	American International Group
BHC	Bank Holding Company
BIS	Bank for International Settlements
BoA	Bank of America
CAE	Chief Audit Executive
CalPERS	California Public Employees Retirement System
CCC	Carlyle Capital Corporation
CDO	Collateralized Debt Obligation
CDS	Credit Default Swaps
CEO	Chief Executive Officer
CFO	Chief Financial Officer
CLO	Collateralized Loan Obligation
CMBS	Commercial Mortgage-Backed Securities
CRE	Commercial Real Estate
CRO	Chief Risk Officer
CSE	Consolidated Supervised Entities
DCF	Discounted Cash Flow
DTCC	Depository Trust and Clearing Corporation
EESA	Emergency Economic Stabilization Act
EMH	Efficient Market Hypothesis
FCIC	Financial Crisis Inquiry Commission
FDIC	Federal Deposit Insurance Corporation
FHC	Financial Holding Company
FOMC	Federal Open Market Committee
FRB	Federal Reserve Bank
FRBNY	Federal Reserve Bank of New York
FSA	Financial Services Authority (UK)
GAAP	Generally Accepted Accounting Principles
GLBA	Gramm-Leach-Bliley Act
GREG	Global Real Estate Group
ISDA	International Swaps and Derivatives Association
LBIE	Lehman Brothers International (Europe)

LBSF	Lehman Brothers Special Financing Inc
LTCM	Long Term Capital Management
MBS	Mortgage-Backed Security
MIS	Management Information System
MMF	Money Market Funds
NYSE	New York Stock Exchange
OCC	Office of the Comptroller of the Currency
OLA	Orderly Liquidation Authority
OTC	Over-the-Counter
OTCFX	Over-the-Counter Forex
OTS	Office of Thrift Supervision
OTTI	Other Than Temporary Impairments
PDCF	Primary Dealer Credit Facility
RMBSs	Residential Mortgage-Backed Securities
SEC	Securities and Exchange Commission
SIFIs	Systemically Important Financial Institutions
TSLF	Term Securities Lending Facility
USPAP	Uniform Standards of Professional Appraisal Practices
VaR	Value at Risk

From Cotton Trader to Investment Banker: 1844–2008

A brief history

On 29 January 2008, Lehman Brothers Holdings Inc reported record revenues of nearly $60bn and record earnings of over $4bn for its fiscal year ending 30 November 2007. Just eight months later, on 15 September 2008, Lehman Brothers sought Chapter 11 protection in the largest bankruptcy ever filed. Its collapse sent shock waves around the world. Everyone remembers the name, Lehman Brothers. Many regard its collapse as the cause of 2008's financial crisis.

The later stages of the existence of Lehman Brothers were dominated by Dick Fuld, one of the longest-serving chief executives on Wall Street. Fuld's dominance of the company, which he had built up and which he regarded as almost a personal possession, was one of the causes of its ultimate failure.

Lehman Brothers' long history began with three brothers, immigrants from Germany, setting up a small shop in Alabama, selling groceries and dry goods to local cotton farmers. Their business soon evolved into cotton trading. Henry, the eldest brother, died at the age of 33 in 1855; the two younger brothers headed the firm for the next four decades. The firm began to expand, setting up a commodities trading business in New York in 1858. That gave Lehman a foothold in Manhattan's financial community, a fact which was of especial importance after the Civil War, when the firm had to rebuild itself, selling bonds for the state of Alabama, servicing that former Confederate state's debt and interest payments. In 1870 Lehman Brothers led the way in the formation of the New York Cotton Exchange, the first commodities futures trading venture. Mayer Lehman was appointed to the Cotton Exchange's first board of directors. Lehman Brothers' commodities futures trading business grew to include other goods, and the firm also helped to set up the Coffee Exchange and the Petroleum Exchange.

This was followed in the 1880s and 1890s by Lehman Brothers' development of the Southern railroad system, just as JP Morgan and Kuhn Loeb led the financing of the Northern railways. Lehman observed the trend of issuing bonds to raise capital, and expanded its commodities business to include the trading of securities.

Raising capital during the Great Depression and the 1930s was obviously extremely difficult. Lehman was one of the first firms to develop a new form of financing, now a standard practice known as private placement. The loans between blue-chip borrowers and private lenders included strict safeguards and restrictions concerning lender safety, enabling borrowers to raise much-needed capital and lenders to receive a suitable level of return. Lehman Brothers continued to be an innovative firm, willing to take the risks of investing in new areas of commerce. It was one of the early backers of retail firms such as Sears, Woolworth's and Macy's, and then the entertainment industry, including 20th Century Fox and Paramount Pictures. The company then turned to oil, financing the TransCanada pipeline, and oil servicing companies such as Halliburton. When electronic and computer technology became drivers of the economic expansion of the 1950s, there was Lehman, still seeking investment opportunities. In the 1960s, Lehman Brothers developed its capital market trading capacity, especially in commercial paper. It became the official dealer for US Treasuries.

The last member of the Lehman family to have actively led the company (which he did from 1925), Robert Lehman, died in 1969, having steered it through an important period of growth in a period in which new developments had dramatically changed the world. Lehman began to expand globally, opening offices in Europe and Asia, eventually merging with a leading investment bank, Kuhn, Loeb & Co. Following the death of Robert Lehman, the firm struggled under the leadership of Frederick Ehrman, who had been at Lehman Brothers since World War II. He was replaced by Peter Peterson, a former US Secretary of Commerce in the Nixon administration, who had little experience of banking, still less as a trader. Nevertheless, he turned the company around, and in the last five years of his stewardship the company became extremely profitable. His chief problem was Lew Glucksman, head of trading, who worked long hours and regarded the bankers (as opposed to the traders) with disdain. Peterson tried to keep Glucksman on-side but neither the additional bonuses nor shared leadership prevailed. Glucksman wanted to run the firm himself, but patently lacked the skills to do so, appointed his own people to important positions, pushed out some partners from the seventy-seven and others decided to go, each taking their capital with them. Dick Fuld, Glucksman's protégé, was in charge of all trading, but was unable to answer questions about his strategy at partners' meetings.

Glucksman had been determined to take over the firm, but

it did not seem to occur to him that he did not have the skills ... He put his own people in the firm's important position ... The biggest bonuses went to Glucksman and Fuld with $1.6 million each. He pushed some partners out, while others decided to go, taking their capital with them. If many more went, Lehman Brothers would have little capital to work with.[2]

Glucksman had put Dick Fuld in charge of all trading.

At a meeting called to discuss the key issue of capital, Fuld was asked how he could help boost capital in the future. 'How did you make money in your trading operations over the last five years, and how are you planning to make money over the next several years?' asked one partner. 'I don't know how I made it over the last five years', he replied. He was also unclear about the future. He had 'hired some people to study the matter'.[3]

Glucksman tried to explain it all away by saying that Fuld had difficulties with communication. It seems that he did not learn all that much more about communication, from all accounts. Fuld was subsequently described as the 'Gorilla', intimidating people by his height, appearance and sometimes inarticulate responses.

As partners left the company, the remaining partners pushed Glucksman into looking for a partner with capital. That, however, was only part of the story. Glucksman and Peterson were jointly running Lehman Brothers, but, it seems, Glucksman's resentment and anger with Peterson grew and intensified over time, as well as his ambition.

It irritated him when Peterson said ... I didn't have a detailed grasp of that part of our business that was increasingly important – trading, futures, brokerage, commodities. This angered Glucksman because these trading functions were then generating two-thirds of Lehman's profits. And now that trading was getting its day in the sun, he feared Peterson was angling within a few years to sell the firm for a substantial premium over the current share price.[4]

The two men were the same age, and both would be obliged to sell their stock when they reached the age of 60. Glucksman fought on and eventually forced Peterson to sell and retire. Glucksman himself only lasted a few months at the helm. In effect he was forced to find a buyer, because rumours began to circulate and were published in *Fortune* to the effect that Lehman Brothers were 'peddling the firm'. If the rumours persisted they would be forced to sell the firm for a fraction of its real value.

American Express was there to take Lehman Brothers on, having recently purchased Shearson, a large brokerage rather than an investment bank. Lehman Brothers would add a touch of class to the new company. In 1984, Glucksman made $15m. by selling his shares, and set up his own consultancy in Wall Street. Glucksman and others had destroyed Lehman's independence. Dick Fuld was bitterly disappointed at the American Express takeover, but stayed on as head of trading. The new company then merged with EF Hutton in 1987 with a combined net value of $1bn, becoming Shearson Lehman Hutton. During that period, the firm aggressively built its leveraged finance business. But Harvey Golub, who became the CEO of American Express in 1993, began to divest the company of its investment and broking arms. Shearson's was sold to Primerica, the precursor of Citigroup, merging with its retail broking business. American Express also disposed of Lehman Brothers with a little capital, having finally recognized that it never sat well with the credit card company. American Express announced to the world at large that it would inject $1.09bn to make the newly independent firm financially viable and ensure that it had an A rating. In exchange, American Express would have a share of Lehman's profits and Lehman's employees would pay $160m. for newly issued shares, so that the total capital infusion would be $1.25bn.[5]

However, Fuld had run the trading division so successfully that when American Express divested itself of the company, the CEO asked him to take over running it as Chairman and CEO. Lehman Brothers emerged as a limited company in 1994, rather than a partnership. Fuld did not want any repetition of in-fighting between partners, which had caused so much damage in the past when partners were leaving the company taking their capital with them. Fuld insisted that the firm's employees had to take a large amount of their salary and bonuses in shares, which they would not be able to sell for several years.

Lehman Brothers had regained its independence, but if it was to retain this independence, given the extent of its losses and assailed as it was by many rumours of takeover throughout the 1990s, then changes would have to be made. Fuld began the process of restructuring the company so that it consisted of three major operating units: investment banking, equities and fixed income. He refocused the company's activities on high-margin business such as mergers and acquisitions, bringing in experienced senior staff to manage the business. This was reinforced by the compensation arrangements in January 1997, when Fuld approved $48m., of which only $2.4m. was for fixed income, with the rest for the equities, investing and banking divisions in January 1997. Changing the company's focus and image for the outside world took time.

The new company had a narrow range of offerings. Its share trading had declined after the 1987 stock market crash. It was without a wealth management unit. Its income from banking came from arranging company takeovers and was $800m. a year, whereas its trading department brought in double that. Chapman notes that it had one feature which would be significant in the future. It was second only to Morgan Stanley in selling mortgage bonds.[6]

In another portent for the future, Lehman extended the range of its business activities by moving into commercial real estate. Mark A Walsh was Lehman's head of global real estate in 1997. He was widely regarded as Wall Street's most successful property financier, having arranged some very large deals in 1997. ITT Corporation, which concentrated on hotel and gaming businesses, had been Lehman's client for a long time, and was then up for sale. Barry Sternlicht, head of Starwood Hotels and Resorts, wanted to buy ITT, but needed to raise $7bn very quickly, otherwise he would lose the deal. Walsh promised him that it would be done, but Sternlicht still needed reassurance. Later, Sternlicht said: 'Dick Fuld sat there in my living room and said, "You have our word. It will be done".'[7] Lehman beat Goldman Sachs to the deal, earning $20m. as the fee. During that year, Walsh made other important deals, such as the sale of the Chrysler and Woolworth Buildings. He was to continue with deals of that nature, ignoring the fall in commercial real estate prices until 2008.

Fuld successfully steered his company through the Asian financial crisis, the collapse of Long Term Capital Management and 9/11, when Lehman lost its headquarters but almost all of Fuld's staff survived. When Lehman Brothers moved to their new headquarters in 2002, the chief operating officer at the time, Bradley H Jack, grouped the bankers by industry group, so that bankers specializing in everything from stocks to bonds and convertibles worked alongside each other in 'pods', each representing a different industry. The aim was to ensure that bankers working for the same client communicated with each other and were in a position to offer creative solutions. 'Before the spin-off in 2004', Fuld told *Business Week*, 'success was measured by what each individual accomplished. Today, it's all about the team.' That is the way in which he viewed his management style.

He gained the support of his staff by keeping their salaries in line with earnings. The ratio of compensation costs to gross revenues remained at 51 per cent.

Even in 2001, Lehman allocated $544m. for stock-based pay, which accounted for 15.8 per cent, as compared with the 6.4 per cent allocated for employees at Merrill Lynch. Fuld's message to new recruits was that if they joined the firm, he would make them rich, perhaps seriously rich. The strategy which Dick Fuld and Bradley Jack developed in the aftermath of 9/11 began to pay off in the summer of 2002. *Business Week* recorded what happened when Williams Cos, an energy trading company facing bankruptcy, asked for Lehman's assistance in raising $3.4bn. Hugh 'Skip' McGee, then head of Lehman's energy-banking group in Houston, with a team of 30 bankers, worked night and day to raise enough capital by selling assets such as pipelines and arranging finance from Warren E Buffett and banks secured by natural gas reserves. They saved the company.

McGee then moved to New York as head of investment banking, where he continued to develop the policy of rewarding his bankers for finding solutions for clients, instead of selling products. Staff were constantly reminded that 'investment banking is a team sport – use all the resources'. McGee's policy seemed to work, since net income increased 74 per cent to $1,699m. in 2003, and Lehman's share price rose from $53.29 to $79 at one point, ending the year at $77.22.

Something of Fuld's commitment to his work was demonstrated in an article in Bloomberg's *Business Week*:

> It was late December but the holidays were not on the mind of Lehman Brothers Inc Chairman and Chief Executive, Richard S Fuld Jnr. On his desk, next to a tall Starbucks Mocha Frapuccino, was a list of hundreds of banking clients. He was determined to reach every person by New Year's Day. 'When something is on my list', he said, 'it will get done'.[8]

He reached almost everyone. Lehman Brothers had advised on $99bn in US mergers and acquisitions announced last year, increasing its market share by an enormous 6.2 per cent to 18.9 per cent. Lehman had beaten Credit Suisse First Boston, Merrill Lynch and JP Morgan Chase, putting the company in fourth place, up from ninth in 2002. In 2002, Lehman also raised $314bn in debt and equity issues for companies, making it the No 2 underwriter of securities in the USA. Moody's was quoted as saying that, 'It is a much more diversified shop than it was five or six years ago, and it operated in an extremely disciplined fashion'.

Lehman was often described, dismissively, as a 'bond house', low in the Wall Street pecking order. That remained true in a sense. 'He chose to exploit that area of strength, building the firm into a fixed income juggernaut and benefitting mightily from the seismic decline in interest rates over the past decade. Today, Lehman derives 48 per cent of its revenue from fixed income." At the same time, however, when Lehman advised AT&T on its $89bn acquisition of BellSouth, it brought in its capital-market experts to advise on financing, share buybacks and liability management. 'Richard Fuld personally committed his time and all the resources of the firm to us, and that made a big impression', said AT&T CEO, Ed Whitacre.[10] The article also quotes one of Fuld's former colleagues, who said that, 'People talk about how successful Dick has been and the great job he has done, and that's all true. But what I find amazing is how he had learned and mastered every part of this business.' Doubts had been expressed about the fixed income business without a falling interest rate environment. Dave Goldfarb, Lehman's chief administrative officer pointed out that in 2000, there was $16 trillion of global fixed-income securities; in 2005, that increased to $27 trillion, and in 2009, he expected that number to climb to $38 trillion.

Perhaps here lies a hint of troubles to come: an over-optimistic view of the future. All would be to Lehman's advantage.

Lehman's acquisitions

Acquisitions in 2003

At the same time, Fuld made a series of acquisitions, designed to lessen Lehman's dependence on fixed-income trading, and focus attention on mergers and acquisitions, investment banking and raising capital. The purchase of Neuberger Berman in 2003 was designed both to rescue Lehman from the volatility of the bond trading market and to establish its position as a leading Wall Street firm. Morgan Stanley, Merrill Lynch and Goldman Sachs already had significant money management operations, regarded as an essential element of an elite Wall Street firm. Neuberger Berman had $63.7bn under management, a respected range of funds and wealthy clients. The deal was completed at the end of 2003, giving Lehman Brothers $100bn under management, but still far below its main rivals, Merrill Lynch, Goldman Sachs and Morgan Stanley. Neuberger Berman had been founded by Roy R Neuberger in 1939, and the sale was agreed on his 100th birthday. At least its employees were about to join an even older firm, and Fuld also sought to retain as many of its employees as possible, setting aside a bonus pool of $120m. as well as seeking to ensure that the 30 top fund managers stayed with the firm by having them sign a three-year non-compete agreement and restricting the amount of shares they could sell. The plan apparently worked, since as part of the bankruptcy proceedings, Neuberger Berman's senior executive team and its fund managers took the company back again in a management buy-out in December 2008.

In 2003, however, Fuld's purchase was designed to enable the company to diversify its sources of revenues, with fee-based income expected to account for 21 per cent of its revenues, up from 13 per cent, and cost savings and revenue gains to total $50m. in 2004 and $100m. in 2005 as the business and back-office operations were combined. During a conference call, Fuld explained to the *New York Times* that 'Neuberger Berman is one of the largest and most respected, independent, high net worth managers. When Neuberger is combined with our existing wealth and asset management group, Lehman Brothers will emerge as one of the leading providers to a highly desirable marketplace.'[11]

The extent to which those expectations were realized is revealed in the quarterly report for the last quarter of 2003 and the annual report for 2004. The description of the company's activities reflected both the move away from fixed income trading, and Fuld's ambitions for Lehman Brothers. The 'customer flow model' was based on the company's principal focus of facilitating client transactions in all major global capital markets, products and services. Customer flow revenues were generated from institutional and high net worth clients by (i) advising on and structuring transactions specifically suited to meet client needs; (ii) serving as a market-maker and/or intermediary in the global marketplace, including having securities and other financial instrument products available to allow clients to rebalance their portfolios and diversify risks across different market cycles; (iii) providing asset management services; and (iv) acting as an underwriter to clients. The investment management business segment consists of the private investment management, with fees from high net worth clients and asset management business lines. The latter generates fees from customized investment management services for high net worth clients and asset management fees from institutional investors and others. By the end of the financial year in November 2004, the total net revenues from these two sources had increased by 87 per cent to $1,694m. from $907m. in 2003, justifying the purchase of Neuberger Berman.

In 2003, Lehman purchased the Crossroads Group and Lincoln Capital Fixed Income. The aim was to boost Lehman Brothers' global private equity franchise to about $7bn in private equity assets under management. Another aim was to strengthen Lehman's position as a leader in private equity management. Michael Odrich, global head of Lehman Brothers Private Equity Division, stated that it emphasized the firm's commitment to expanding its private equity and asset management franchise. Lincoln Capital was acquired to be part of the wealth and asset management group. All three acquisitions were essential, in Fuld's mind, to end the company's dependence on fixed income markets, enabling it to offer a variety of services and to be seen as an equal, if not more so, of Goldman Sachs, JP Morgan, Merrill Lynch and Bear Stearns.

At that time, critics thought that the then expected downturn in the bond market would show that Lehman still had not ended its dependence on the fixed income market. But Blaine A Frantz, a senior credit officer at Moody's told *Business Week*, 'It is a much more diversified shop than it was five or six years ago, and is operated in an extremely disciplined fashion'.[12] The final results for 2003 showed that Lehman had advised on $99bn in US mergers and acquisitions, raising its market share by 6.2 per cent to 19 per cent, putting it in fourth place, up from the ninth place (and overtaking Merrill Lynch and JP Morgan Chase). The company also became the second largest securities underwriter in 2003, up from fourth in 2002.

Acquisitions in 2004

Acquisitions did not stop there. In 2004, Lehman purchased California-based BNC Mortgage, having already taken a stake in the company in 2000. Other acquisitions included Finance America LLC (which merged with BNC in 2005) and Aurora Loan Services LLC, which it acquired in 1997. BNC Mortgage specialized in making subprime loans, while Aurora Loan Services specialized in Alt-A loans, that is, loans made to borrowers without full documentation. In the first half of 2007, Aurora originated over $3bn a month of such loans. Through BNC Mortgage, Lehman stood at No 11 in a list of 25 subprime lenders with a loan volume of $47.6bn between 2005 and 2007.

In addition to owning subprime lenders, Lehman was also a leading underwriter for subprime mortgages for other companies, to the tune of some $221bn between 2000 and 2007. In August 2007, Lehman announced that it was closing BNC Mortgage, although it would continue to make loans through its subsidiary, Aurora Loan Services. With regard to BNC, Lehman gave as its reasons, the 'poor market conditions', which necessitated 'a substantial reduction in its services and capacity in the subprime space'. In its regulatory filing for the three months ending on 31 May 2007, Lehman said it had 'unrealized' losses of $459m, but that these losses were offset by gains in corporate bond and equity holdings as well as derivative contracts.

Acquisitions and developments in 2005

Mortgage loans were not the only area into which Lehman Brothers expanded during those two significant years, 2006 to 2007. Established in February 2005, Ospraie had become one of the leading specialist commodities funds, and Lehman had taken a 20 per cent stake in the fund from the beginning. Lehman had the rights to 20 per cent of Ospraie's profits and access to the investment opportunities the fund would provide. In return, Ospraie had access to Lehman's prime brokerage and other trading opportunities.

These developments were all part of Fuld's strategy. In July 2005, in an interview with *Euromoney*, he stated, 'What we focus on in the executive committee is increasing our revenues from around $12bn to $15bn or $20bn', and indicated that such gains might come from 'a strong acquisition'. Despite the efforts to increase diversity, Lehman still earned about 60 per cent of its revenues from the fixed income business, whereas for Bear Stearns the figure was 50 per cent, and for Merrill Lynch 25 per cent. The article stressed that Lehman's fixed-income business was one of the strongest and most diversified on Wall Street, which, 'combined with the bank's more conservative approach to risk management, helped it to report solid second quarter earnings in the face of severe dislocation in the markets'.

Fuld also stated in the article that his staff were expected to have as much responsibility for how the company was run as he had. 'I expect everyone at the firm to be a risk manager', and for all twelve members of the executive committee: 'All twelve of us are focussed on all parts of the business. It's all about risk management. If it's just about me, then we're in trouble.' This interview took place before Fuld adopted what has been described as a more 'aggressive business strategy', but some of the groundwork had already been carried out in 2005. During the course of the interview, he was asked why, although Lehman was already a large underwriter of mortgage-backed securities, the company had invested in mortgage origination platforms and that 55 per cent of the MBS deals came from their own mortgage platform. Fuld replied that adding mortgage originations created a fully integrated business for the firm from a captive source for generating mortgage loans. It also provided additional fees and ensured quality control, so that loans were underwritten to appropriate standards. By 2005, Lehman realized that it was missing the vast profits other Wall Street banks were making by slicing residential mortgages and selling them on to investors as mortgage-backed securities or collateralized debt obligations, ignoring warnings about the growth of subprime mortgages. Lehman took comfort from the fact that they had the largest portfolio of commercial real estate on Wall Street. The firm regarded itself as an expert in financing commercial real estate, but it had paid high prices just before prices of commercial real estate began to decline. But management continued to take an optimistic view that this market was safe, in spite of the emerging evidence to the contrary – with disastrous consequences.

Rather than the major acquisition hinted at in the *Euromoney* article, Fuld turned to what seemed a lucrative and growing market: subprime loans. As the housing market strengthened, the strategy looked robust as Lehman turned more loans into mortgage-backed securities. In 2006, Lehman made a deliberate business decision to pursue a higher growth strategy, as he had already stated in the *Euromoney* interview. To achieve this objective, and noting that his main competitors had increased their revenues through the subprime mortgage market, Lehman moved away from a low-risk brokerage model to a higher-risk capital-intensive banking model. The groundwork for this had already been done through BNC Mortgage and Aurora and by the purchase of mortgage origination platforms. The switch may not therefore have been as drastic as it has sometimes been presented. Before 2006, Lehman acquired assets to 'move' them to third parties as mortgage-backed securities, but in 2006 Lehman started to retain the assets, both residential markets and commercial real estate, as its own assets. The risk and return remained with Lehman.

The effects of this policy were that Lehman had to continually roll over its debt because of the mismatch between short-term debt and long-term illiquid assets. The company had to borrow billions of dollars on a daily basis. Its business risk was increased because of its investments in long-term assets – residential and, especially commercial real estate, private equity and leveraged loans. To provide for this growth in risk, a 13 per cent growth in revenues and an even faster (15 per cent) increase in its balance sheet and total capital base was required. In late 2007, the company held assets of $700bn on equity of $25bn with $675bn of liabilities, most of which was short-term. As the subprime crisis began to develop, Lehman trebled its holdings in illiquid investments from $87bn in 2006, to $275bn at the end of the first quarter of 2008.

Why did Fuld decide to pursue this aggressive growth strategy at that point in time? The company had grown and developed remarkably under his leadership since he took over as Chairman and CEO in 1994. He had been named 'Best CEO' in 2004 by *Institutional Investor*. One long-standing former director at Lehman Brothers said that Fuld seemed determined to change from his family-orientated and relatively modest lifestyle (despite his millions, he did not own a yacht or a private jet, and went to the same part of Italy with family every year), and wanted to join the very rich club. That change also apparently affected his approach to management, becoming more detached and dictatorial. He had been described by many on Wall Street as an 'unbelievable competitor', 'obstinate, determined and unaccountable' and by others as 'obstinate, confrontational and blunt'. His nickname was indeed the 'Gorilla', which he seemed to enjoy. He was often criticized by former employees for being remote, staying on Floor 31 of the headquarters in New York's 7th Avenue, where he and his No 2, Joe Gregory, discussed the business 'at least 20 times a day'. Andrew Gowers, who left the *Financial Times* to become Lehman's head of corporate communications in London in 2006, noted that

> Fuld had become insulated from the day-to-day realities of the firm and had increasingly designated operational authority to his number two, a long-standing associate [President and Chief Operating Officer Joe Gregory], who was not a detail man or a risk manager, who actively urged divisional managers to place even more aggressive bets in surging asset markets such as mortgage business and commercial real estate.[13]

By the third quarter of 2007, Lehman Brothers had some thirty-five guaranteed subsidiaries in all the major markets, employing about 30,000 staff worldwide, including around 10,000 at the head office in New York. That was quite different from the early days of Fuld's tenure as Chairman and CEO, when he had only twenty-two managers reporting to him. He knew the staff at headquarters individually, was often seen in the trading rooms and was accessible to his staff. As Lehman Brothers grew, that inevitably meant that Fuld's commitments, both in travelling to set up new offices or new subsidiaries, meetings and interviews, took up so much of his time that the camaraderie and personal oversight of the trading room had gone. Many employees had worked at Lehman Brothers for a long time, and they remembered the sense of belonging to a family, which Lehman encouraged. It also involved its employees in the company through the 'culture of ownership', in which staff received a disproportionately high percentage of their pay in Lehman stock and options. When the firm went public, employees owned 4 per cent of the firm worth about $60m., but by 2006, they owned about 30 per cent equivalent, equivalent to $11bn. Of course, by September 2008 their shares were worthless.

Between 1994 and 2007, Lehman Brothers' market capitalization increased from $2bn to $45bn, and its share price went from $5 to $86, providing shareholders with an average annual return for shareholders of 24.6 per cent. It grew to 26,200 employees, with more than 60 offices in over 28 countries by the third quarter of 2007. It is small wonder that any sense of belonging to a family disappeared, with the exception of a small band of senior executives who met together on Friday mornings. That could be part of the reason for the perception that Fuld was remote and inaccessible on Floor 31. One of his former executives indicated that, apart from the inevitable increasing burden of meetings for any CEO of a global company, the firm itself may have grown beyond the capacity and management skills of the CEO. For Fuld, in particular, it may have been especially difficult to realize that the management of the company he had built up was perhaps beyond the capability of one man, since he had devoted his life's work to that task, and had succeeded in keeping the company going when many thought it would fail through extremely difficult times. Instead of being 'too big to fail', the time had come to consider the risk that a global bank with a vast network of subsidiaries, many of which focused on different aspects of financial services, might have become 'too big to manage', unless the management structure was well-designed with clear reporting lines and highly competent managers at every level. Much more work needed to be done to find ways of making the inevitable pyramid structure function effectively.

From Hubris to Nemesis: January to September 2008

January 2008: outlook rosy

In its financial report for the fiscal year ending 30 November 2007, published on 29 January 2008, Lehman Brothers reported record revenues of nearly $60bn, and record earnings in excess of $4bn. The highlights of the report included net revenues of $19.3bn (a 10 per cent increase over the previous year and the fifth consecutive record) and a net income of $4.2bn (a 5 per cent increase over the previous year and the fourth consecutive record). Earnings per share came in at $7.26, a 7 per cent increase over the previous year and a record for the fourth consecutive year, and a return on equity of 20.8 per cent.[1] These achievements were somewhat marred by the fact that Lehman's share price had declined for the first time in five years, perhaps due to the much more difficult economic environment in the second half of the year. Fixed income had been hit by tough credit markets and the housing downturn had affected their mortgage origination and securitization business to such an extent that they had closed BNC Mortgage, a subprime lending unit, with the loss of 1,200 jobs, as well as the Korea Central Mortgage business. None of these were mentioned in the introduction to the company's report. Instead, Dick Fuld referred to the disruption in the mortgage market, the sharp decline in liquidity and the slowing of corporate and institutional activity. He added, 'We have successfully navigated difficult markets before. We have benefited from our senior level focus on risk management and, more importantly, from a culture of risk management at every level of the Firm'.[2]

The annual report made a good start to the year, many observers concluded. It was followed by the first quarter report, published on 17 March 2008. Their press release reported a net income of $489m for the first quarter, ending on 29 February, which was 57 per cent lower than the $1.15bn for first quarter of 2007. The press release also highlighted record client activity in their capital markets businesses, record net revenues in investment management, and that Lehman ranked second in global M&A transactions for the first two months of 2008. The company maintained its strong liquidity position, with the holding company having a liquidity pool of $34bn and unencumbered assets of $464bn, with an additional $99bn at their regulated entities. The liquidity pool was one of the business highlights listed in the press release.

The impact of the fall of Bear Stearns

Lehman's March results were announced shortly after the news that Bear Stearns had had to arrange emergency funding from JP Morgan and the New York Federal Reserve, amid a deepening liquidity crisis. The immediate trigger was its stake in Carlyle Capital Corporation (CCC), a $22bn hedge fund exposed to mortgage-backed securities. The fund was suspended in Amsterdam, after it revealed that it had substantial additional margin calls and default notices from its lenders. As Bear Stearns was the founder of the fund and owned 15 per cent of it, its shares fell by 17 per cent when CCC collapsed on 13 March. Investors had become increasingly anxious about Bear Stearns and its exposure to CCC and other troubled hedge funds. By the end of 2007 Bear Stearns' balance sheet showed $395bn in assets supported by $11.1bn in equity, a leverage ratio of 36:1. Nothing was done to improve the situation and the bank failed to raise additional funding. In March it began to face a run on the bank, as one firm after another sought to withdraw its funds, and hedge funds requested that a Swiss bank take over trades where Bear Stearns was the counterparty. In one week, Bear Stearns had lost $18bn of its reserves. By midday on 13 March, it was clear that the firm might not last until the next business day. A conference call was held the following day with Timothy Geithner, President of the Federal Reserve Bank of New York, and Ben Bernanke, Chairman of the Board of Governors of the Federal Reserve Bank, and JP Morgan agreed to purchase Bear Stearns.

With the support of the Federal Reserve Bank to the tune of $30bn, on 16 March JP Morgan offered to buy Bear Stearns for $2 per share; the price was subsequently raised to $10 per share for the purchase of 95 million shares to ensure the agreement of Bear Stearns' board. The Federal Reserve's $30bn special financing associated with the transaction depended on JP Morgan Chase taking the first $1bn of losses associated with any of Bear Stearns' assets being financed, and the Federal Reserve agreed to fund the remaining $29bn on a non-recourse basis to JP Morgan Chase. The collapse of Bear Stearns and its subsequent rescue had shocked the market.

The Federal Reserve explained its actions in its press release of 16 March 2008. On 13 March, Bear Stearns advised the Federal Reserve that it did not have enough funding or liquid assets to meet its financial obligations the following day, and would be unable to find a private sector source of funding. Given 'its large presence in several important financial markets' such as mortgage-backed securities and the securities clearing services, and the 'potential for contagion', the Federal Reserve took the view that it should provide a bridge loan through JP Morgan Chase Bank to Bear Stearns on 14 March. This was insufficient, and by the weekend it became clear that the bank would be bankrupt by Monday 17 March. JP Morgan Chase emerged as the only viable bidder bank for Bear Stearns. To facilitate the merger, the FRBNY created a limited liability company, Maiden Lane LLC, to acquire Bear Stearns' assets. Maiden Lane LLC then managed the assets, having purchased approximately $30bn from Bear with a loan of $29bn from the FRBNY. The details of the loan and the order in which repayments from the assets were to be made to the Federal Reserve were set out in the press release. Both the bridge loan and the loan to Maiden Lane LLC were made 'under the authority of Section 13(3) of the Federal Loan Act, which permitted the Board, in unusual and exigent circumstances, to authorize Reserve Banks to extend credit to individuals, partnerships and corporations.'[3] That makes it difficult to understand the subsequent claims made by Ben Bernanke, Timothy Geithner and Henry Paulson, that they lacked the legal authority to bail out Lehman Brothers by such means.

Many expected Lehman Brothers to be the next to fall. Its stock declined by 20 per cent the day after the bail-out of Bear Stearns, with more than 40 per cent of its shares changing hands. During that quarter, bond risk spreads had widened considerably and equity values had fallen sharply. However, Richard Fuld was able to announce, 'Our results reflect the value of our continued commitment to building a diversified platform and our focus on managing risk and maintaining a strong capital and liquidity position.' This presentation of their results seemed to allay investors' fears about the company's ability to withstand the turmoil in the financial markets caused by the collapse of Bear Stearns. Lehman's share price shot up by 48 per cent, the biggest surge it had ever experienced.[4] But this was simply a recovery from what had been lost the previous day because of fears that it would be the next investment bank to fail after Bear Stearns.

Lehman saw the price of CDSs (credit default swaps) on its bonds jump from $228,000 to $398,000 between 3 March and 10 March. On 11 March, the Federal Reserve introduced an important measure, the Term Securities Lending Facility, aimed at lending as much as $200bn in Treasury securities to banks and primary securities dealers and the major investment banks, by pledging capital, such as investment grade mortgage-backed securities and all securities eligible for tri-party repurchase agreements for a period of 28 days, instead of overnight. Primary dealers had increased difficulties in obtaining funding and so were less able to support broader markets. This facility was designed to improve conditions in the financial markets more generally.

Doubts emerge about Lehman's March financial statement

Lehman's March financial statements, announcing a profit of $489m., came as a great relief. However, the euphoric market reaction to the first quarter results did not last. Suspicions about the accuracy of Lehman's financial statement emerged, aided and abetted by David Einhorn's critique of the company's 'accounting ingenuity' in his presentation to the Ira W Sohn Investment Research Conference on 21 May. As the founder and President of Greenlight Capital, a very successful long-short value-orientated hedge fund with $6bn in assets, founded in 1996, Einhorn commanded the attention of the markets. He made it clear that Greenlight 'was short on Lehman'. Some three weeks after the press release and the accompanying conference call in which Einhorn had participated, Lehman filed its 10-Q with the SEC for the quarter.

Einhorn presented his analysis of the press release alongside the 10-Q. Both refer to 'other asset-backed securities' with an exposure of $6.5bn. At first, there had been little reference to collateralized debt securities, but in the footnote it was explained that the 'other asset-backed securities' were in fact CDOs, 'primarily structured and underwritten by third parties' and that about 25 per cent of the positions held at 27 February 2008 and 30 November 2007 were 'rated BB+ or lower'. In other words, the whole $6.5bn consisted of CDOs and synthetic CDOs. They were not based on residential mortgages, but on commercial real estate. A write-down of only $200m. was much too small on a $6.5bn pool of CDOs, of which at least $1.6bn were below investment grade. Lehman also had $59bn of exposure to commercial mortgages at the end of the year, in which the Triple-A rated commercial mortgage-backed securities declined by 10 per cent in the first quarter, and lower-rated bonds fell even further, so Lehman's write-down should have been more that 10 per cent, instead of which it was less than 3 points. These and other discrepancies spelt out in Einhorn's presentation meant that Lehman should deleverage and raise capital 'before federal taxpayer assistance is required'. The effects of the presentation and the extensive media coverage began to emerge a few days later.

On 27 May, *Forbes* reported that the 'bears are prowling around Lehman Brothers'. The 'puts' were in $30 contracts expiring in June, which meant that many traders saw Lehman's shares falling by 16 per cent in June, whilst others saw the stock falling to $17.50 by then, and a few contracts were out on $5 January options. The article noted that the 'speculation is also being aided' by David Einhorn as a result of his speech. On 4 June *The New York Times* noted that he had 'pilloried the venerable Lehman Brothers in an effort to drive down the bank's stock price, which he is betting against'. He was succeeding. The stock had already fallen by 59 per cent over the previous twelve months. While he was criticizing Lehman Brothers, he was also working with a financial public relations company to promote his book, *Fooling Some of the People All of the Time: a Long Short Story*. As with many others, Greenlight Capital suffered losses of 22 per cent on longs, but made 17 per cent on shorts in a year in which the firm 'made too many mistakes'.[5] However, in 2009, it recouped all of its losses, which had more to do with macroeconomic and market developments than its investment strategy.

Lehman had sold assets worth $100bn during the previous few months in order to shore up its finances. All this was of no avail when the second quarter results were published on 9 June, which revealed a much greater loss than expected of $2.8bn. This was the first loss Lehman had experienced since becoming a public company in 1994. The bank also announced that it would raise $6bn in common and preferred shares to strengthen its financial position. Erin Callan, Lehman's chief financial officer, stated that the bank did not really require the new capital but it would be used to seize market opportunities in the future. But Lehman Brothers revealed that it had booked $17bn in write-downs since the credit crisis began. These included $11bn in mortgage and asset-backed securities, about $3.5bn in commercial mortgages and $2bn in leveraged loans, but these were offset by hedging benefits of approximately $7.5bn, although some of the hedging had not been as beneficial as expected. Hedging would be continued. Lehman also disclosed that its liquidity pool had increased from $35bn to $54bn, decreasing its gross assets by $130bn by the end of May. As a result, its exposure to mortgages and real estate investments decreased by 15–20 per cent, while its exposure to leveraged business was 35 per cent lower.[6]

The results were released a week early in an effort to reduce investor anxieties, following intense speculation about the state of Lehman's finances. This did little to assuage market fears, and Lehman's shares fell by another 10 per cent. On 13 June, still facing a credibility crisis with investors, Dick Fuld took the classic way out by sacking his lifelong friend Joseph Gregory as his No 2, and demoting

Erin Callan to the investment banking division, replacing them with two other long-standing Lehman staff, Bart McDade and Ian Lowitt as his deputy and chief finance officer respectively. This did not help either. The shares continued to fall. The collapse of Bear Stearns was seen by many as a turning point in the crisis, but the apparent decline of Lehman Brothers continued to worry investors and Wall Street. However, hopes had been raised that the worst was already over.

An internal classification memorandum produced by Citibank gives an interesting and perhaps more considered analysis of Lehman at the time and on the basis of the information provided by the company. S&P and Moody's rated Lehman Brothers as A and AA respectively in 2007. In March 2008, after the collapse of Bear Stearns, S&P revised its outlook from negative to stable and from June, A/negative/A-1. Moody's remained as AA until September 2008. The Q1 results enabled the rating agencies to reaffirm their ratings, based on Lehman's 'abundant liquidity and strong risk management'. But Lehman's credibility suffered when the company raised capital three times following its January statement that it did not require any more. On 2 June the rating agencies downgraded Lehman's unsecured rating, as well as those of Merrill Lynch and Morgan Stanley, as part of a review of the global securities industry. Before the Q2 results were announced, several analysts had revised their estimates on the grounds that the company had used special one-time charges and gains to artificially inflate its first quarter results, and that it had not disclosed its holdings of collateralized debt obligations before the first quarter. Lehman had not valued its commercial mortgage related assets based on current market prices. Lehman however claimed that they were very aggressive in writing down their commercial real estate assets and selling them. Analysts were not convinced at the apparent failure to write down their commercial real estate, which should have revealed that the company would have to raise further capital.[7]

Lehman's claim about the size of its liquidity pool, some $45bn, the highest on record, was accepted by analysts and the markets. To bolster liquidity and to help the financial markets function more effectively, the Federal Reserve had established the Primary Dealer Credit Facility. This was an overnight loan facility to provide funding to primary dealers in exchange for any tri-party eligible capacity. Lehman had access to that and to the Term Securities Lending Facility, which allowed firms to swap certain types of agency collateral for Treasury securities. It was designed to increase liquidity in the funding markets by increasing the ability of dealers to obtain cash in the private market by enabling them to pledge securities temporarily as collateral for treasuries, which are relatively easy to finance. It was supposed to reduce the need for dealers to sell assets in illiquid markets, as well as preventing a loss of confidence amongst lenders. As well as being able to use these facilities, Lehman was also thought to have access to funds at the European Central Bank through Lehman Bankhaus AG as lenders of last resort.

However, although their bond research analyst was less concerned than others about Lehman Brothers, Citibank adopted a risk mitigation strategy in their dealings with the bank. Since it transacted regularly with Lehman globally, Citibank advised its traders' desks that they would not approve the extension of trades or long-term trades, as part of an effort to reduce their exposure to subprime and Alt-A loans. Citibank was Lehman's global securities clearing bank, with over $20bn of lines approved, and wanted to reduce the limits to about $12–13bn. Lehman agreed to maintain a 'good faith' deposit of $2bn. This is interesting, as the memorandum is dated 13 June, before the detailed announcement of results in its quarterly SEC 10-K on 16 June, yet it shows concerns about dealing with Lehman, despite its analyst's report.[8]

Using the Primary Dealer Credit Facility

Lehman was one of the first banks to use the Primary Dealer Credit Facility when it was announced, immediately after the rescue of Bear Stearns. The New York Federal Reserve Bank stated that the overnight funding was intended to provide funding for a 'specified range of collateral', including 'investment-grade corporate securities, municipal securities, mortgage-backed securities and asset-backed securities for which a price is available'. Richard Fuld, who had convened an emergency board meeting at the weekend, issued a statement on 18 March, stating that 'the Federal Reserve's decision to create a lending facility for primary dealers and permit a broad range of investment grade securities to serve as collateral improves the liquidity picture and, from my perspective, takes the liquidity issue for the entire industry off the table'.[9]

However, it appears that Lehman had no intention of sticking to investment grade securities. Lehman immediately seized the opportunity to dump illiquid assets, accessing the PDCF seven times in the liquidity stress period, describing these as 'tests' both internally and to third parties, although 'witnesses' from the Federal Reserve Bank of New York stated that these were instances in which Lehman drew upon the facility for liquidity purposes. In the same month, Lehman packaged 66 corporate loans to create the 'Freedom CLO'. It consisted of two tranches: a $2.26 billion senior note, priced at par, rated single A, and designed to be PDCF eligible, and an unrated $570m equity tranche. The loans that Freedom 'repackaged' included high-yield leveraged loans, which Lehman had difficulty moving off its books, and included unsecured loans to Countrywide Financial Corporation. On three occasions – 24, 25 and 26 March 2008 – Lehman pledged the Freedom CLO to the Federal Reserve Bank, New York on an overnight basis and received $2.13bn for each transfer, or $6.39bn in total.[10] Later, Chairman Bernanke commented that the Federal Reserve assessed the value of the collateral and imposed extra haircuts on the loans to the brokerage. The Federal Reserve was repaid in full.[11]

The New York Federal Reserve Bank was aware of the possible use of the 'Freedom CLO' on 20 March, since Jan Voigt of the FRBNY reports that

> during the same March 20 meeting, the Freedom CLO came up near the end of the conversation. We were surprised when they noted that their debt structure team had converted unencumbered corporate loans into an investment grade facility (pending rating review), with internal pricing assuming a range of 10–30 per cent haircuts on the underlying assets. The corporate loans had been financed using cash capital at the holding company level ... The Lehman management team also noted that while there was confusion about the purpose and utility of the PDCF, they saw this as an opportunity to move illiquid assets into a securitization that would be PDCF eligible. They also noted that they intended to create two or three additional PDCF eligible securitizations. We avoided comment on the securitization but noted the firm's intention to use the PDCF as an opportunity to finance assets they could not finance elsewhere.

Lehman did not intend to market its Freedom CLO or any other securitizations to investors. Indeed an internal presentation of Freedom CLO and subsequent securitizations was marked 'not meant to be marketed'. The Freedom CLO and other securitizations were specifically created to pledge to the PDCF, which Lehman treated as a 'warehouse' for its illiquid leveraged loans. It appears that the Federal Reserve Bank of New York was aware that Lehman 'intended to use the PDCF as both a backstop and a business opportunity ... to move illiquid assets into a securitization that would be PDCF eligible. We avoided comment on the securitization but noted the firm's intention to finance assets they could not finance elsewhere'.[12] It is also entirely clear that the Department of the Treasury knew what was happening. Phillip Swagel, then an assistant secretary to the Treasury, sent an e-mail to his colleagues, one of whom, Neel Kashkari, was an aide to Henry Paulson at that time, stating that 'Lehman has already done number 4 to game the PDCF – they securitized their illiquid CLOs and got a rating agency to say that some large fraction of it was investment grade. And then poof they get access to tens of billions of dollars from the Fed's PDCF'.[13] The 'Freedom CLO' was pledged three times before 9 April, when the Federal Reserve started talking to the bank about the CLO's underlying assets. Lehman received $2.13bn for each transfer, $6.39bn in total. The purpose was, of course, to make Lehman's balance sheet look better than it was. It is clear that Lehman's position regarding the PDCF was recognized at the highest levels, yet no further action was taken, apart from the provision of the cash.

The PDCF credit offered by the Federal Reserve was fully collateralized and, initially, eligible collateral was limited to investment grade securities. These included fixed income instruments and equity shares, unsecured debt issued by the Treasury, federal government agencies and government-sponsored enterprises, mortgage-backed securities and collateralized mortgage obligations issued by government-sponsored agencies and private corporations, and non-securitized loans granted to various borrowers. The list is a comprehensive one, but the weakness lay with the credit rating, which was defined as 'a composite credit rating for the pledge collateral based on ratings information used by the borrower's clearing bank'. But the Federal Reserve's acceptance of the clearing bank's valuation of the assets offered by the investment banks and others was marred by the fact that the clearing banks held similar assets themselves.

Willem Buiter, now Chief Economist at Citibank, commented:

> This arrangement is an invitation to primary dealers and their clearers to collude to rip off the Fed by overvaluing the collateral, including using false markets and/or internal pricing models as part of their range of pricing services (what are pricing services anyway?). They can then split the difference. If the Fed wants to be mugged, why not let the primary dealers themselves price the collateral they offer the Fed? For all collateral that is not priced in verifiable, liquid markets, the Fed should arrange its own auctions to discover the reservation prices of those offering the collateral. Leaving it to the clearers is a written invitation to be offered dross at gold valuations.[14]

That was the position when the facility was first introduced on 17 March 2008, but from 15 September 2008, collateral eligibility was extended to include a broad range of securities transacted in tri-party repurchase agreement transactions, including unrated securities.[15] The purpose was simply to provide overnight funding. The terms of the loans included a requirement that primary dealers would be subject to a frequency-based fee after they exceeded 45 days of use, which was based on an escalating scale. The Federal Reserve statement states that the facility was closed on 1 February 2010 and that 'all loans extended under this facility were repaid in full, with interest, in accordance with the terms of the facility'.

Lehman was not the only bank to make use of the facility. The data released by the Federal Reserve Bank in 2010 showed that Goldman Sachs, Morgan Stanley, Citigroup, Bank of America, JP Morgan Chase, and foreign banks such as Barclays, UBS and BNP Paribas had used the PDCF extensively.[16] Morgan Stanley borrowed from the PDCF 212 times between March 2008 and 2009, perhaps an indication of the difficulties the bank faced. Goldman Sachs used it 84 times and Bear Stearns used the facility almost daily from April 2008 to late June 2008, after JP Morgan bought the bank in March 2008 but before the extra funding from the government finished. Commercial banks such as Citibank and Bank of America also used the PDCF frequently. These two banks used it almost every trading day through its investment banking unit, with Citibank borrowing as much as $17.9bn in late November 2008 and Bank of America using it between 18 September and 12 May 2009, more than 1,000 times in total. At one time Bank of America borrowed $11bn in 2008, also taking almost $10bn on several occasions. A spokesman for Goldman Sachs pointed out that in late 2008, many of the US funding markets were clearly broken. 'The Fed took essential steps to fix these markets and its actions were very successful.'[17] The Bank of America took a similarly robust approach:

> The programs helped our customers, such as borrowers, auto dealers, depositors and money-market fund investors, continue to do business as usual despite virtually unprecedented disruptions in the financial markets. We have repaid, with interest, all of the borrowings except some of those whose terms have not expired.[18]

Lehman looks for buyers

As the markets continued to decline, and the financial services industry limped from one bleak quarter to the next, Lehman Brothers began to lay off another 1,500 members of staff in a fourth round of cutbacks, which would constitute about 6 per cent of the workforce. Lehman had already laid off 6,000 employees since June 2007. It was not alone in this, as job losses in banks and securities firms amounted to over 100,000 in 2008. The cutbacks for Lehman as well as other firms began in the mortgages and securitization businesses, but as the demand for merger advisory services, initial public offerings and debt underwriting began to decline, so the cutbacks spread to investment banking. As far as banking analysts were concerned, poor results for Lehman Brothers were expected, but they wanted to hear what the firm planned to do about its huge portfolio of troubled securities. In the days before the announcement of its third quarter results, Lehman's shares were very volatile, falling by 13 per cent on one day and rising by 16 per cent on another. Overall, however, the shares lost 73 per cent of their value over the period from the beginning of 2008.

Lehman had been urgently seeking bids for the company. What seemed a promising avenue was the possibility that the Korean Development Bank would come to the rescue. The KDB had visited New York in May to discuss the possible purchase of 50 per cent of Lehman Brothers, but had concluded the price was too high. Then the KDB proposed buying 25 per cent of Lehman Brothers together with private Korean financial institutions, but all the major financial institutions, such as Kookmin Bank, Woori Finance Holdings, Shinhan Financial Group and Hara Financial Holdings refused to join in a consortium, due to local economic uncertainties. Then Jun Kwang-woo, Chairman of South Korea's Financial Services Commission, whose approval of the purchase was required by the KDB, stated that the talks had ended. That was reported on the Dow Jones Newswire on 9 September. Lehman's shares fell by 38.1 per cent in early trading, recovering by 9.10 per cent by the end of the trading day.

Lehman's third quarter results

It was against this background that Lehman Brothers released their earnings report at 7.30 am on the morning of 10 September in an attempt to present the results in as favourable a light as possible, and to emphasize the actions they were taking to preserve their 'core' business. They needed to stem rumours about their liquidity after the talks with the Korean Development Bank had failed. Their press release was headed 'Lehman Brothers announces preliminary third quarter results and strategic restructuring'. The newly appointed chief finance officer, Ian Lowitt, sought to present the results in the best possible light, referring to the intense market pressure and scrutiny of their legacy residential and commercial real estate assets and speculation about their strategic alternatives. He pointed out that their total shareholder equity had increased in the third quarter by 8 per cent to $28bn, with net leverage reduced to 10.6 times from 12.1 times, and Tier 1 capital ratio approximately 11 per cent as compared with 10.7 per cent in the second quarter. Their commercial real estate and real estate held for sale had been reduced to $32.6bn, down from $39.8bn. 'Fair value' had been realized for buyers by providing 'lengthy asset-specific diligence on each position'.[19]

Part of the strategy was to move $25–30bn of commercial assets, including SunCal, a Californian land developer and Archstone, an apartment developer, into Real Estate Investments Global (REI Global), which would account for all its real estate assets on a hold-to-maturity basis, which would enable the new company to manage assets without mark-to-market volatility. Lehman would provide equity capital of 20–25 per cent and provide debt financing for 75–80 per cent of the total. The pool of assets was expected to generate cash flow of $5bn per annum for the next three to five years. The company had conducted extensive stress tests on the portfolio and was confident that there was sufficient equity to survive even under severe stress. Their residential mortgage exposures had been reduced from $24.9bn in the second quarter to $13.3bn in the third quarter. That figure included the sale of $4bn in UK residential assets, which Blackrock was due to sell. The remaining portfolio consisted of residential mortgages in various markets in Asia and Europe and included US Alt-A and subprime mortgages. Plans to sell a majority stake in parts of their investment management division were also announced, including the sale of Neuberger Berman. The result of all these changes, as Dick Fuld put it, would be a 'clean' Lehman, but the announcement referred to plans, not completed deals or agreements.

By 30 June, total stockholder equity was about $28bn and their long-term capital was $135bn. Gross assets had been reduced by 6 per cent to about $600bn and net assets by 5 per cent from $238bn to about $311bn. Lehman stated: 'Our third quarter Tier 1 ratio is well above our target level and the total capital ratio was well in excess of the 10 per cent minimum regulatory threshold.' However, the media and other analysts were not impressed by the plans proposed, or with the results.

Despite the efforts to focus on the firm's strategy, the media headlines on 10 September 2008 were that Lehman Brothers' earnings showed a loss of $3.9bn: 'Lehman Suffers Nearly $4bn loss' (*CNN Money*); 'Lehman Shares Plunge 45 per cent: Firm to Release Earnings Early' (*Washington Post*); 'A Battered Lehman Fights for Survival' (*New York Times*); 'Lehman Faces Mounting Pressure. Stocks Drop 45 per cent as Capital-Raising Talks Falter' (*Wall Street Journal*, 10 September, followed by 'Lehman's Revamp Plan Draws Doubters', 11 September). The *Wall Street Journal* commented that 'after suffering nearly $7bn in losses in the last two quarters, Mr Fuld was left with no choice but to shed most of Lehman's real-estate assets, sell half its money-management business and slash its dividend.'

The *Wall Street Journal* also quoted an analyst from the Bank of America Corp., who said that the plans might 'require Lehman to raise an additional $6bn in capital to plug further holes in its balance sheet', adding that its remaining $20bn in 'risk exposures are still too high to instil confidence that the worst is behind us'. Another analyst quoted by *CNN Money* pointed out that 'Lehman was being forced to make hard decisions now that the various options on the table have narrowed and balance sheet concerns start to bite'. In other words, the early presentation of the third quarter results and the conference call with its announcements of its strategy to restructure the bank did nothing to inspire confidence in the media or the market. The end would come within a few days.

The failures of the SEC's Consolidated Supervised Entity programme

Annette Nazareth, former SEC Commissioner, was reported as stating that:

> the investment banks requested consolidated supervision from the SEC and did not opt into the Federal Reserve's Financial Holding Company regime (even though the investment banks could have done this, and this would have satisfied the requirements of the EU Directive). Her view was that the investment banks didn't want bank-type supervision from the Federal Reserve. They wanted to be regulated by the SEC, which had been their functional regulator for 70 years.[20]

This does put the position as stated by Erik Sirri, Director of Market Regulation, Securities and Exchange Commission, in a somewhat different light, but does not undermine the basic point that proper regulation of the investment banks did not exist. In his testimony, Sirri pointed out that no regulator in the Federal Government was given explicit authority and responsibility for the supervision of investment bank holding companies with bank affiliates in the Gramm-Leach-Bliley Act. The five largest investment bank holding companies were ineligible because they had specialized bank affiliates. Goldman Sachs, Lehman Brothers, Merrill Lynch and Morgan Stanley owned Industrial Loan Companies, which accounted for 1.0, 0.6, 7.2 and 1.2 per cent respectively of the consolidated assets of each firm. Three of the firms, Lehman Brothers, Merrill Lynch and Morgan Stanley, also owned thrifts, which accounted for 3.3, 1.7 and 0.1 per cent of their assets respectively. There was at that time absolutely no provision in the law that required an investment bank to compute capital measures and maintain liquidity on a consolidated basis, nor did the law provide for a consolidated supervisor, who would be an expert in their core securities business.[21]

The point is that when Congress passed the Gramm-Leach-Bliley Act, it failed to give the SEC or any other agency the authority to regulate certain large investment banks. The CSE programme had no explicit statutory authority to require the investment banks in the programme to report their capital, maintain liquidity or submit to leverage requirements. Christopher Cox, then Chairman of the SEC, referred to the scheme as being entirely voluntary.

These requirements enabled Christopher Cox to argue that during the week of 10–17 March, 'Bear Stearns had a capital cushion well above what is required to meet the Basel standards', and that 'its consolidated capital and its broker-dealers' net capital exceeded relevant supervisory standards'. He added that 'what neither the CSE regulatory approach, nor any existing regulatory model, has taken into account is the possibility that secured funding, even if it is backed by high quality collateral, such as US Treasury and Agency securities, could become unavailable.'[22] Liquidity risk was not on the regulatory agenda. The SEC was not in a position to extend credit or liquidity facilities to any regulated entity. That was in the hands of the Federal Reserve.

Erik Sirri's stringent criticisms of the weak regulatory structure turned out to be entirely justified, but why was this situation not remedied by the regulatory authorities putting the case to Congress and seeking to extend existing laws appropriately? Typically, weak supervision leads to a bank taking undue risks and failing to maintain sufficient capital against a constellation of risks.

Robert Colby, deputy director of Market Regulation at the SEC, described their prudential regime as allowing the Commission to 'monitor for, and *act quickly in response to financial or operational weaknesses in a* CSE *holding company*' or any of its affiliates, which the SEC manifestly failed to do. Colby outlines the nature of the 'prudential regime' in some detail. The investment banks 'are required to maintain and document a system of internal controls', which the Commission must approve. The SEC must also examine the 'implementation of these controls'. The Commission was supposed to monitor the investment banks (the consolidated supervised entities (CSEs) continuously for financial and operational weaknesses; require the CSEs to compute a capital adequacy measure at the holding company that is consistent with the Basel Standard and ensure that the CSEs maintained significant pools of liquidity at the holding company. Such supervision looks impressive on paper, but the 'monitoring' largely consisted of monthly meetings with senior management and two members of the SEC staff on-site. Decisive enforcement action was entirely lacking.[23]

Erik Sirri's description of the rapid deterioration at Bear Stearns provides an interesting insight. The SEC confronted the rapid deterioration of liquidity at Bear Stearns during the week beginning 10 March 2008:

> This was the first time that a major investment bank that was well-capitalized and fully liquid experienced a crisis of confidence that resulted in a loss not only of unsecured financing but also short-term financing. This occurred even though the collateral it was able to provide was high quality, such as agency securities and had a market value that exceeded the amount to be borrowed.[24]

The impression given is that it was simply rumours about liquidity problems at the firm, which intensified during that week. There appears to have been no specific event which gave rise to them, although factors included 'naked' short selling and a rapid rise in activity involving credit default swaps. These intensified when some over-the-counter derivatives counterparties sought to replace their trades with the company by entering into new contracts with other dealers. Then some of Bear Stearns' prime brokerage clients decided to move their cash balances elsewhere, which obviously influenced other market participants. Ultimately, counterparties would not deal in derivative transactions with Bear Stearns, and lenders would not lend stock or enter into tri-partite repurchase agreements with the company. By 15 March, Bear Stearns had to either file for bankruptcy or be acquired by another company.

What seems to be left out of these accounts is the context in which the 'rumours' occurred. After all, in 2007, it had not been rumours about the two hedge funds, the High-Grade Structured Credit Fund and the Credit Enhanced Leverage Fund managed by Bear Stearns Asset Management, which had led to their near collapse. Bear Stearns had tried to raise about $3.2bn in loans to bail out the larger fund. In the end, Bear Stearns lent the High Grade Fund $1.5bn, which, it was thought, could help it meet its margin calls while it liquidated its position. It also suspended redemptions from the fund. The company also had to advise investors in the funds that it was suspending redemptions. On 17 July, investors were advised that the Credit Fund had lost over 90 per cent of its value, leaving about $1bn dollars, and that the Credit Enhanced Leverage Fund had lost virtually all of its investor capital. On 31 July the two funds had filed for Chapter 15 bankruptcy. It was widely acknowledged at the time that their collapse was due to the slump in the housing market and the continuing fall-out from the subprime mortgages.

That led to the first quarterly loss for the three months ended in November 2007. In other words, it was obvious that Bear Stearns was exposed to the subprime market through increasingly illiquid mortgage-backed securities and collateralized debt obligations (CDOs), and that there had been serious management failures as well as too little capital.

Looking at what actually happened with Bear Stearns and then with Lehman, the question which immediately arises is: where exactly was the SEC? What had they been doing over the past four years? Had anyone carried out any of the supervisory activities so carefully described by Mr Colby? Chairman Cox appeared to believe that all was well. He described Bear Stearns as a 'well-capitalized and apparently fully liquid major investment bank that experienced a crisis of confidence, denying it not only unsecured financing, even when the collateral consisted of agency securities with a market value in excess of the funds to be borrowed.'[25]

A few months later, Chairman Cox was to declare that the programme was 'fundamentally flawed from the beginning', which he attributed to its being a voluntary scheme, although it was not entirely voluntary, given the European Union dimension. Its flaws lay elsewhere. It was an attempt to fill a regulatory gap, but one which left the SEC without the statutory powers it needed. The SEC's regulations exempted the five largest investment banks from the net capital rule, a 1975 rule for computing the minimum capital standards at broker-dealers. The investment banks were allowed to use their own mathematical models of asset and portfolio risk to compute their appropriate capital levels in accordance with Basel II rules. As a result, leverage ratios rose sharply from their 2004 levels, as the banks' models indicated that they had sufficient capital, being allowed to increase to 40:1. Basel II relies heavily on credit ratings to assess the quality of the capital held, and did not really take short-term secured lending into account. The rules did not charge for illiquid trading positions at the brokers, did not control overnight funding, nor did they limit leverage. Short-term funding of the balance sheet by tri-party repo agreements, structured demand notes and short-dated commercial paper increased as a source of funding without any interventions by the SEC. Instead the SEC applied the Basel II ratios in a rather mechanistic way, assuming that the Basel capital ratio of 10 per cent was sufficient, and hence there had been no anxieties when Bear Stearns' capital ratio decreased from 21.4 per cent to 11.5 per cent between April 2006 and March 2008. For the CSE programme, part of the problem lay in the awkward combination of a mission that stressed *ex post* enforcement over *ex ante* prudential guidance and its non-statutory nature, which left it without enforcement tools.

On 25 September 2008 David Kotz, the SEC's Inspector General, issued a controversial report, 'Audit of SEC's Oversight of Bear Stearns and Related Entities:

The Consolidated Supervised Entity Programme.' Here, it is important to note the management's response, even though the SEC's Trading and Market Division accepted all of the Recommendations in the Report, except Recommendations 13, 15 and 16. For example, the Report claims with regard to Bear Stearns that, although the Trading and Markets (TM) division became aware of the firm's concentration of mortgage securities, high leverage, shortcomings of risk management in mortgage-backed securities, and lack of compliance with Basel II standards, no action was taken to limit these risk factors. No leverage ratio limit for CSE firms was required. The senior management of the SEC and the TM division, which had the prime responsibility for regulating and supervising the investment banks, insisted that the Inspector General both misunderstood the nature of the regulations and had not consulted with the senior officials, a claim which the Inspector General firmly rejected.[26] In response, the Inspector General pointed out that 'over the five months of fieldwork, OIG auditors had weekly and sometimes daily conversations with TM management, including senior officials, on all issues relating to the audit work. In many cases, TM management did not provide full responses to questions posed and issues raised by the OIG.'[27] Despite such disagreements, TM accepted 20 of the 23 recommendations addressed to them in the report, although TM often states that the recommendation is based on misunderstandings, or is 'fundamentally flawed', or the work is already in progress.

TM rejected Recommendation 13 regarding an internal and external communications strategy as not being a regulatory requirement, although, perhaps an effective strategy of this kind might have helped Bear Stearns during the crisis. Recommendation 16 recommended that TM should complete the inspection process before allowing another consolidated supervised entity to use the alternative capital method, although TM explained that the SEC was clearly informed of the findings before that status was granted.

The SEC's Corporate Finance (CF) division accepted only one of the recommendations but rejected the other two which involved establishing guidelines for the timeliness of reviewing reports on the grounds that Bear Stearns had released in its filings (10-Q, 8-K and 10-K) in October, November and December 2007 and January 2008, improvements in its disclosures about subprime mortgage securities in response to CF's comment letter of September 2007. Similar letters were sent to Goldman Sachs, Morgan Stanley, Lehman Brothers and Merrill Lynch well before the end of their fiscal years. Comment letters and responses were posted 45 days after the completion of a filing review.

However, in his response the OIG points out that, although the CF was correct in pointing out that its approach to timeliness was dictated by the requirements of section 408 of the Sarbanes-Oxley Act 2002, this still meant that reviews of high-risk companies should be carried out more quickly. Its 2006 10-K filing showed the high risks of the company, since it indicated the company's exposure to subprime loans.

Despite all the controversy surrounding the Report, it did show the weaknesses in the SEC's management of the CSE programme. It is clear from other evidence that the CSE programme was understaffed, given the size and complexity of the companies involved. It had ten to twelve people in teams of three (with some overlap) to monitor risk at the five investment banks and also at Citibank and Chase. The main focus was on the holding companies, but since Citibank and Chase were refused exemption from the net capital rule, the SEC relied on the Federal Reserve to regulate them. The CSE staff would take reports received from the CSEs at face value and 'work from there'. The CSE staff did not perform audits or in-depth examinations, but verified the Basel II calculations (for example, the capital the investment banks had), verified the controls, analysed and questioned the management of these banks. At first, examinations were conducted by the SEC's Office of Compliance Inspections and Examinations, which seemed to be more concerned with finding violations than checking controls. Perhaps owing to tensions between the two divisions, TM division was given authority to conduct examinations and hire additional staff. The numbers of CSE staff remained too small to supervise the five investment banks, which between them controlled over $4 trillion in assets.[28] The SEC's then head of Market Regulation, Annette Nazareth, had promised to hire highly skilled supervisors to assess the riskiness of the investment banking activities, but did not. Instead, economists and financiers were added to the team. When Christopher Cox became Chairman in 2005, he closed the risk management office and the SEC did not complete a single large-scale inspection of a major investment bank during the eighteen months leading up to the collapse. In her interview with the Financial Crisis Inquiry Commission (FCIC), Annette Nazareth indicated that they had observed the trends towards subprime mortgages but had not seen how the quality of the underlying assets had changed. Their focus had been on the liquidity of the investment banks, not the extent of the leverage.[29]

The SEC adopted Basel II in terms of the minimum capital requirement, based on the use of the investment banks' internal models and risk management structures. The SEC required full information about the affiliates of the broker-dealers, financial and risk information about holding companies, affiliates of broker-dealers, and certain off-balance sheet items of broker-dealers, their holding companies, and their affiliates through risk assessment rules and meetings with and reports from members of the Derivatives Policy Holding Group. The CSE was required to compute group-wide capital and allowances for market, credit and operational risk, on a monthly and quarterly basis. It was also required to implement and maintain a consolidated and comprehensive internal risk management control system and procedures to monitor and manage group-wide risk, including market, credit, funding, operational and legal risks. That was all subject to Commission Review. Then, along with the tentative net capital requirements, the CSE was able to use its own internal mathematical models to calculate some of its market and credit risk charges for risk measurement, including internally developed value-at-risk models or scenario analysis. The CSE was obliged to adhere to strict rules regarding its group-wide risk management control, designed to ensure the integrity of risk measurement, monitoring, and management process, and to clarify accountability, at the appropriate organizational level, for defining the permitted scope of activity and level of risk.

Both Bear Stearns and Lehman Brothers apparently complied with Basel II on paper. But both acted in such a way that questionable levels of capital were maintained. Bear Stearns had a system whereby each division of the company used separate VaR numbers for each portfolio of assets. This inconsistency in VaR numbers prevented adequate enterprise-wide risk assessments from being made; indeed, the system allowed Bear Stearns to choose the most favourable VaR numbers for calculating its capital charges. Nor did the company mark down stressed assets, in order to avoid the inevitable capital charges.[30]

Some of the SEC's internal memoranda of the Risk Management Reviews make it clear the SEC knew what was going on. In April 2006, staff commented that 'problems are surfacing at subprime originators. The CSEs purchase whole loans with the intention of securitizing them, but are having difficulty in arranging "put backs"', that is, returning the defective loans to subprime originators. It was also noted that Bear Stearns had a 'significant amount of loans in inventory with outstanding claims with a disproportionate number involving a relatively small number of originators'. But the SEC decided to 'follow up on the corrective action taken in this area', rather than require any action and a specific timetable.

Having adopted Basel II, the SEC should have been equally clear about its Second Pillar, the Supervisory Review Process. Although the evidence of the SEC's supervision is somewhat unclear, it is doubtful that the full application of the review process could have been undertaken, given the demands of the process and the lack of staff or that the nature of the supervisory process was understood or that the recommendations for action were not part of the SEC's CSE programme. In stressing the importance of the supervisory review, Basel points out that supervisors are expected to evaluate how well banks are assessing their capital needs relative to their risks and 'to intervene where appropriate'. Increased capital is not the only option, and 'strengthening risk management', applying internal limits, strengthening the level of provisions and reserves, or improving internal controls, must be considered, and, indeed, required of banks. Liquidity risk is also noted, with the requirement that banks should have adequate systems for measuring, monitoring and controlling liquidity risk, and should evaluate the adequacy of their own capital, given their own liquidity profile and the liquidity of the markets in which they operate. Later the SEC would claim that lack of liquidity was the cause of the collapse of Bear Stearns and Lehman Brothers, but little attention seems to have been paid to this issue by SEC staff as far as the CSEs were concerned. The programme required regular inspections of the banks' management systems, but the SEC failed to use its powers to enforce compliance.

The SEC did not even inspect the VaR models before approval, and never issued a formal approval of Bear's VaR modelling. The internal memoranda reviewed by the OIG indicate that the SEC was aware of the problems, but accepted management's agreement to improve them.[31] At each meeting throughout 2006, Bear Stearns required a separate discussion; for example, in October 2006, it was noted that the Mark-to-Market Committee had asked for a complete review of the firm's mortgage residual positions, adding that 'due to the magnitude of these positions, we have asked for a detailed briefing', but that was all. By January 2007, the SEC noted that several CSE firms had 'potential credit exposures to subprime originators that have failed or are in distress through warehouse lending facilities'. The possibility of a credit loss existed if they were unable to repurchase the loans or provide other collateral. The increase in default and delinquency rates for subprime notes was noted. The situation at Bear Stearns worsened in 2007, when the firm absorbed a $58m. writedown on mortgage assets in January and the managers advised the SEC that 'these events reflect a more rapid and severe deterioration in collateral than anticipated'.[32]

The reviews required under Basel II all lead to 'supervisory action', which, in the first instance, means that the bank has to demonstrate that it has carried out all the changes set out by the supervisor. Penalties follow if the bank has failed to implement the necessary changes. But there is no evidence that the CSEs were required to agree to substantial changes in risk management, nor of any penalties.[33] In the case of Bear Stearns, there had surely been sufficient cause for concern and action following the collapse of its two hedge funds in July 2007 and then its reported losses, its first quarterly loss in its eighty-four-year history, which included a \$1.9bn write-down on its holdings of mortgage assets, followed by substantial falls in its share prices. Inaction with regard to Lehman Brothers will be set out in the following chapters.

Looking back on it all, Mary Shapiro, who became Chairman of the SEC in January 2009, accepted the inadequacies of the CSE programme, due in part to a 'siloed financial regulatory framework that lacked the ability to monitor and reduce risks flowing across the regulated entities and markets; and the lack of an adequate statutory framework for the oversight of large investment bank holding companies on a consolidated basis'. She added that

> [the] consolidated oversight of these holding companies was more prudential in nature than SEC's traditional rule-based approach for broker-dealer regulation … a profoundly different approach to oversight and supervision for the Commission. Properly executing the programme called for a correspondingly significant expansion in human, financial, technological and other resources devoted to the oversight and examination of the CSE holding companies and their subsidiaries.[34]

She and others have stated that the SEC was not a prudential regulator, which is undoubtedly true, but this simply emphasizes the fact that regulation of the investment banks was taken far too lightly by all the banking regulators. Mary Shapiro became Chairman of the SEC on 27 January 2009, and, although she had many reservations about the Office of the Inspector General's report, she instituted a wide range of reforms to the Commission's structure. These included modernization of the SEC's technology and upgrading of its case management system, the creation of specialized enforcement units, a successful enforcement programme and new corporate disclosure units. She also brought in experts in risk management and created the agency's first Office of the Chief Operating Officer, to name but a few. She stepped down in December 2012.[35]

However, whether or not the Inspector General's report was wholly accurate or not, whether or not the SEC had sufficient resources or was prepared to take decisive action, or whether or not the SEC was sufficiently aware of the changing circumstances surrounding the investment banks as the subprime mortgage market began to collapse, all went by the board. The day after the publication of the Report, Christopher Cox, then Chairman of the SEC, announced the abandonment of the Consolidated Supervised Entities programme, blaming the lack of an explicit supervisory authority to require the five investment banks to report their capital, maintain liquidity, or submit to leverage requirements and on the fact that it was a voluntary scheme (despite the EU requirements already described). The programme ended on 26 September, the day after the publication of the report.[36]

Immediately after the forced sale of Bear Stearns, Chairman Cox wrote to the then Chairman of the Basel Committee on Banking Supervision, Dr Nout Wellink, about 'Sound Practices for Managing Liquidity in Banking Organizations'. He provided data on Bear Stearns which showed that its capital and its broker-dealers' capital 'exceeded supervisory standards. Counterparty withdrawals and credit denials, which resulted in a loss of liquidity – not inadequate capital – caused Bear's demise.'[37] This was disingeneous, to say the least. Interestingly enough, the then CEO of Bear Stearns offered exactly the same explanation in his statement to the Senate Banking Committee when he stated that 'during the week of March 10, even though the firm was adequately capitalized and had a substantial liquidity cushion, unfounded rumours and attendant speculation began circulating in the market that Bear Stearns was in the midst of a liquidity crisis'. The 'impetus for the run on Bear Stearns was . . . a lack of confidence, not a lack of capital or liquidity'.[38] It is unusual for the regulator and the regulated to agree, almost word for word, on the failure of a regulated company, as happened in this case.

On the issue of liquidity, the CSE programme was designed to ensure that, in a stressed environment, a firm could withstand the loss of its unsecured financing for up to a year, on the assumption that secured funding for its liquid assets would be available. It also assumed that any assets in the regulated entity could not be used elsewhere in the conglomerate. These guidelines were insufficient and it appears that Bear Stearns was aware of that, so the firm's liquidity planning involved developing a 60-day cash inflow and outflow analysis to track cash flows on a daily basis. This analysis did not assume that secured funding was always available, but assumed the existing credit lines would not be withdrawn. The firm therefore realized that the one-year period was unrealistic and that secured funding might not be available in times of stress. This may have helped the company in 2007, but was not sufficient in March 2008.[39]

That was not the only weakness in the CSE programme. Chairman Cox described what happened to Bear Stearns as unprecedented, describing the bank as being 'well-capitalized and apparently fully liquid', yet it found itself being denied 'not only unsecured financing, but also short-term secured financing even when the collateral consisted of agency securities with a market value in excess of the funds to be borrowed'. These decisions by counterparties and prime brokerage clients in turn influenced others to reduce their exposure to Bear Stearns.[40] Bear Stearns' capital, according to the CSE programme monitoring, was well above the requirements of Basel II. Cox declared that 'capital is not synonymous with liquidity', but in times of stress, the ability of a securities firm to withstand market, credit and other types of stress events is linked to the amount of capital, but, in addition, the firm also needs enough liquid assets in the form of US Treasuries and other high-quality instruments to meet its financial obligations. The CSE programme also required substantial liquidity pools and funding procedures so that the holding company had enough stand-alone liquidity to meet its expected cash flows in a stressed liquidity environment. The loss of liquidity to Cox was entirely unprecedented, and obviously came as a shock. He added that 'Bear's extensive participation in a wide range of critical markets meant that a chaotic unwinding of its positions could have cast doubt on the financial positions of some of Bear Stearn's thousands of counterparties, placing additional pressures on the financial system.' That was in April 2008, and Chairman Cox was entirely oblivious to the approaching storm.

Cox was correct to refer to the link between capital and liquidity, since a bank's capital base and its holdings of liquid assets enable the bank to withstand certain types of shocks. But he should have been aware of the general principles. A bank should hold a buffer of liquid assets to mitigate against the risk of liquidity crises caused where other sources of funding dry up. The assets which a bank holds includes loans, such as mortgages, lending in the wholesale market, secured or unsecured together with liquid assets. A bank should hold a buffer of liquid assets, such as cash, central bank reserves and government bonds, which should be increased if the bank has invested in risky assets. Liquidity is linked to both sides of a bank's balance sheet, relating to the mix of assets a bank holds and the various sources of funding for the bank, in particular, the liabilities which should in due course be repaid. Banks may face two kinds of liquidity risk: insufficient cash or collateral to make payments to its counterparties or customers as they fall due, and market liquidity risk. The latter is the risk that an asset cannot be sold in the market quickly, or, if quickly, then only at a heavily discounted price. Instead of a concern about general principles, Chairman Cox and his staff should have been aware of the nature and extent of the assets held by Bear Stearns and Lehman Brothers, but they were not. It was the quality of the assets which initially caused the run on both banks.

Lehman had invested extensively in mortgages – even in 2007, when the cracks in the housing market began to appear. It underwrote more mortgage-backed securities than any other firm, accumulating an $85bn portfolio, four times its shareholders' equity. Its leverage ratio was 31 in 2007, but its vast mortgage securities portfolio made it vulnerable to deteriorating market conditions. Bear Stearns' was the second largest portfolio, and was subject to the same issues until it was bailed out. Nor was it just the risks involved in poor-quality assets, but the extent of the leverage of all the five large investment banks. But as the Joint Economic Committee pointed out in its analysis of the financial meltdown,

> To achieve the high returns on equity to which the independent investment banks were accustomed, the leverage ratio at independent investment banks ballooned relative to the average leverage ratio at commercial banks and savings institutions. At the end of the first quarter in 2008, the leverage ratios at Morgan Stanley, Lehman Brothers, Merrill Lynch and Goldman Sachs were 31.8, 30.7, 27.5 and 26.9 respectively, compared with an average of 8.8 for all U.S. commercial banks and savings institutions.[41]

That was always high, but between 2004 and 2007, the average ratio of assets to equity rose from 25:1 to 30:1. If the SEC was aware, no action was taken. Small wonder that Chairman Cox abruptly ended the CSE programme on 26 September 2008.

Later, Chairman Bernanke would admit to the regulatory failures, but the initial problem was that he did not appreciate the impact of the increases in subprime lending and the abandonment of sensible underwriting standards. He described the advantages of subprime lending as making 'homeownership possible for households that in the past might not have qualified for a mortgage and has thereby contributed to the rise in homeownership [from 65 per cent in 1995, reaching 69.2 per cent by the first quarter, 2005, falling back to 63.9 per cent in the fourth quarter, 2014].' But by May 2007, as the Federal Reserve observed the continued rise in delinquencies and foreclosures in subprime mortgages, Bernanke concluded that together with other regulators and Congress, the Federal Reserve 'must evaluate what we have learned from the recent episode and decide what additional regulation or oversight might be necessary to prevent such an occurrence … but, at the same time, we do not want to curtail subprime lending or close off options that would be beneficial to borrowers.'[42] By August 2007, Bernanke seemed to have recognized that the situation was more serious that his earlier, somewhat complacent assessment. He referred to the 'marked deterioration in the performance of the subprime mortgage market', to the intensification of investors' concerns about mortgage credit performance, and the declines in investor demand for asset-backed commercial paper and unsecured commercial paper. He did not, however, see any of this as requiring any action on the part of the Federal Reserve:

> It is not the responsibility of the Federal Reserve … to protect lenders and investors from the consequences of their financial decisions. But developments in financial markets can have broad economic effects felt by many

outside the markets and the Federal Reserve must take these into account when determining policy.

In its 7 August meeting, the Federal Open Market Committee reiterated its view that inflation was its predominant policy concern, but just ten days later the Federal Reserve Board cut its discount rate by 50 basis points and allowed for term financing for as long as thirty days, renewable by the borrower.[43] These speeches show that Bernanke was slow to recognize the enormity of the problems facing them. Reflecting on the financial crisis long after the event, he realized that other and more forceful actions should have been taken. The Joint Economic Committee refers to the beginning of the global financial crisis on 9 August 2007, when 'both commercial and investment banks incurred significant credit losses on subprime residential mortgage loans and write-downs on subprime RMBSs and tranches of CMOs'.[44]

In a speech to the American Economic Association on 3 January 2010, Chairman Bernanke admitted the serious failures of regulation and supervision, which should have focused on problems with underwriting practices and lenders' risk management, since these 'would have been a more effective and surgical approach to constraining the housing bubble than a general increase in interest rates'.

In his testimony to the Committee on Financial Services, later in the same year, Bernanke's views about the role of the Federal Reserve in banking supervision actually shows some of the major failings of banking supervision with references to the need to adopt a multi-disciplinary approach in order to 'better understand the linkages between firms and markets' using horizontal reviews that look across a group of firms to identify common sources of risks and best practices for managing those risks, and the use of models and data analysis to identify vulnerabilities at the firm level and for the financial sector as a whole.[45] It was the lack of understanding of the linkages which led to the calamitous decision to allow Lehman Brothers to fail.

One can only speculate on what might have been if the Big Five investment banks had been placed under the Federal Reserve's Consolidated Supervision in 2004. All the blame for the collapse of Bear Stearns, Lehman Brothers and the rescue of Merrill Lynch cannot be laid at the door of the regulators. In all cases the banks brought their downfall on themselves.

The Fateful Weekend

Lehman's last efforts to save the company

On 10 September 2008, Dick Fuld presented what would be the firm's last earnings report, announcing the loss of $3.9bn, the second quarterly loss after June's loss of $2.8bn:

> This is an extraordinary time for our industry, and one of the toughest periods in our Firm's history. The strategic initiatives we have announced today reflect our determination to fundamentally reposition Lehman Brothers by dramatically reducing balance sheet risk, reinforcing our focus on our client-facing business and returning the Firm to profitability.[1]

The early announcement included an increase in total stockholders' equity of $28.4bn, up from $26.3bn, an estimated liquidity pool of $42bn, and plans to sell a majority stake in its asset management unit. Lehman also revealed that it would separate off a 'vast majority of the firm's commercial real estate assets from our core business by spinning off those assets to our shareholders and to an independent, publicly traded entity which will be independently capitalised'. The plan was to place between $25bn and $30bn of its $32.6bn portfolio in SpinCo, or REI Global as the company would be called. Lehman had reserved the name in Delaware on 4 September. Fuld acknowledged that the 'losses created by these concentrated legacy assets have clouded the underlying value of our franchise', adding that while the firm's clients and trading partners 'continue to stand with us, we nevertheless cannot put the strength of our franchise and their continued trust at risk'.[2] Fuld also claimed that they were in the final stages of raising capital with the sale of a majority stake in their investment management division, whilst retaining the Lehman and the Neuberger Berman brands. A potential deal with a Korean sovereign wealth fund, the Korean Investment Corporation, which would have provided Lehman Brothers with $5bn, had fallen through in August 2008. Negotiations had then taken place with the Korean Development Fund

(KDF). It was thought that the fact that negotiations had taken place with KIC would not affect the discussions with KDF, as its CEO, Min Euoo-Sung, was head of Lehman's Korean operations for three years until 2007. However, the relationship did not help.

All of the proposed actions were no more than plans, as opposed to completed deals or agreements. They did not inspire confidence. On the same day, Moody's announced that it had placed 'on review with uncertain direction' the long-term ratings of Lehman Brothers Holdings Inc (as well as its principal rated operating and guaranteed subsidiaries). The ratings review reflected the 'fluidity' of the current situation, as well as Moody's assessment of the likelihood of the sale. Blaine Frantz remarked that 'a strategic transaction with a stronger financial partner would likely ... result in a positive rating action'.[3] The effect of this on 10 September was to encourage a further fall in Lehman's shares, which having risen gently during the day, fell by 6.9 per cent to $7.25 at 4.00 pm in the New York Stock Exchange composite trading. The next day was no better, as analysts, having had time to study the Real Estate Investment Global proposal, were not convinced, to say the least, and advised their clients accordingly. It failed to impress JP Morgan or other potential investors. The new company would require $8bn of equity from Lehman, with the remainder to be borrowed from Lehman and outside investors. The advantage for Lehman was that it would be able to hold the commercial real estate assets, since as 'a new company it would not have to mark-to-market, allowing its assets to be monetized in an orderly manner over time, with more negotiating leverage and at prices which maximize returns'. Lehman's shares, which at one time had been worth $66.73 and had averaged in the high to mid-fifties at the beginning of 2008, continued to plummet, closing at $4 on 12 September.

It was now clear that action would have to be taken, and in the form of a buyer. Indeed, this is just what Paulson had been advising Fuld ever since the rescue of Bear Stearns and throughout the summer. 'With all the attention on the GSEs, I still kept an eye on Lehman's travails, speaking regularly with Dick Fuld about his options. The best of these was to sell his firm, and the Bank of America was the most likely buyer.'[4]

The gathering storm

The pre-announcement of Lehman's earnings did not reassure the market. Geithner commented that Fuld did not seem to realize that 'the endgame had began. We still hoped to find a last-minute buyer, but my team had began drawing up a "Lehman liquidation game plan".' Bank of America agreed to give Lehman another look, but did not have a due diligence team. Lewis was already in a dispute with Countrywide and wanted written assurances. Geithner refused, and Ken Lewis then agreed to send his team.[5]

On Thursday 11 September, Geithner confirmed to Fuld that Barclays was still interested in bidding for the company. Eventually, Robert Diamond, CEO of Barclays Capital and President of Barclays plc, advised Dick Fuld that he and his team would arrive in New York to examine Lehman's books. This had already been agreed with Tim Geithner and Hank Paulson. Indeed, Paulson recalls telling Diamond that he did not think that he could give Barclays a leg-up, and nor could Lehman's, but 'because the government couldn't put any money into the transaction, Barclays should focus on Lehman's troubled assets so we could discuss realistically how they could get a deal done'.[6]

Meanwhile, both Paulson and Geithner hoped that Ken Lewis, CEO of Bank of America, would buy Lehman Brothers, but both made it clear that the Government would not finance the deal, but would assist by encouraging 'others in the industry to help finance the part that you weren't going to take. It would be just like the LTCM consortium'.[7] Lewis was not going to take LTCM as an example, having recently observed the Federal Reserve assisting JP Morgan to acquire Bear Stearns, but he agreed to put a proposal together for consideration by the other Wall Street CEOs. All that happened was that the situation for Lehman deteriorated, because JP Morgan reiterated its $5bn collateral call, with the possibility of another $10bn by the weekend. The company had borrowed $230bn overnight on the repo market, short-term funding which could be withdrawn at a moment's notice. That just added to the underlying major problem, that Lehman had overvalued its assets so that for the Bank of America and Barclays, the risks were too high without financial support from the Federal Reserve. Paulson and Geithner had discussed a liquidation consortium which might subsidize the sale of Lehman, if the Bank of America or Barclays refused to complete the purchase on their own, but the proposal had not yet been worked out. This was further discussed with Ben Bernanke, then Chairman of the Federal Reserve and Chairman Cox of the SEC, and all four concluded that it was to be a private-sector solution and that there would be no public money.[8] That was the clear message. Hence on Thursday evening, Michele Davis, Paulson's Director of Communications, briefed journalists off the record that there would be no bail-out.[9]

On Friday 12 September, Paulson began the day by reading the press, where the message he had wished to convey had not been expressed in clear enough terms. It was supposed to be 'no more bail-outs'. Although the front-page story in the *Washington Post* said, 'The Government is looking for an agreement that would not involve public money', what was said by the *Wall Street Journal* and the *New York Times* mattered most. The front page story on the *Wall Street Journal*, 'Lehman Races to Find a Buyer', left the door open, although it also reported that the 'Federal Reserve and Treasury Department had been working with Lehman to help resolve the bank's troubles, including talking to potential buyers . . . Federal officials currently aren't expected to structure a bail-out along the lines of the Bear transaction'. Paulson records that 'Michele quickly went to CNBC to reiterate that there would be no public money'.[10] But in his response to questions from James Stewart which appeared in the *New Yorker* in 2009,

> Paulson now acknowledges, as some in the room suspected, that the Government was more amenable to funding a rescue than it let on. 'We said no public money', he told me. 'We said this publicly. We repeated it when these guys came in. But to ourselves we said, "If there's a chance to put in public money and avert a disaster, we're open to it."'[11]

These remarks should perhaps be seen as wishful thinking only a year after the events of September 2008. In his own account, five years later, he says that he would 'continue to believe that we did the only thing we could have done'.[12]

Geithner and Paulson had agreed that the only solution was to call all the Wall Street CEOs together at 6.00 pm to the New York Federal Reserve Bank. Telephone calls were made after the markets closed at 4.00 pm The CEOs would be urged to provide a private market solution. The Bank of America's proposals were complicated, since their due diligence had shown that Lehman's capital hole was about $20bn. Ken Lewis explained that if he bought the investment bank it would have to leave about $40bn of assets. His bank would then split the first $2bn in losses 49 per cent to Bank of America and 51 per cent to the Government. The Government would have to absorb 100 per cent of all the other losses on the remaining assets, and the BoA would give the Government warrants to buy its shares.[13] Barclays began its own due diligence, according to the minutes of the meeting of the board of directors, 12 September 2008. The Examiner also notes that Lehman posted $5bn cash collateral at JP Morgan's request on 11 September and that Citibank had amended its Direct Custodial Services Agreement to strengthen its lien on Lehman's assets. Lehman calculated that its easily monetized liquidity pool was $2bn. John Varley, chief executive of Barclays advised Paulson that Barclays' board was prepared to consider a possible bid for Lehman.

Meanwhile at the Friday evening meeting on 12 September, the CEOs were divided into groups, to each of which was assigned one of the following: minimizing the effects of Lehman's bankruptcy, focusing on unwinding Lehman's derivatives, secured funding and tri-partite repo transactions. One group would consider how the industry could buy all of Lehman Brothers and liquidate it over time, while another would consider how to finance those parts of Lehman Brothers that a prospective buyer did not want. Geithner then told the CEOs to return on Saturday morning and 'be prepared to do something'. Paulson first noted the absence of any Lehman representatives and then made it clear that federal money would not be available to rescue Lehman, but a failure to find a solution would have an impact on the whole industry.[14]

The Examiner noted that Diamond stated that he had told Fuld that there would not be a deal at the 'current market price' because of the risk and the current situation, and that Barclays' only interest was as a 'rescue situation', that is, at a 'very, very distressed price'.[15] Some members of the Lehman team felt that 'Diamond was contemplating the purchase of the whole firm.' It is understandable that their hopes were raised, but it is doubtful that Barclays was seriously considering such a purchase.

It is worth noting that the teams working for BoA and Barclays took only a few hours to assess the extent of the poor-quality assets Lehman held, and to find the holes in the balance sheets. Tom Russo, Lehman's Vice Chairman and Chief Legal Officer, pointed out that the capital hole was discovered by Lehman's competitors, but later the existence of such a large hole was contested. Of course, the SEC did not have such a large contingent of highly skilled staff, but they did have time and should have been aware of the market signals, as the defaults continued to rise in the subprime market.

Saturday 13 September 2008

Paulson and Geithner arrived at the New York Federal Bank at 7.00 am, where Paulson first spoke with Ken Lewis, who reported that Lehman's assets were worth even less than they had estimated the previous day. That confirmed Paulson in his view that Lewis did not really want to buy Lehman Brothers. That was followed by a conference call with Barclays' Chairman Marcus Agius and CEO John Varley, in which they expressed serious concerns about some of Lehman's assets, stating that Barclays would have to reject the problematic commercial mortgages, allegedly worth $50bn. They were also concerned about other investments, including undeveloped land and Chrysler bonds.

The meeting began at 9.00 am Paulson indicated that Barclays was the most likely buyer. The assessment for any decisions to be made was carried out by Brady Dougan of Credit Suisse, who reported that the real estate assets were worth between $17 and $20bn instead of the $41bn. Paulson was shocked by the disparity of $20bn between what Lehman said its assets were worth and 'their true value'.[16]

The meeting ended without any decisions being made. Paulson records that as he left the meeting and crossed the main lobby, he observed teams of lawyers, bankers, chief risk officers, specialists on lending and private equity, one for each of the banks represented, so that a 'war-room atmosphere' was developing. Geithner and Paulson decided to meet with Lloyd Blankfein (Goldman Sachs), Jamie Dimon (JP Morgan Chase) and John Thain (Merrill Lynch). Paulson knew that if Lehman Brothers collapsed, Merrill would be the next to go, as it had a weak balance sheet.

The next meeting with the Bank of America was fruitless, as their deal team had unearthed yet more bad assets, totalling between $65 and $67bn, including $33bn of commercial mortgages and real estate and $17bn residential mortgage-backed securities. They believed that Lehman's valuation of its own commercial real estate positions were too high. Lewis referred to a Lehman black hole of $66bn. These shortfalls would destroy Lehman's equity of $28.4bn. They were not prepared to fund any of these without government assistance to offset the undesirable assets, which effectively ruled them out as a contender. However, it is possible that Lewis did not want too close an examination of his own assets, after the purchase of Countrywide Financial Corp in January 2008, a deal which would come back to haunt him in later years. In May 2008, Lehman and Bank of America Strategic Ventures and Barclays Capital had jointly provided a $4.7bn loan for a leveraged buy-out of the Archstone-Smith REIT, together with Tishman Speyer, according to SEC filings. Prices started to fall soon after the deal was completed, making it difficult for the three banks to sell the equity, leaving them with the much of the bridge loan. Perhaps Lewis's involvement in the Archstone deal meant that he had more insight into the value of Lehman's commercial real estate investments than he cared to admit. Apparently, Lewis then began talks with Merrill Lynch about a potential merger, without telling anyone, having already sent his due diligence team home.[17]

On his way to the next meeting, Chris Flowers stopped Paulson and advised that AIG, the large insurance company, was, according to the company's own projections, going to run out of cash in ten days. Geithner and Paulson agreed to meet with Robert Willumstead (CEO of AIG) during the day. Paulson went to the next meeting with Geithner, Dimon and Blankfein to discuss a private sector consortium. He thought these CEOs would come up with a plan, and hoped that Barclays would play its part as a result of the various telephone calls which took place during the day. It all seemed so simple: Barclays focusing on the quality of Lehman's assets and the Financial Services Authority's expectation that the bank had an adequate capital plan in place. Then Bob Diamond suddenly raised the issue of a shareholder vote being required to approve the merger, which would take between 30 and 60 days to organize, and which would require the Federal Reserve to guarantee Lehman's trading book during that period. Geithner did not promise this, but stated that if Barclays came up with a plan, then the Federal Reserve would consider its options.

After that meeting, two other potential crises emerged. If Lehman Brothers did collapse, then Merrill Lynch would be the next in line. Paulson recommended that John Thain should look to Bank of America as its buyer and then returned to Barclays. By the middle of the evening with the CEOs, Barclays would not take the overvalued assets and wipe out Lehman's shareholders. A consortium of Wall Street firms would agree to lend up to $37bn to a special purpose vehicle to hold these assets. The firms would lose collectively some $10bn, but Barclays would also contribute some of its own shares to mitigate the loss to some extent.

Paulson left the New York Federal Reserve at 9.00 pm feeling that the day had been well spent. The solutions would be finalized the following day. Geithner's take on the day differed from Paulson's. He was satisfied that Merrill Lynch would be rescued by the Bank of America, and they were in talks about a deal. It appeared that Ken Lewis preferred Merrill's army of retail stockbrokers, which explained his lack of interest in Lehman. Geithner records the same optimism. 'Barclays looked like it was ready to move on Lehman. There were still some unanswered questions – and last-minute Fed assistance still seemed possible to me – but I thought we had a decent chance to avoid the trauma of a default.'[18]

Geithner begins his description of the weekend by referring to Hank Paulson's clear and consistent message in his private calls to the market: the Government would not subsidize the purchase of Lehman. Paulson's views were all over the media on Friday 12 September. Geithner reports major papers, news wires and business TV channels detailing the Government's unwillingness to use taxpayer funds to rescue Lehman, all citing sources close to Hank. However, Geithner's own view was, 'Whatever the merits of no-public money as a bargaining position, I didn't think it made much sense of public policy'.[19]

Sunday 14 September 2008

On his arrival at the New York Federal Reserve office, Paulson learnt that, following Barclays' board meeting at 7.15 am New York time, Diamond had discovered problems with its regulators, the Financial Services Authority (FSA). Less than an hour later, Diamond and Varley informed Geithner, Christopher Cox and Paulson that they had just discovered that the FSA would not support the deal. Barclays, Paulson pointed out, had assured them that they were keeping in touch with their regulators. Subsequently, Geithner and Cox conferred with Callum McCarthy, then the FSA chairman, who provided a cautious statement of the FSA's position. The FSA had neither approved nor disapproved of the deal, but required further due diligence, to see Barclays' plans to raise capital to fund the acquisition and a guarantee for Lehman's trading book during the shareholder vote. This caution apparently came as a surprise to Paulson and Geithner, but the FSA's statement of 20 January 2010 indicates that they should have expected the response they received. It sets out the communications between Varley and Hector Sants, CEO of the FSA, Callum McCarthy, FSA Chairman and Geithner on 10 and 11 September at that time when Barclays had not yet drawn up a proposal. Again on Friday 12 September Paulson had spoken to Alistair Darling, then UK Chancellor of the Exchequer, and he had advised that the US Treasury was considering two prospective buyers but that it was unclear whether any transaction could be structured without external support. In response, Darling had advised Paulson that no transaction with Barclays would be possible if the level of risk for Barclays was inappropriate. This was the same cautious message as the one both Sants and McCarthy had given to Geithner. Paulson observes that at that time he did not understand Darling's words as a 'red flag'. McCarthy's conversation with Geithner seems to have been more explicit.[20]

On Saturday 13 September discussions continued throughout the day between the FSA and Barclays over the possible terms of an acquisition. Neither the FSA nor the board wanted Barclays to take on the assets proposed by Lehman's for REIGlobal, though Barclays were advised by the US authorities that a consortium of banks would take on these assets. Barclays also wanted the continuation of the Primary Dealer Credit Facility (PDCF). During the following day, 14 September, the FRBNY expanded its access to its PDCF, but Lehman was told that it was ineligible to access it. The UK FSA was especially concerned that since Barclays was and is one of UK's clearing banks, it was important that it should not take on risks which might have a wider systemic impact on the UK financial system.

During the afternoon, the FSA discussed the importance of cooperation between the regulators if Lehman was going to go into Chapter 11. Later that evening Barclays advised that the Federal Reserve Bank of New York had asked Barclays to guarantee Lehman's financial obligations in the time leading up to the closing of the acquisition, a guarantee which would remain in place even if the deal did not go ahead. This was obviously a key point for the board, but Barclays sought confirmation that, given the size and nature of the interim guarantee, the UK Listing Rules would require it to obtain prior shareholder approval. There was a final telephone call at the end of 13 September, in which McCarthy inquired about the state of negotiations, but also said that no specific proposal had been brought to the FSA by Barclays, but if one was, it would raise very significant issues.

On Sunday 14 September 2008, the FSA spent most of the day discussing the possible acquisition, despite having no specific proposal from Barclays. The key issue was the guarantee, to be taken on by the regulatory authorities or a consortium of banks. If the assets were guaranteed, then Barclays would have to show a robust capital position and sufficient liquidity. In those circumstances, the FSA could in theory waive the requirement for prior shareholder approval, even though this would compromise one of the fundamental principles of the FSA's listing regime. At 1.00 pm (British Summer Time), McCarthy contacted Geithner and advised him of the FSA's concerns and the issue of shareholder approval under the Listing Rules. He also advised that such a waiver would be unprecedented.

Geithner then asked if an acquisition could be restructured in the available time, but McCarthy confirmed that this was unlikely since the FSA had not yet seen a Barclays' proposal. If that was the case, Geithner replied then the US would bring forward Chapter 11 plans. Bill Rutledge, Executive Vice President of Banking Supervision at the New York Federal Reserve telephoned Sants to ask what the FSA required for the Barclays bid to be successful, and was advised once more that Varley had not provided him with a proposal. By early afternoon, Barclays had completed its scenario analysis and had concluded that it could meet the FSA's capital requirements. The FSA continued to have doubts about Barclays' ability to retain the core Tier 1 capital ratio, and concluded that the aggregate level of risk could still be unacceptable.

Later that afternoon, Cox contacted McCarthy to discuss if there was any flexibility in waiving the Listing Rules; McCarthy explained again that no specific proposal from Barclays had been received, and that the problems about capital and funding remained. This was followed about an hour later by Varley's telephone call to Sants advising him that Barclays and the New York Federal Reserve that negotiations had ceased since an acceptable proposal could not be put together in time. He also confirmed that Lehman's long-term liquidity position was uncertain and that the Federal Reserve could not offer funding or liquidity support beyond the inauguration of the next President.

The FSA evidence indicates that their concerns about a Barclays bid had been shared with Geithner and Paulson and members of their team at an early stage. Alistair Darling had telephoned Paulson on Friday 12 September in the early afternoon, a call which Paulson says he did not see as a 'red flag' at the time. Later, by 14 September, he realized that what he had taken as 'understandable caution should have been taken as a clear warning'. In his account of his days as Chancellor, Darling recalls the discussion with Paulson as one in which Paulson told him that they had three options: (i) a wind-down; (ii) an industry consortium; or (iii) a straight take-over, of which he preferred the second. This is where Barclays came in. Darling states that: 'I made it clear that I was not against a takeover or investment by a British bank in principle but I needed to be certain that Barclays was not taking on more risk than it could manage.'[21] Darling further points out in his book, that there was no clear deal on the table. The Bank of America had pulled out of the purchase of Lehman, but the reasons for that were not given to the UK. Nor was any financial support being offered. The US wanted to override the requirement for a shareholder vote. On Sunday 14 September, Darling had another conversation with Paulson, by which time, Darling had concluded that, 'not only would we have to stand behind Barclays ... but we would be overriding the rights of millions of shareholders who might get cleaned out'. He added that 'there was no deal on the table ... and we could not stand behind a US bank that was clearly in trouble'. This telephone call settled the matter for Paulson, who had been exasperated by conversations with Callum McCarthy, who had raised countless objections but had not said 'No' unequivocally. Darling notes that in his conversations with John Varley, he 'got the impression that the board was divided over whether to buy Lehman, given the risks involved and the lack of US government support'. John Varley told Darling that he would understand, if we decided not to support the deal, and if that was the case, 'Barclays would not proceed.'[22]

Diamond must have been aware of the Listing Rules and the requirement for a shareholder vote, and if he had decided to overlook it, then his team of advisers would have reminded him. The fact is that Diamond did not have a plan of any kind and did not produce even an outline proposal during the weekend. Thus the possibility of Barclays rescuing Lehman Brothers disappeared with a series of telephone calls when Geithner contacted Varley and Diamond after the Barclays board meeting at 7.15 am New York time, and were told that the FSA refused to approve the deal. They claimed not to understand why. Geithner and Cox then spoke separately with Callum McCarthy and once again the FSA said that it neither approved nor disproved the merger, but needed more due diligence. But Barclays' plans to raise more capital and the shareholder vote all meant delay, and time was simply not available. The final decision to allow Lehman to collapse had to be taken. Lehman could not open for business unless it had a major financial institution to guarantee its trades. The die was cast.

That only left the decision to be taken by Lehman's board, but even that was problematic. Lehman was in no hurry to file, and Cox, the SEC's Chairman, was working on a press release to advise and reassure Lehman's broker-dealer customers that they would be protected. It fell to Paulson to ensure that Lehman filed for bankruptcy. Paulson comments: 'I understood that it was unusual and awkward for a regulator to push a private sector firm to declare bankruptcy' but it was necessary 'for the good of the rest of the system'.[23] Finally, Cox, along with Thomas Baxter, General Counsel of the New York Federal Bank, together with other staffers from the SEC and the Federal Reserve, called just after 8.00 pm to reiterate that there would be no government rescue. A late-night conference call confirmed that Lehman would shortly file for bankruptcy under Chapter 11, but that Lehman Inc. would be kept afloat by the Federal Reserve. The FSA asked if this funding would be kept available for Lehman Brothers International (Europe), but this was refused. Lehman did not file for bankruptcy until 1.45 am on Monday 15 September 2008. LBIE, Lehman Brothers Ltd, Lehman Brothers Holdings plc and LIB UK Holdings Ltd entered into administration in the UK, and Lehman into Chapter 11 at 7.56 am on that day.

The Examiner notes that on 14 September the FRBNY made it clear that it would no longer keep on funding Lehman. On the same day, the FRBNY both broadened the collateral eligible to be pledged at the PDCF but excluded Lehman from using it to continue its normal operations, perhaps to ensure that the firm did file for bankruptcy immediately. The FRBNY advised Lehman it would provide up to two weeks' overnight secured funding through the PDCF to allow LBI to have an orderly liquidation.[24]

As far as Lehman was concerned, the bankruptcy affected about 8,000 subsidiaries and affiliates, with $600bn in assets and liabilities, over 100,000 creditors, and about 26,000 employees, triggering defaults in many derivatives contracts. It led to 80 insolvency proceedings of its subsidiaries in 18 countries.

It had, of course, much wider ramifications through the entire global financial system.

One day later, on 16 September 2008, the Federal Reserve Bank announced that it would step in to save AIG with an $85bn loan collateralized by AIG's assets, to be repaid with the proceeds of the sale of those assets. That gave the Government a 79.9 per cent equity interest in AIG.

Many questions have been asked about that infamous September weekend. They range from whether or not Lehman had a huge capital 'hole', Lehman's over-valuation of its real estate assets, to whether or not the bank was solvent, should the Federal Reserve have bailed out Lehman, was Alistair Darling, the UK Chancellor of the Exchequer, alone in blocking the Barclays deal, and was it true that the Federal Reserve did not have the legal powers to rescue Lehman? The issues of Lehman's valuation of its assets and its capital were thoroughly explored by the Examiner's Report, the subject of the following chapter.

Was the Barclays' deal a real deal?

Diamond failed to produce a detailed proposal during the whole weekend. But given the fact that the weakness of Lehman Brothers was known, and that many in the market expected Lehman to be next after the collapse of Bear Stearns and the extent of the losses announced in June and September, he would surely have concluded that the chances of buying Lehman Brothers might be extremely high. One insider stated that there was never any intention to acquire Lehman Brothers, but only to cherry-pick assets, whilst avoiding some of the worst business risks that would inevitably have followed if they had.[25]

Diamond might well have shown greater interest to the Federal Reserve than he actually felt in order to give him good standing when some of the options provided a partial way out. That is, of course exactly what happened. Just two days after Lehman filed for Chapter 11, Barclays announced that it would acquire Lehman Brothers North American investment banking and capital markets operations and supporting infrastructure. That included Lehman Brothers' New York headquarters and two data centres, all for $1.75bn, a price which the *New York Times* described as a 'fire sale' and which was much less than Lehman expected.

Lawyers acting for the Lehman estate claimed that Barclays had improperly reaped an $11bn windfall from the deal by secretly negotiating a discount for Lehman's North American operations, and pursued this case through the courts.

In his 103-page decision Judge James Peck of the United States Bankruptcy Court in Manhattan rejected the claims. 'The sale process may have been imperfect but it was still adequate under the exceptional circumstances of Lehman's collapse'. Judge Peck also rejected a separate claim by a federal trustee assigned to the Lehman case, that Barclays owed his office about $7bn. Lehman had sought to amend the sales order that Judge Peck had approved just days after the investment bank filed for bankruptcy. The Lehman estate contended that Barclays benefited from a $5bn discount that they had been given during the completion of the sale. The judge rejected their arguments, stating that these new facts 'do not change the essence of the approval process and would not have made any difference to the court's ruling'. He concluded that the purchase of Lehman's investment bank had been done in good faith, and denied Lehman's request to recover an alleged $11bn windfall. He added that the perception at the time was that the

> transfer to Barclays benefitted all interested parties, mitigated systemic risk and helped to save everyone of us from an even greater calamity. Nothing in the voluminous record presented to the court in these protracted proceedings has done anything to change that undoubtedly correct perception.[26]

The case took several months in the courts and was finally decided on 22 February 2011.

Could Lehman have been saved?

Before moving on to the question of why the Federal Reserve allowed Lehman to fail, it is worth considering the role of the Federal Reserve, together with the Treasury, prior to the fateful weekend. Thomas Baxter in his evidence to the FCIC, stated that after the Bear Stearns episode in March 2008, it was clear that some primary dealers were in difficulties. The Federal Reserve introduced the Term Securities Lending Facility (TSLF) to help primary dealers with their access to term funding and collateral and introduced the PDCF at the same time. As part of the process,

> the New York Fed sent small teams of two monitors into each of the four remaining investment banks-something it had never done before ... Let me again emphasize that we were not intending to conduct supervisory activities with our personnel, nor were we attempting to displace the SEC, the primary regulator of the investment banks. To the contrary, we were acting as a potential

lender to these potential borrowers and we wanted to know our new borrowers better.[27]

On 10 March, Geithner advised the Federal Open Market Committee (FOMC) that, 'If we have evidence, directly or through the supervisors, of some material erosion in the financial business of those institutions from a solvency perspective, that will cause us to reflect on what we do with those institutions going forward.' But perhaps to guard the Federal Reserve against any criticism, he added, 'I wish it were the case that we could condition this step on a change in the regulatory regime that would give us that capacity.'[28]

The role was strictly limited and set out by Vice Chairman Donald Kohn in his testimony before the Subcommittee on Securities, Insurance and Investment on 19 June 2008. The on-site monitors were expected to:

> ensure that any credit that the Fed extended to the investment banks would be repaid and to ensure that the investment banks did not become too dependent upon Federal Reserve Credit and would continue to work on improving their liquidity positions and financial strength.

A few weeks after that testimony, on 7 July 2008, the SEC and the Federal Reserve signed a Memorandum of Understanding which agreed on information-sharing and cooperation to assist the SEC in its supervision and the Federal Reserves to carry out their responsibilities. The SEC and the Federal Reserve would share information and analysis of the financial condition, risk management, internal controls, capital, liquidity and funding resources of those firms. Mr Angulo reported, 'We have accessed information from these companies through the PDCF and TSLF, so we'll share that with the SEC.'[29]

If effective, the monitoring should surely have revealed the serious weaknesses in Lehman's position, and perhaps have enabled Lehman to alter its strategy even at that late stage. No doubt the efforts Lehman made did improve its position to some extent, although Baxter insisted in his statement that 'at no time, however, did any one at the New York Federal Reserve believe that Lehman had sufficient liquidity to withstand what was to come in September', which included the decision to take Fannie Mae and Freddie Mac into conservatorship on 8 September. Both supervisors and monitors seemed to limit their role to that of observing a slow-motion train crash, rather than taking any corrective or enforcement actions to prevent it at an earlier stage. The actions of the Treasury and the Federal Reserve Bank of New York after the collapse of Bear Stearns, and especially over the summer months, repay close scrutiny.

Lehman pre-announced its first loss since going public on 9 June 2008. Yet the on-site monitor, Kirsten Harlow stated in her email to several officials that there was 'no adverse information on liquidity, novations, terminations or ability to fund either secured or unsecured balances has been reported'. She also reported that Lehman had taken steps to improve liquidity, increasing its liquidity pool to $45bn.[30] Two days later, she reported that there were trading issues with four financial institutions, including Santander, Westpac and the Commonwealth Bank of Australia, and that Citi had decided to reduce clearing/settlement lines to Lehman from about $20bn to around $10–12bn. The FRBNY Senior Adviser in the Division of Banking Supervision and Regulation, Tim Clark, replied: 'this is not sounding good at all'. Of course it was not; but nothing else happened.

Later in June, the FRBNY undertook liquidity stress testing of Lehman Brothers, which led to the conclusion that 'Lehman's weak liquidity position was driven by its relatively large exposure to overnight CP [commercial paper] combined with overnight secured funding of less liquid assets and that any downgrade would result in significant collateral calls'. The report concluded that Lehman should improve its liquidity position by $15bn.[31] In July, Pat Parkinson, Deputy Director of the Research and Statistics Division commented that although other firms had pulled their Repo lines from Lehman, 'there are other such reports but overall LB's funding seems to have held up thus far. Lots of anxiety nonetheless.' During August, New York Federal Reserve officials begin to consider how to deal with a potential Lehman failure.

Throughout June, July and August, Treasury officials worked on various scenarios to clarify the extent of Lehman's over-the-counter (OTC) derivatives and tri-party repos. These activities took place in the summer of 2008, a full year after Standard & Poor's and Moody's downgraded securities backed by subprime mortgages, placing a large number on credit watch. Two Bear Stearns hedge funds involving CDOs collapsed, Countrywide announced a large increase in subprime mortgage defaults and was bought by Bank of America in January 2008, against a background of rising defaults and house prices continuing to fall. The point is that against that background, the Federal Reserve and the Treasury should already have had sufficient information about the risks Lehman Brothers was taking, and if they had acted on it in 2007 and 2008, then perhaps the company could have been rescued.

In the months before Lehman collapsed, there was much discussion between regulators and Treasury officials, focusing on Lehman after the Bear Stearns debacle. On 6 February 2008, Erik Sirri, Director of Markets and Trading at the SEC, received a risk management review of the CSEs from the SEC's Office of

Prudential Supervision and Risk Analysis. This was based on discussions with senior risk managers over a four-week period. They claimed that they were reducing risks and hedge positions as the economy continued to slow down, but the underlying risks were increasing, with fewer ways of offsetting losses. Mounting concerns were expressed about monolines and credit default swaps, and what would happen in the case of a default. Lehman had raised its risk appetite limit to $4bn and its firm-wide VaR limit to $150m. All of this information was gathered, but it appears that no further action was taken, nor was it shared with the Federal Reserve and the Treasury at this stage.

In May 2008, an email to Stephen Shafran, one of Paulson's former colleagues at Goldman Sachs and then senior adviser to Paulson at the Treasury, discussed the possibility of discovering more about their tri-party repos and OTC derivatives. Treasury officials planned to ask Lehman about their OTC derivatives positions directly, but also to set up the private-sector default management group, and ask them to advise on the information required from a troubled dealer to assess the potential impact of close-out of a dealer's OTC derivatives books on its counterparties and on the financial markets, and to assess the potential risks and returns for an acquirer.[32] Again, it is not clear if the requested information was ever given, or what use was made of the information in, for example, assessing the risks Lehman faced.

On 17 June 2008, Donald Kohn, as a board member of the Federal Reserve Bank, proposed that both the TSLF and PDCF should be extended until the end of the year, and that the matter should be discussed with the Federal Open Market Committee.[33] This was agreed by the FOMC. In July, the New York Fed, via further email exchanges, discussed the possibility of providing liquidity to Lehman through the PDCF function.

The plan was reiterated in July when Geithner circulated a paper in which the PDCF would step in if a dealer should lose the confidence of its investors or the clearing bank, both by providing overnight financing and then also by replacing the credit provided by the clearing bank during the day. By such actions the Federal Reserve would hope to support market confidence in the dealer and by continuing the smooth function of the market, in the tri-party repo itself. Information on Lehman's repo collateral was finally received, and its exposure was $236.4bn.[34] Bill Dudley of the New York Federal Reserve put the 'good bank, bad bank' idea on the table, but that was not pursued. The use of the PDCF was rejected partly because there were doubts about its legality, and also because Lehman's clearing bank would be aware very quickly that confidence in the bank had been lost, and would refuse to unwind the previous night's repos, thus creating more problems. By 19 August staff at the New York Federal Reserve still had not received sufficient information, and were reluctant to dig deeper, as the meeting with Lehman 'caused a stir ... and we had to assure them that our questions were not institution specific'.[35] On 9 September, an email from Meg McConnell requested a note for Geithner on 'what's different and what's the same' (Bear Stearns and Lehman) for his discussion with Bernanke later that day. Lehman's tri-party repo book was much larger than Bear's, and investor concentration was high with the top-10 counterparties providing 80 per cent of the financing. These estimates were based on the assumption that Lehman itself had an accurate assessment of its assets, as was later revealed in the Examiner's Report. All of this should have been known, assessed and action taken months, if not a year, earlier. But even then, 2007 was hardly a tranquil year for the markets.

It was marred by the 'panic of 2007'. Between June and September, a whole series of events, including Bear Stearns' announcement that two of its funds were liquidated even though the firm had spent $3.2bn in bailing them out, BNP Paribas suspended three investment funds, rising defaults hit Countrywide and its share prices plunged amid fears of bankruptcy. The Federal Reserve Board reduced the primary credit rate to 5.75 per cent, as well as increasing the borrowing term to 30 days. The FOMC issued a press release observing that the 'downside risks to growth have increased considerably'. As the foreclosures on subprime mortgages continued to rise, home loan providers filed for Chapter 11 bankruptcy, fears mounted, leading to panic as banks stopped lending to each other. That was only the beginning of the panic in the markets. Worse was to come in 2008.

But did the Federal Reserve and the Treasury understand the full extent of the collapsing valuations? Their own valuations seemed to be too conservative. A relatively new index, the ABX group, provided a respected measure of the collapsing valuations in the subprime mortgage market. The ABX.HE family of indices are based on credit default swaps (CDS) written on US home equity loans (HEL MBS), tracking the price of credit default insurance on a basket of such deals. Declining risk appetite and rising concerns were a significant cause of the collapse in ABX prices from the summer of 2007 onwards. The ABX began 2007 at 153 basis points (bps), close to the historical average. By March, the spread was 552 bps, 669 bps by, 1,738 bps by the end of July and continued its steady rise throughout the second half of 2008 until it reached 9,000 by the end of the year. The asset-backed commercial paper (ABCP) market fell apart in the late summer of 2007. Investors expect to be able to access their funds on demand at par value, but even limited concerns about risk can give rise to a flight from the market. The ABCP market grew slightly in the first half of 2007 to almost $1.2 trillion, but fell by $190bn in August and then fell another $160bn during the rest of 2007, when the lack of any good news continued to drag the asset-backed markets and the financial institutions down.

It was not only the markets for MBSs that were affected in 2007. Asset-backed commercial paper (ABCP) contracted by some $350bn in the last five months of 2007. It is not entirely clear why this happened, although mortgage originators had used ABCP to bridge the financing gap between origination and securitization and the write-downs on mortgage-related assets made investors wary. The country was sliding into a recession, so assets depending on a firm's performance, such as credit card receivables, auto loans and leases, student loans, trade receivables and equipment loans and leases, were at risk as well. Between early 2005 and July 2007, the amount outstanding had doubled, reaching $1.2 trillion, and debtors extended the maturity of their borrowings so that investors had to wait for repayment. As the market collapsed, some conduits, special purpose vehicles usually set up by banks to purchase and hold financial assets by selling asset-backed commercial paper to investors, such as the money market mutual funds (MMMFs) were affected as well. Investors became increasingly unwilling to roll over ABCPs, especially at maturities of more than a few days. As the sponsors of the programmes, the banks, also provided liquidity, investors became increasingly worried that banks would be unable to support them, so they began to withdraw their funds from MMMFs invested in CP and turned to those only invested in US Treasuries. The investors were particularly spooked by an announcement by a large overseas bank that it could not value the ABCP held by some of its money market funds and, as a result, had suspended redemptions from those funds. Then the banks, in order to protect their liquidity and balance sheets, became less willing to lend to others, including other banks, thus exerting considerable pressures on both overnight and term interbank funding. On 10 August 2007, the Federal Reserve provided liquidity by temporary open market purchases, thus heading off that particular potential crisis. The Federal Reserve acted promptly, but in the role of a fire fighter: once that fire was put out, another would spring up, demanding attention and action. In fact, the fires were only smouldering, ready to burst into flames again at any moment.

The point here is that it might have been possible to save Lehman, if the SEC through its CSE programme had carried out its role in supervising the investment banks; if the Federal Reserve and the SEC had communicated about the state of Lehman, and if the Federal Reserve and the Treasury had been fully aware of the state of the markets and the implications for the value of Lehman's 'assets'. Some of the proposals outlined above might have worked a few months earlier, but by mid-2008, it was too late.

Even as late as August 2008, it was clear that Treasury and Federal Reserve officials had little knowledge of Lehman, and although they had a 'game plan', it was not clear that it could be activated on the basis of the information they then had. On 8 August, Parkinson set out the plan in an email to Steve Shafran:

1. Identify activities of the firm whose liquidation (Chapter 11) could have a significant effect on financial markets and the economy.

2. Gather additional information about those activities so as to assess more accurately the potential liquidation to have such an effect.

3. Then to identify actions that the firm, its counterparties or the government could take to mitigate the risk.

4. Most likely causes of systemic risk are tri-party repo borrowings and OTC derivatives. But are there other activities?

5. We have given considerable thought to what might be done to avoid a fire sale of tri-party repos but the risks are risks of moral hazard, Fed/taxpayer, but we are still at the early stages of assessing the potential systemic risk from the close-out of OTC derivatives.

He had also suggested that they should use an industry group to obtain more information about Lehman. This received a cool reception from Steve Shafran:

My worry is that while this would make sense in a less stressed market, that the timing right now is problematic. If we ask, will we see anything in time to deal with some of the immediate issues that concern us?

Further emails from Patrick Parkinson to Steve Shafran and others on 19 August pointed out: 'We keep coming up against same quandary (lack of knowledge) . . . I still think it is worth engaging with the industry group'. Others who had met with Lehman advised that they 'had not really got much new information that will push the agenda forward'. He asked for a more detailed game plan. Parkinson forwarded Shafran's email to William Brodows, banking supervision officer at the New York Federal Reserve, who agreed that asking for an industry group would be 'less provocative' than gathering information from a single firm. Parkinson then forwarded Brodows' reply to Shafran, and Paulson eventually agreed to Parkinson's ideas on 28 August: 'Can confirm that his [Paulson's] preference is to do this in a way that minimizes disruption and concerns.'

It is clear from these emails that neither the Treasury nor the Federal Reserve had any idea of the size of the problems they were about to face. On 5 September,

Parkinson circulated a draft letter requesting information from Lehman's CEO. Geithner would ask Gerald Corrigan, the former New York Federal Reserve President, who had co-chaired the Counterparty Risk Management Policy Group, to form an industry group to advise on the information required from a troubled investment bank. New York Federal officials were also 'very reluctant' to request copies of the master agreement that would shed light on Lehman's derivatives counterparties, because that request would send a 'huge negative signal'. All of these activities were wasted.

Geithner, Paulson and their officials went into September knowing little about the state of Lehman's finances and were ill-prepared to handle what happened in September. The FCIC report comments that, 'as they now realised, regulators did not know nearly enough about over-the-counter activities at Lehman and other investment banks'. Investment banks only disclosed the total number of OTC derivative contracts, the total exposure and their estimated market value, but not the terms of the contracts or the counterparties. 'There was no way of knowing who would be owed how much and when payments would have to be made.'[36] All of this means that bailing out Lehman would have been a far more costly exercise than Geithner and Paulson realized.

Was there any intention to bail-out Lehman?

Geithner argues that the Federal Reserve was unable to bail out Lehman. Even at the time, this claim seems difficult to believe, especially in the light of the AIG rescue on 16 September. In his book, Geithner states that, 'in the end, I am confident that the Fed would have helped finance a deal with a willing buyer . . . But the Fed assistance would not have diminished the risk to Barclays, much less the British requirement for a shareholder vote.' He adds,

> We had shown that we could push the boundaries of our authority to take some modest risk, but the Fed's emergency authorities limited how much risk we could take; we were the central bank of the United States and we weren't going to defy our own governing law to lend into a run.[37]

Giving testimony before the Financial Crisis Inquiry Commission on 2 September 2010, Bernanke, Chairman of the Federal Reserve, admitted that the decision to allow Lehman to fail had been taken for practical and legal reasons. According to Bernanke, the Federal Reserve was not allowed to lend without a reasonable expectation of repayment. The FCIC report also quotes from an email sent by Bernanke on the afternoon of Sunday 14 September 2008, in which he indicated to Governor Warsh that more that $12bn in capital assistance would have been required to prevent Lehman's failure. The email read: 'In case I am asked: how much capital injection would have been needed to LEH as a going concern? I gather $12bn or so from the private guys together with Fed liquidity support was not enough.'[38] What is odd about that email is that Bernanke seems to be so out of touch with what was happening.

Furthermore, the reference to the Federal Reserve's alleged lack of powers was not upheld by Chairman Bernanke when it came to his testimony to the FCIC, following testimony from a Fed official, who stated that it was only necessary for the Federal Reserve's Board of Governors to have adopted an appropriate resolution. There were other ways of preventing the collapse. The White House could have invoked the International Emergency Economic Powers Act 1977. It would have been possible for President Bush to have ordered whatever was required, such as guaranteeing Lehman's trades or financing the acquisition of Lehman's toxic assets.[39] Wide powers are granted to the President, provided the international emergency is international in scope and is also a threat to national security. Since President Bush gave full support to Hank Paulson, had he requested executive action, then it might well have been forthcoming. Such a request would have required Paulson and others to understand the international dimensions of the crisis, however, and it appears that they did not.

As the FCIC pointed out, this was quite different from the evidence Bernanke had given to the Senate Banking Committee in 2008. Then, he had said:

> The failure of Lehman posed risks. But the troubles at Lehman had been well known for some time, and investors clearly recognized – as evidenced, for example, by the high cost of insuring Lehman's debts in the market for credit default swaps – that the failure of the firm was a significant possibility. Thus we judged that investors and counterparties had had time to take precautionary measures.[40]

It is hard to see how that belief could have been sustained at the same time precisely as the extent of the troubles at AIG emerged over the weekend. If that was indeed the judgement made then, it was one that was not based on the realities of the situation at that time.[41]

What was said at the time of the rescue of Bear Stearns was even more relevant to the collapse of Lehman Brothers. Then Christopher Cox stated that the Fed's

> decision to provide funding for Bear Stearns through JP Morgan was made because – as you have heard Chairman Bernanke testify – Bear's extensive

participation in a range of critical markets meant that a chaotic unwinding of its positions not only could have cast doubt on the stability of thousands of the firm's counterparties, but also created additional pressures well beyond the financial system through the real economy.[42]

The press release issued by the Board of Governors of the Federal Reserve System, regarding Bear Stearns, JP Morgan Chase and Maiden Lane LLC, set out the powers of the Federal Reserve in such situations, when the loan to Maiden Lane LLC was extended 'under the authority of Section 13(3) of the Federal Reserve Act, which permitted the Board in unusual and exigent circumstances, to authorize Reserve Banks to extend credit to individuals, partnerships and corporations.' The impact of allowing Bear Stearns to fail, as described by Christopher Cox, applied even more so to the impact of the collapse of Lehman.

Jim Wilkinson, chief of staff at the Treasury, emailed Michele Davis, assistant secretary for public affairs at the Treasury, on 9 September 2008 at 5.20 pm: 'We need to talk . . . I just can't stomach us bailing out Lehman. Will be horrible in the press don't u think?' Just some twenty minutes previously Paulson had convened a telephone call with Cox, Geithner, Bernanke and Treasury staff to 'deal with a possible Lehman bankruptcy'. The contents of the telephone call were not revealed at the time, but in his autobiography, Paulson said: 'Lehman has been hanging like a dead weight in the market.' They discussed ways to forestall a Lehman collapse. Geithner was still thinking in terms of the 1998 rescue of Long Term Capital Management. Doing something similar would involve getting Lewis, CEO of Bank of America, interested, allowing him to buy what he wanted and convincing an industry consortium to take on the remaining assets. 'Of course, the alternative, Lehman's demise was far worse.'[43]

On Thursday 11 September, Federal Reserve officials, including Jamie Anderson, circulated a document to Tobias Adrian, Beverly Hirtle and Michael Schussler, proposing that a representative group of Lehman counterparties and creditors should make plans in the event of a bankruptcy filing by Lehman. The purpose of the group was to reach agreement by the members of the group to hold off fully exercising their contractual rights to close out their trades with the defaulting counterparty. The document set out three possibilities for the weekend: first, a single institution taking over; second, a consortium taking over; and third, bankruptcy. It emphasized:

> unless we have credible bankruptcy plan our negotiating position, the subsidy in the liquidity consortium option will be weak. Consequently planning for bankruptcy will reduce some of the expected costs of bankruptcy and

externalities imposed on the financial system as a whole, and make it a more viable alternative.

The group would also be required to review their options for agreement on netting offsetting agreements, reaching 'common valuations' for contracts post-bankruptcy.

This does not read as though it is a contingency plan, but rather as if it was designed to try and ensure the bankruptcy should go as smoothly as possible. The outcome was to be a public statement of the framework to which the members would have agreed, to be issued on the Sunday evening. The document also refers to the timing, stating that

> contingent on the anticipated bankruptcy filing by Lehman, on Friday evening, after the markets have closed, issue invitations to the chief risk officers of the member firms. The meeting would convene at 9 a.m. on Saturday at the FRBNY, and continue through to the Sunday evening.

Their only hope of avoiding bankruptcy was to find a buyer, but many of the officials involved realized that it was unlikely that a buyer would be found. A bail-out was not on the cards. On 10 September 2008, the Senior Vice President of the New York Federal Reserve, Patricia Mosser, wrote that the

> reputation cost of [another bail-out] is too high. If the Fed agrees to another equity investment, it signals that everything the Fed did in March in terms of temporary liquidity backstops is useless. Horrible precedent; in the long run MUCH worse than Option 3, bankruptcy, would be a mess on every level, but fixes the moral hazard problem.[44]

That was not the view of all the Federal Reserve Banks' officials, according to a recent article in the *New York Times*:

> [Some] believed that the government had the authority to throw Lehman Brothers a lifeline, even if the bank was nearly broke ... we had lawyers joined at our hips, and they were very helpful at framing the issues. But they never said we couldn't do it ... It was a policy and political decision, not a legal decision.

The article adds that members of the teams said that Lehman had considerable assets that were liquid and easy to value, such as US Treasury securities. The question was Lehman's illiquid assets – primarily a real estate portfolio that Lehman had recently valued at $50bn. By Lehman's account, the firm had a surplus of assets over liabilities of $28.4 bn. While the Fed team did not come up with a precise value for Lehman's illiquid assets, it provided a range that was far more generous in its valuations than the private sector had been.

> It appears that neither Geithner nor Paulson were informed about such research, with the suggestion in the article that they were both distracted by AIG. The legal position was clear that in 2008, the Federal Reserve Bank Act provided that 'in unusual and exigent circumstances' the FRB could lend to any institution as long as the loan was 'secured to the satisfaction of the Federal Reserve Bank' (Section 13–3). For the FRB that meant that a firm must be solvent and have adequate collateral to lend against it, and that was the responsibility of the NYFRB, some of whom thought that was the case. It is noteworthy that the legal argument only emerged later on October 7th after criticisms of the decision emerged that Chairman Bernanke stated that, Neither the Treasury nor the Federal Reserve had the authority to commit public money in that way.[45]

In his autobiography, Paulson made his position clear: 'Moral hazard is not something I take lightly . . . I did not want to suggest that we were powerless. I could not say, for example, that we did not have the statutory authority to save Lehman-even though it was true.' If he had said that, then that would have been the end of Morgan Stanley, which was already under an assault that would dramatically intensify in the coming days.[46] He was repeating what he had said at a White House press conference on 15 September 2008, when he said that 'he never once considered it appropriate to put taxpayer money on the line in resolving Lehman Brothers'.[47] Michele Davis said that Henry Paulson and officials at the Treasury were consumed with trying to find a solution, but had little time to react without the necessary authority. 'You had this outpouring of stuff from the Hill of: No bail-outs, No government money, No nothing.'[48]

Later, Harvey Miller was to comment that 'Post the Bear Stearns bail-out, he was subjected to such criticism both from various Congressional personnel, from conservative groups, that he was scarred'.[49] It is interesting to note that, whereas a Parliamentary form of government involves the selection of Cabinet ministers from members of the ruling party, who have learnt to handle the political flak, this is much more difficult for Cabinet ministers who are drawn from senior business positions, but lacking political experience to take such hard public decisions.

It is worth noting also that analyses of the fateful weekend differ:

> Bankers involved said that they did not recall Paulson talking about Lehman's impaired collateral . . . Buyers walked away for one reason: because they could not get the kind of government backing that facilitated the Bear Stearns deal.[50]

Paulson did, however, admit that he could have seen the subprime problem coming earlier, but that did not mean that he would have done anything differently. The kind of pressure he was under concerning 'moral hazard' is clear from an article in *Forbes* on 15 September 2008 in which Greenspan cautioned Washington against viewing the Fed as a 'magical piggy bank'. William Poole, former President of the Federal Reserve Bank of St Louis, regarded Lehman's failure and the forced sale of Merrill Lynch as a price worth paying: 'If there had been Federal Reserve money, the issue would have been raised immediately with AIG and Washington Mutual'. No doubt they were shattered by 16 September's announcement of the 'seizure' of AIG.

Tom Russo, General Counsel for Lehman Brothers, had 'a lengthy discussion with a room full of government officials during the Lehman weekend', trying to make it clear what the ramifications of letting Lehman go would be. His input clearly had little impact.[51] On 15 October 2008, Russo heard a speech given by Chairman Bernanke, who stated that Hank Paulson had

> never once considered that it was appropriate to put taxpayer's money on the line with ... in resolving Lehman's Brothers' 'huge hole on its balance sheet' that he realized the inconsistencies in the statements made about the alleged lack of legal powers. He also referred to the Government's lack of legal power, but if Paulson had never considered such a move, how did concerns about legal power enter into the conversation?[52]

Russo then argued that most lawyers believed that

> any court would have deferred to the Federal Reserve on an interpretation of its statutory powers, especially given the unprecedented circumstances ... The standard set forth in the applicable provision, Section 13(3) of the Federal Reserve Act, refers to 'unusual and exigent circumstances' ... and the lending standard was 'secured to the satisfaction of the Federal Reserve Bank'.[53]

The lack of powers has been given by Geithner, Paulson and Bernanke as the reason for letting Lehman go, but this appears to be a post hoc view. At any rate, Russo argue, most bail-outs, that is, infusions of capital into institutions holding assets that are permanently valueless – are limited and rare. Most often what happened was that the Fed lent against assets that would ultimately pay off but that no one wanted to buy or lend at the time. 'With mark-to-market accounting, institutions had to treat those holdings as losses but the real problem was that they were not liquid, not that they didn't have value as a credit matter'. The reason given by the Federal Reserve and others was that Lehman had a 'capital hole' which he denied existed.[54]

Were the effects of allowing Lehman to fail known at the time?

No doubt with so many problems on their hands in September 2008, neither the Federal Reserve, including the Federal Open Market Committee and the New York Federal Reserve, nor the Treasury looked beyond the domestic scene at the global implications of allowing Lehman to fail. Even at that late stage, too many players failed to understand that the root of their problems was the nature and extent of subprime mortgages, even as foreclosures and delinquencies continued to rise and the markets failed to respond to the actions the Treasury and Federal Reserve had already taken.

Rita Proctor, assistant to the Chairman, provided him with an update on the state of the market to prepare him for a conference call on 11 September 2008. The report was gloomy enough, yet still did not set out the full extent of the damage that the collapse of Lehman would cause both nationally and internationally. The update stated that Lehman's share price had declined 45 per cent to $4 in the pre-open, and its CDS price widened 200 basis points to 775 as market participants voiced concern over the viability of Lehman as a going concern. Moody's also cited the market's 'crisis of confidence' concern with Lehman to suggest that ratings downgrades could come quickly unless there was swift progress to shoring up Lehman's capital base.

The report also indicated that if Lehman failed, it would be much more difficult to unwind their positions, since at the end of 2007, Lehman's net positions in derivatives were about $54 bn, or nearly twice as much as Bear Stearns. A worst-case scenario for Lehman Brothers would push more hedge funds towards their NAV (net asset value) triggers.[55] Although the email stated that

> funding from money funds [*sic*] are likely to be adversely impacted by a ratings downgrade [for Lehman]. We've spoken with several large money funds since Lehman's preannouncement and received somewhat mixed reports in terms of new shifts in providing funding to Lehman. Of the funds that we have spoken with thus far, all but one were continuing to roll overnight repo for steady amounts.

There was no warning that the damage done by the Lehman bankruptcy would actually 'break the buck' of a large money market fund, although the end of the email does refer to 'pressures in the funding markets'. The rest of the email is redacted.

The recently released full minutes of Federal Open Market Committee (FOMC) meetings suggest that in the early months of 2008, Federal Reserve officials did not seem to be aware that the country had already entered into recession, but at an emergency meeting, officials concluded that 'substantial additional policy easing in the near term might well be necessary'. Bernanke and Mrs Yellen took a more pessimistic view, which was not shared by all of their colleagues. Richard Fisher of Dallas had discussed the state of the economy with a cross-section of 30 CEOs in his district, and found that none of them 'see us going into recession.' A few days later, on 21 January, the Federal Reserve cut the benchmark interest rate by 75 basis points, the largest cut in over two decades.

By 30 January 2008, the FOMC cut the benchmark rate by a further 50 basis points, to 3 per cent. The accompanying statement read: 'financial markets remain under considerable stress, and credit has tightened further for some businesses and households.' Anxiety about inflation was a dominant theme in the discussions in the Committee, but then inflation is part of the Federal Reserve's mandate. Bernanke, four days after the rescue of Bear Stearns, commented that

> I think we are getting to the point where the Federal Reserve's tools, both its liquidity tools and its interest rate tools, are not by themselves sufficient to resolve our troubles. More help, more activity, from Congress and the Administration to address housing issues, for example, would be desirable.[56]

That help was not forthcoming until it was too late.

William Dudley, Vice President of the Markets Group at the New York Fed, gave his analysis of the Bear Stearns rescue, which was that 'an old fashioned bank run is what really led to Bear Stearn's demise . . . in this case, it was customers moving their business elsewhere and investors' unwillingness to roll over their collateralized loans to Bear'.[57] His description of the market turmoil suggests that he was well aware of the extent of the disruption in the markets. But Geithner's remarks after Bear Stearns are interesting: 'People who know this stuff quite well, who are reasonably calm people, say "This is possibly the worst financial crisis in 50 years, and the most challenging set of pressures facing the central bank in 20 or 30 years" . . . It is no surprise that we disagree.'[58] Earlier in the meeting, he said: 'The hardest thing in this balance now is to make sure that it's a backstop that's so attractive that they come.'[59]

The transcripts of the meetings of the FOMC convey the impression that the rescue of Bear Stearns, the opening of the Primary Dealer Credit Facility and a further cut in interest rates to 2 per cent indicate that members and officials considered that sufficient actions had been taken to arrest the crisis and stave off recession. The FOMC even predicted modest growth during the rest of 2008, and faster growth in 2009. The April meeting was dominated by concerns about inflation, due to a rise in the price of oil and other commodities.

At the June meeting, William Dudley refers to Lehman Brothers, reporting that its second quarter losses were larger than expected, but that its short-term financing counterparties 'have generally proved to be patient', with the PDCF encouraging them to keep their financing lines in place.[60] Other members were not quite so complacent. President Rosengren of the Federal Reserve Bank, Boston pointed out that

> [the] recent flurry of articles on Lehman before their announcement of their capital infusion highlights continued concerns about investment banks, despite our new liquidity facilities. As a result, I continue to view the downside risk of further financial shocks as being significant.[61]

A further shock came along quite quickly in July when it became clear that Fannie Mae and Freddie Mac were undercapitalized and soon required Paulson to announce emergency measures to prevent the disruption of the availability of mortgages to the market, and to stabilize the financial markets. To realize these objectives the Treasury would purchase equity in either of the two agencies. None of these proposals settled the market and by September, both Fannie Mae and Freddie Mac were taken into conservatorship.

The August meeting of the FOMC did not reflect the turmoil in the markets, but focused on the need to extend the liquidity provisions beyond the end of the year and to agree on how that should be done. The risk was of draining the Federal Reserve's balance sheet. Once again William Dudley spelt out the extent of the problems:

> The housing legislation [regarding Fannie Mae and Freddie Mac] raised the debt limit substantially. There is now about $1.2 trillion of headroom under the debt limit compared with only about $400bn previously ... I wouldn't say I am confident that we could handle any eventuality – after all, the tri-party repo system provides trillions of dollars of funding to the primary dealers. In the unlikely event it all came to us, we wouldn't have the capacity to fully offset it at present. But we could accommodate hundreds of billions of dollars of demand if that proved to be necessary.[62]

It is perhaps against this background that Paulson's decision not to bail out Lehman should also be understood. At the 16 September FOMC, two members were very supportive of the decision. Mr Lacker:

What we did with Lehman I obviously think is good. It has had an effect on market participants assessment of the likelihood of other firms getting support ... We're likely to see a lot more disruption this week ... but the silver lining to all the disruption ... is that it will enhance the credibility of any commitment that we make in the future to be willing to let an institution fail.[63]

Mr Bullard said:

My sense is that three large uncertainties looming over the economy have now been resolved – the GSEs and the fates of Lehman and Merrill Lynch. Of these, the resolution of the GSE uncertainty seems most pivotal. By denying funding to Lehman suitors, the Fed has began to re-establish the idea that markets should not expect help at a difficult juncture.[64]

Others, such as President Rosengren, were much more cautious:

I think it's too soon to know whether what we did with Lehman is right ... But we took a calculated bet. If we have a run on the money markets funds or if the nongovernment tri-party repo market shuts down, that bet may not look nearly so good.[65]

Mr Warsh took the view about the Lehman situation that

no matter what judgement we made this past weekend about whether or not to provide official-sector money, it's not what's driving the markets. What's driving the broader uncertainty are questions about institutions like AIG that were rated AAA ... If in a matter of weeks that AAA rating and that security turns out to be worthless, then firms will reduce their exposure and question the reliability of other insurance companies.[66]

But that caution was not shared by Chairman Bernanke. His lack of awareness of the global effects of allowing Lehman to fail is demonstrated in his testimony to the House Committee on Financial Services on 24 September 2008. Bernanke struggled to explain why AIG was rescued but not Lehman's:

Whilst perhaps manageable in itself, Lehman's default was combined with the unexpectedly rapid collapse of AIG, which together contributed to the development last week of extraordinary turbulent conditions in global financial markets ... These conditions caused equity prices to fall sharply, the cost of short-term credit – where available – to spike upward, and liquidity to dry up in many markets.[67]

The rescue of AIG took place on 16 September, and made a nonsense of Paulson's stand on moral hazard and no more government bail-outs. The Federal Reserve had known for months that the AIG had problems with its Financial Products division which had sold credit default swaps, insurance for CDOs, containing subprime mortgages, but had done nothing. The rescue of AIG, the insurance giant, at the initial cost of $85bn, took place because it was too large (with assets over $1 trillion), too global and too interconnected to fail. With Lehman's the focus was too narrowly on Wall Street, and ignored the international effects. After facing the international reaction to taking Fannie Mae and Freddie Mac into conservatorship, it seems odd that nothing of the sort was considered either before, during or immediately after the fateful weekend.

The impact of the collapse of Lehman Brothers

The failure of Lehman was widely reported. Media reporting varied from the dramatic to the pedestrian. From *The New York Times* (Dealbook): 'There will be blood: Call it the Weekend that Changed Wall Street', to the London *Financial Times*: 'Lehman Brothers files for Bankruptcy'.[68] Stock markets fell around the world, especially the Dow Jones, which fell by at least 504 points on fears that AIG would be next. The dollar fell against the yen, the euro, and the Swiss franc. UK and European central banks injected a total of $50bn into the financial system.

The bankruptcy of Lehman Brothers, the largest in American history, the fourth largest investment bank by asset size with over $600bn in assets and 25,000 employees, was at the very least the trigger for the ensuing financial crisis. Lenman's bankruptcy led to increased uncertainty, if not panic, and a wave of distressed selling of securities that caused a collapse in asset prices and a drying up of liquidity. This was immediately followed by the AIG collapse on 16 September 2008, the run on the Reserve Primary Fund on the same day, and difficulties in getting the Troubled Asset Relief Plan (TARP) approved by Congress over the following two weeks, which meant that the US Treasury and the Federal Reserve were tied in dealing with any other collapses of financial institutions.

The Financial Products Unit of the American International Group (AIG) was also affected by the collapse of Lehman, since it had written over $400bn of insurance contracts, credit default swaps which had to make payments when subprime mortgages suffered losses. As it seemed likely that AIG would have to make large payments under those contracts, AIG found it impossible to obtain short-term funding. On 16 September 2008, the Federal Reserve had to provide an $85bn loan to keep AIG afloat. The total loans to AIG eventually turned out to amount to over $170bn. This had come as a surprise to regulators and others discussing more effective regulation. However, it is not so surprising when it is recognized that insurance companies are still only regulated at state level, and under differing rules.

On the same day that AIG collapsed, there was a run on the Reserve Primary Fund, a large money market mutual fund. The fund held $785m. of Lehman paper, and when Lehman collapsed, the fund could no longer afford to redeem the shares at par value of $1, thus 'breaking the buck'. The fund lost 90 per cent of its assets.

Bruce Bent, the chairman and founder of the Fund, for a long time had resisted investing in commercial paper but had begun buying it in 2006, and from November 2007 had increased purchases of Lehman securities. The one-year return was 4 per cent above the comparable rate for securities. The Reserve Primary Fund was highly rated, triple AAA by Moody's and S&P, attracting individual and large institutional investors. Its assets reached nearly $63bn, but only about 1.2 per cent ($785m.) were in Lehman commercial paper and other securities. It became public knowledge that the Reserve Fund was exposed to Lehman's bankruptcy. The Fund

> was obliged to pay out $10.8bn in redemptions and faced about $28bn of further withdrawal requests. The run quickly spread to other money market funds with commercial paper, so that within a week institutional investors reduced their investments in money market funds by more than $172bn.[69]

The US Department of the Treasury announced a temporary deposit insurance covering all money market investments, which stopped the run immediately.

The bankruptcy of Lehman and other events of September 2008 greatly intensified the recession in the USA that had started in December 2007. GDP fell by 5.1 per cent between the fourth quarter of 2007 and the second quarter of 2009, but the last three months of 2008 to the first quarter of 2009 showed the largest drop in growth – an 8.9 per cent plunge in GDP, coinciding with the aftermath of the collapse of Lehman.[70] World economic growth fell at an annual rate of 6.4 per cent in the fourth quarter of 2008, worsening to a fall of 7.3 per cent in the first quarter of 2009. This is because a financial crisis widens credit spreads, increasing interest rates for household and business purchases, and so demand drops. The value of collateral also falls, making it harder to borrow. Banks begin the process of deleveraging, which also causes spending to fall, so the economy spirals downwards.

The collapse of Lehman also led to the destruction of trust between banks, which is essential if banks are to lend to each other. Banks could not assess the value of the assets which they all held, and hence were reluctant to take the risk of the borrower being unable to pay back a loan. What had happened to Lehman was a clear warning: the assets had lost value as a result of the accumulating defaults on mortgages and derivative products.

The financial crisis arising from Lehman's bankruptcy led to a significant decline in credit to the private sector, as well as to a sharp rise in interest rates. The failure of many US financial institutions led to the collapse of the equity markets in late 2008 and 2009, although the indices showed a recovery in 2010 as well as a slow down in international trade and industrial production. One of the main channels allowing the crisis to spread was the money markets. Following the bankruptcy, the short-term debt that Lehman had issued became virtually worthless, resulting in panic amongst the various investors and funds that held it. This led to a run on the money market funds which provided lending to the commercial paper market. This increased perceptions of default risk, leading to further panic in the global financial markets. Commercial banks cut back on lending, and central banks made concerted efforts to inject liquidity into the system. Letters of credit, and commercial paper to guarantee goods in transit, which gave trading partners the confidence that they would receive the money owed to them when goods reached their final destination, were no longer readily available. The credit markets froze. This was one of the reasons for the vast reduction in global trade. At the peak of the crisis, in early 2009, exports fell on a year-to year basis by 30 per cent in China and Germany, and by 37 per cent and 45 per cent in Singapore and Japan. The Lehman bankruptcy did not cause the financial crisis, but it was a significant trigger, leading to widespread fear that the global financial system was about to collapse, bringing financial ruin in its wake. It is only as 2009 wore on that fears gradually subsided. The costs of 'No bail-out' were far greater than Paulson, Bernanke and Geithner could ever have envisaged for a single moment. If they had been aware, as they should have been at the time, of at least some of the possible effects, then it is entirely possible that Lehman Brothers would have been rescued.

Regulating the 'Big Five'

This chapter will examine the regulation of the Big Five investment banks in the context of the changes which took place in the structure of banking after the repeal of the Glass-Steagall Act and the introduction of the European Union's Consolidated Supervision Directive in 2004.

Immediately after the financial crisis, various reasons were found for the failure of so many banks, and indeed for the collapse of Lehman Brothers. This is despite the obvious fact that the major investment banks were stand-alone investment banks. One of the most popular scapegoats was the repeal of the 1933 Glass-Steagall Act, which had forbidden commercial banks, their holding companies and affiliates from undertaking investment banking activities, while investment banks were forbidden from accepting deposits and thus acting as if they were commercial banks. The barriers imposed by the Act remained unchallenged until the 1980s, when both commercial banks and investment banks began to offer a wider range of services, including for households, assisting in stock purchases and sales. They also began to offer corporate financial services to businesses, such as the private placement of securities issuances or assistance with mergers and acquisitions. Investment banks encouraged larger corporations to raise capital through bond issuances, rather than through loans from commercial banks. These changes continued throughout the 1980s, when in 1987, the Federal Reserve first allowed commercial banks to undertake a limited amount of underwriting of corporate securities. The limits were further relaxed in the 1990s. 'Finally, Citicorp's 1998 acquisition of the Travelers Group, which encompassed a diverse portfolio of insurance operations and a major investment bank, Salomon Smith Barney, which the Federal Reserve allowed on an interim basis, provided the imminent impetus for Congress to act.'[1]

The Gramm-Leach-Bliley Act 1999 did not 'repeal' the Glass-Steagall Act in its entirety. It is important to be clear about what exactly it did and did not repeal. Only if that is understood is it possible to see that any diagnosis of the causes of the financial crisis which relies on that interpretation will lead to the wrong conclusions about the remedies.

Relevance of the Gramm-Leach-Bliley Act 1999

Resolving many years of controversy about the nature of financial competition and regulation, the 106th Congress passed the Gramm-Leach-Bliley Act (GLBA) by overwhelming majorities in November 1999, and President Clinton signed the legislation a few days later. The Act is very comprehensive, addressing affiliations of banking, insurance, securities firms and regulation of the resulting organizations, securities and insurance regulation, financial privacy and the modernization of the Federal Home Loan Bank System, amongst many other issues. The Act also requires a number of regulatory agencies to develop new regulations to implement it.

What exactly did the Gramm-Leach-Bliley Act repeal?

The view that the Glass-Steagall Act was repealed by the 1999 Act is entirely misconceived.[2] The Glass-Steagall Act is still applicable to banks insured by the Federal Deposit Insurance Corporation (FDIC), and still prevents such banks from underwriting or dealing in securities. It left intact section 16 of the Glass-Steagall Act, which prohibits banks from underwriting and dealing in securities. Under section 16, 'The business of dealing in securities and stock by the association shall be limited to purchasing and selling such securities and stock without recourse, solely upon the order, and for the account of customers, and for its own account, and the association shall not underwrite any issue of securities or stock.'[3]

Section 21 prohibits securities firms from taking deposits. GLBA only repealed sections 20 and 32 of the Glass-Steagall Act, which prohibited member banks from affiliating with organizations dealing in securities.[4] It is important in this context to refer to the usual definition of a bank as an institution which takes deposits that can be withdrawn on demand, and makes loans, and which is chartered by the federal government or national or state authorities and insured by the FDIC. The Act comes with a warning attached to it: 'Before concluding that the GLBA reduced banking regulations and complexity, however, note that the GLBA comprises 144 pages of text. While the new law eliminated many restrictions, it also maintained the practice of delineating allowable activities with a combination of numbing details and vague terms.'[5]

The Glass-Steagall Act was designed to separate banks from the risks which might be created by their affiliates, especially a holding company or any subsidiary or affiliate allowed to engage in securities trading, by strictly limiting transactions between banks and their affiliates so that the safety net of deposit insurance and access to the discount window was not extended beyond banks to their holding companies or their non-bank affiliates, and to protect banks' financial position from the risks taken by their affiliates. The aim was to allow the holding company or even a bank securities affiliate to fail, without endangering the bank. The Act continues to prevent banks from underwriting (that is, assuming the risk that an issue of securities will not be fully sold to investors) and dealing (holding an inventory of securities for trading purposes).

The Glass-Steagall Act did not prevent banks from making investments, that is purchasing and selling securities acquired for investment, nor did it prevent banks from buying and selling whole loans or from securitizing loans. They were allowed to buy and sell securities based on assets, such as mortgages, but they could not deal in or underwrite mortgage-backed securities (MBSs), a restriction which remained in place even after the GLBA, with the only difference being that the GLBA now allowed banks to be affiliated with firms engaged in underwriting or dealing in securities, including MBSs. Glass-Steagall allowed banks to deal in and underwrite US government securities, the securities of Fannie Mae and Freddie Mac[6] and the general obligation bonds of states and municipalities, mostly where these were guaranteed by the government, although Fannie Mae and Freddie Mac's bonds were not guaranteed. They were, however, generally believed to be guaranteed by the government, which turned out to be true when the two companies collapsed in 2008. The point here, however, is crucial to the subsequent debate and the introduction of the Volcker rule, which prohibits banks and their affiliates from engaging in bond trading on their own account. The GLBA repealed only the provisions of the Glass-Steagall Act which referred to affiliations of banks. It did not allow banks to do anything that they were previously prohibited from doing. The 'repeal' of the Glass-Steagall Act had no effect whatsoever on the ability of banks to engage directly in the risky business of underwriting and dealing in securities.

The 1956 Bank Holding Act established the terms and conditions under which a company can own a bank, authorizing the Federal Reserve to adopt regulations to uphold the Act. Most banks in the USA are owned by bank holding companies, and all are supervised by the Federal Reserve Bank. The percentage of banks owned by BHCs rose steadily from the 1980s to 2012, reaching 80 per cent of all banks. Under the 1956 Act a BHC was allowed to engage directly in or establish or acquire subsidiaries that engage in non-banking activities determined by the Federal Reserve to be closely related to banking, such as mortgage banking, consumer and commercial finance and loan servicing, leasing, asset management and financial and investment advisory services. In other words, banks can engage in securities trading for only a very limited category of securities, primarily government securities or those backed by the government, but a BHC or an investment bank is not subject to these restrictions. A BHC is a business corporation which controls a bank. It is not specifically chartered like a bank and is not allowed to take deposits, nor does it have automatic access to the Federal Reserve's discount window, participation in the nation's payments system or deposits insured by the FDIC. BHCs are regulated by the Federal Reserve, whereas most banks and almost all the large ones are regulated by the Office of the Comptroller of the Currency. State chartered banks are regulated by their home state regulators and the FDIC at the federal level.

The GLBA expressly authorizes the broker-dealer subsidiaries of an FHC to underwrite and deal in all types of securities, including corporate debt and equity securities, without limit as to the amount of revenue the subsidiary may derive from underwriting and dealing in bank-ineligible securities. Because a 25 per cent revenue limit applies to each section 29 subsidiary controlled by a BHC, the BHC must conduct their securities underwriting and dealing activities through a single subsidiary, to comply with the 25 per cent rule. FHCs, on the other hand, have the flexibility to establish as many or as few securities subsidiaries as they consider to be appropriate to their business needs. This explains why some of the large banks opted to become FHCs, with 37 US FHCs operating underwriting and dealing activities.

The Act also allows investment banks to set themselves up as FHCs. Politicians and others do not seem to understand the role of investment banks. They facilitate mergers and acquisitions, undertake reorganizations of companies, broker trades for institutions and private investors; create capital for other companies, underwrite new debt and equities, and act as an intermediary for securities issuers and the investing public. Typically, an investment bank also provides guidance to issuers regarding the issue and placement of stock. They assist corporations to obtain debt financing by finding investors for corporate funds as well as pre-underwriting counselling and continuing advice after the distribution of securities. The size of an investment bank is also an asset, since the more connections a bank has, the more likely it is to make a profit by matching buyers and sellers. Even before the GLBA, investment banks were allowed to trade and hold mortgage-backed securities, credit default swaps, derivatives, and collateralized debt obligations. The increase in investment banks' trading portfolios resulted from their increased capital base, as a result of their becoming publicly held companies, as opposed to being corporate partnerships, an arrangement which predated the GLBA.

Investment banks did not wish to set themselves up as FHCs, although they sometimes complained about the ability to do so of the larger commercial banks, as measured by the total assets on their balance sheets, and their willingness to use these to attract clients and to provide low-cost funding by attracting deposits. The Glass-Steagall Act had prevented commercial banks from being affiliated with investment banks. After the GLBA was passed, commercial banks could change their BHCs into FHCs, and so could engage in investment banking activities through their non-bank subsidiaries. No domestically headquartered investment bank, especially not the Big Five investment banks, wished to become an FHC, because they would then have had the Federal Reserve Bank as their over-arching regulator.

> The Federal Reserve does not serve as the primary bank regulator, except for the roughly 15% of banks that are state chartered Fed member banks ... GLBA generally adheres to the principle of 'functional regulation', which holds that similar activities should be regulated by the same regulator.[7]

Under functional regulation, federal and state regulators regulate banking activities, securities regulators regulate securities and insurance regulators regulate insurance. Even immediately after the passage of the Act, the authors recognize the problems in this approach to regulation.

> For example, banking agencies cannot prescribe capital requirements for any functionally regulated securities firms or for any insurance subsidiary that is in compliance with the capital requirements of another federal or state regulator.[8]

The Act also 'exempted certain bank activities that have a "securities" component from regulation by the Securities and Exchange Commission'. The lengthy list of examples includes various traditional banking activities, such as commercial paper, private placements, asset-backed securities and derivatives. The Federal Reserve set out its Framework for Financial Holding Company Supervision a year later.

Limits are imposed by law on the ability of banking regulators to impose capital requirements on a functionally regulated securities firm. Functional regulation where financial companies increasingly offer a wide range of financial services is fraught with problems, as many regulatory authorities, including those of the UK, have discovered. The USA was soon to find that the functional approach would face problems, due to the EU and its introduction of consolidated supervision.

> Commercial banks had to jump through certain hoops in order to be accepted as an FHC; all of a BHC's banking subsidiaries had to be well-managed and well-capitalized. In other words, the GLBA allows existing bank holding companies to acquire full-service securities firms and insurance companies, and it allows securities firms and insurance companies to acquire a bank, and thereby become a bank holding company. Foreign banking organizations subject to the BHC Act may also become FHCs. The Act allows FHCs to engage in or affiliate with any company engaged in a financial activity under the Act, including securities underwriting and dealing, insurance underwriting, insurance agency activities and merchant banking. The Act also authorizes the Board of Governors of the Federal Reserve System in consultation with the Treasury to decide that certain activities are financial in nature or incidental to a financial activity, and thus permissible for FHCs.

How did the Federal Reserve regulate and supervise Financial Holding Companies?

In its Supervisory and Regulatory Letter of 2000, the Federal Reserve set out its guidance and the purpose of its supervisory oversight of FHCs.[10] The Federal Reserve is

> responsible for the consolidated supervision of the FHCs . . . the Federal Reserve will assess the holding company on a consolidated or group-wide basis with the

objective of ensuring that the holding company does not threaten the viability of its depository institution subsidiaries ... [The] depository institution subsidiaries of FHCs are supervised by their own supervisor (federal or state) and those engaged in insurance, securities or commodities are supervised by their appropriate regulators ... Oversight of the FHCs is important at a consolidated level because the risks can cut across legal entities and business lines. The purpose of FHC supervision is to identify and evaluate, on a consolidated or group-wide basis, the significant risks that exist in a diversified holding company. The Federal Reserve will focus on the financial strength and stability of the FHCs, their consolidated risk-management processes and overall capital adequacy.[11]

As part of its supervision, 'the Federal Reserve will develop strong relationships with senior management and boards of directors of FHCs'[12] and access to timely information from them, including assessing the centralized risk management and control processes in order to understand the overall risk profile and determine how risks are being controlled on a consolidated basis.

The Federal Reserve, apart from its own supervisory activities, also works closely with other regulators, depending on information received from them, since the Act also preserved the role of federal and/or state banks, securities and insurance regulators as regulators of the various companies in the FHC. The Federal Reserve became the 'umbrella' supervisor for any FHC owning a bank; under its 'streamlined supervision' remit, the Federal Reserve was limited in its day-to-day authority to oversee functionally regulated non-banking subsidiaries of these holding companies. Safeguards for financial safety and soundness applied through the new holding, with existing firewalls being extended to provide further protection for banks within FHCs. The Act envisaged functional regulation, that is, by activity rather than the institution. In spite of its reliance on the functional regulators, the important point here is that the Federal Reserve is ultimately responsible for the consolidated supervision of the BHCs and FHCs.

This examination of the laws governing banks and holding companies and their affiliates is crucial. It makes it entirely clear that the GLBA did not remove any of the provisions of Glass-Steagall forbidding commercial banks from engaging in underwriting and dealing in securities, which remain in force. The financial crisis cannot be attributed to a departure from the Glass-Steagall Act, a conclusion which would amount to a failure to take into account the banking laws prevailing at the time of the crisis, and to understand their implications.

Did the Gramm-Leach-Bliley Act cause the crisis?

Many have argued that the GLBA caused the crisis to a large extent because they thought it repealed the Glass-Steagall Act in its entirety. Richard Parsons, a former director of Citigroup, made such a claim two days after he stepped down from office, saying that to some extent, the crash of 2007 and 2008 had been a result of its repeal, 'because we haven't gotten our arms around it yet. I don't think so because the financial services industry moves so fast'.[13] Others have argued that banks were undermined through their connection with investment banking, which many regard as 'casino' banking. Vince Cable, the UK Business Secretary, described the UK's concerns that 'retail banking is being tied up with investment banking which some people call "casino" banking'. This was 'the government's anxiety about the future stability of banks'.[14]

Such a view bears some relationship to the Dodd-Frank Act para 619, known as the Volcker rule after the former Chairman of the Federal Reserve Bank and President of the President's Economic Recovery Advisory Board, which prohibits insured commercial banks and their affiliates from engaging in 'proprietary trading' of all securities except US government debt by all 'bank-related entities'. The Volcker rule, on the one hand, is thus more restrictive than the Glass-Steagall Act. On the other hand, it allows commercial banks to engage in underwriting, making markets and hedging, provided they are acting solely for their customers or for their own hedging transactions. The distinction proved very difficult to define clearly, causing extensive delays in its implementation by the regulators, so that the final rules were not completed until 13 December 2013, with the date for full implementation by national banks being July 2015. Governor Tarullo admitted that the

> fundamental challenge is to distinguish between proprietary trading, on the one hand and either market-making or hedging on the other. The difficulty in doing so inheres in the fact that a specific trade may be either permissible or impermissible, depending on the context and circumstances within which that trade is made.[15]

That difficulty may prove to be insurmountable.

The trouble with this analysis and the proposed solution in terms of the Volcker rule, which clearly has been very difficult to articulate and even more difficult to enforce, is that it misses the point. As noted above the GLBA's repeal solely of the affiliation provisions of the Glass-Steagall Act did not permit banks to do anything that they were not previously prohibited from doing.

The 'repeal' did not have any effect whatsoever on the ability of banks to engage directly in underwriting and dealing in securities.[16] It is necessary to look elsewhere for the causes of the collapse of some of the banks and their financial weakness. The GLBA did not alter that. Where banks failed or got into difficulties, it was because their investments were unwise and the banks did not exercise due diligence, relying on the rating agencies to do their work for them. With the encouragement of successive Administrations, the banks lent to those who were not in a position to repay the loans, underwriting conditions were abandoned, loans were sold to Fannie Mae and Freddie Mac, so that the discipline of retaining loans on their books disappeared. In addition, banks invested in mortgage-backed securities that pooled subprime and other low-quality mortgages. More exotic securities were created out of the subprime loans, such as collateralized debt obligations (CDOs). When house prices began to falter in mid-2006, subprime borrowers began to default and mortgage-backed securities fell in value, because they had been over-valued in the first place by the rating agencies. The failures were amongst the banks and thrifts, large investment banks and the two government sponsored-entities, Fannie Mae and Freddie Mac, all of which were too highly leveraged.[17]

What about the 'Big Five' investment banks?

None of this affected the Big Five investment banks, Goldman Sachs, JP Morgan, Merrill Lynch, Bear Stearns and Lehman Brothers. Understanding exactly what effect the repeal of the Glass-Steagall Act had on the American banking system is to see that it was not only irrelevant as far as the financial crisis is concerned, but also that it did not affect the status of these stand-alone investment banks. All the Act did was to give the Big Five investment banks the opportunity to continue as stand alone banks without becoming FHCs which would have brought them under more effective regulation and supervision.

The SEC's focus has always been on the securities broker-dealer, for which the key rule is rule 15c3-1 of the Securities and Exchange Act 1934, the 'net capital rule' which is intended to protect customers and other market participants from broker-dealer failures and to enable those broker-dealers to liquidate in an orderly fashion without the need for a formal proceeding or financial assistance from the Securities Investor Protection Corporation'. Rather than considering the appropriate means of supervising a financial conglomerate, the SEC merely sought to adapt its existing rules without a specific focus on the holding company or the fact that the holding company was an investment bank.

None of that was of any use to the investment bank holding companies, operating in the European Union. EU Directive 2002/87/EC requires financial conglomerates operating in the European Union or the European Economic Area (EEA) to have a single supplementary supervisor to provide oversight of the group, in particular with regard to solvency and risk concentration, intra-group transactions, internal risk management processes at the conglomerate level, and fit and proper management. Article 3 of the Directive set out the thresholds for identifying a financial conglomerate, and Articles 6–17 set out the way in which supplementary supervision was to be exercised.

The Directive required any conglomerate to have a single lead supervisor in place by 1 January 2005. The supervisor had to provide a level of oversight equivalent to that provided by European regulators. SEC Director Annette Nazareth, in her testimony to the House Committee on Financial Services, stated that

> several US securities firms had advised the Commission that they were concerned about the EU Directive as the EU's 'equivalence' determination might lead to the view that the SEC's supervision at holding company level might not meet EU standards and that this would increase the cost of their doing business in Europe.[18]

It might lead to higher capital and risk control requirements than an EU-based firm or the creation of a sub-holding company in the EU. Hence, the five investment banks had to obtain an appropriate level of supervision at the level of the holding company or undertake reorganization of companies operating in the EU, which would have been costly and time-consuming.

As a result, the SEC formally adopted amendments to the 1934 Securities Exchange Act in August 2004. These amendments permitted the non-bank affiliated holding companies of the US broker-dealers the alternative of 'voluntarily' committing themselves to having the SEC as supervisor. They then became 'consolidated supervised entities' (CSEs) and continued to operate in the EU and the EEA. All of the Big Five US investment banks became CSEs.

Regulations for the consolidated supervised entities

The new regulations for the five stand-alone investment banks are set out in the Federal Register, although the term 'investment bank', for the ultimate holding company, does not appear there.[19] It is worth examining the way in which the SEC adapted its long-standing rule, 15c3-1, the net capital rule, in order to establish a voluntary, alternative method of computing capital for certain broker-dealers. The new rules came into force on 20 August 2004. They consisted of 'alternative net capital requirements for broker-dealers that are part of consolidated supervised entities',[20] which included allowing the broker-dealer to use mathematical models to calculate net capital requirements for market and derivative-related risk. A broker-dealer using the alternative method of computing net capital would have to hold a higher level of net capital. If the tentative net capital should fall below $5bn, the Commission would have to be informed immediately. The SEC would then have to consider whether appropriate remedial action should be taken.

In addition, the SEC required firms to maintain an overall Basel capital ratio at the consolidated holding company level of not less than the Federal Reserve's 10 per cent well-capitalized standard for bank holding companies.[21] The broker-dealer had to have in place comprehensive internal risk management procedures for market risk, credit risk, liquidity, legal and operational risk. To be able to use the alternative calculations, the holding company had to provide the SEC with extensive financial information, including financial, operational and risk management information, group-wide allowable capital and allowances for market, credit and operational risk calculated in accordance with Basel II standards, along with many other reports on a monthly, quarterly and annual basis. The broker-dealer's ultimate holding company and its affiliates also had to agree to group-wide supervision.

These rule changes were designed to 'help ensure the integrity of the broker-dealer's risk management (and other) procedures'. At the same time, the 'ultimate holding company' had to provide information about 'its own financial and operational conditions' as well as the information about risk exposures from its senior risk managers. It also had to comply with rules regarding the implementation and documentation of a comprehensive, group-wide risk management system, which identified and managed market, credit, liquidity, legal and operational risk. The holding company had to compute the group-wide allowable capital and allowances for the specified risks in accordance with Basel Committee on Banking Supervision requirements.

In the course of presenting the rule changes for CSEs, the SEC noted that the ultimate holding companies might own many other companies, including both broker-dealers and non-broker-dealer companies operating on a global basis. (Indeed, they all owned broker-dealers, which were already supervised, as separate subsidiaries by the SEC.) Any one of these could become insolvent and so affect a broker-dealer's access to short-term funding, or the broker-dealer's capital might be diverted to prop up an ailing firm. The more sophisticated broker-dealers had already been pressing the SEC to allow them to use models to measure risk and compute capital levels along the lines of those being adopted by the more advanced banks under the (then) new capital adequacy rules. They would have to agree to their holding company being supervised on a group-wide basis, which meant additional reporting, record-keeping and the examination of all its entities, including the parent company and affiliates, by the SEC.

The final rules are convoluted indeed. Their purpose is to help the Commission 'to maintain the integrity of the securities markets, by improving the oversight of broker-dealers and providing an incentive for broker-dealers to implement strong risk management practices ... and to reduce costs for broker-dealers by allowing very highly capitalized firms which have developed internal risk-management practices' to use them. The broker-dealer may only use the alternative method of computing net capital, if it maintains tentative net capital of at least $1bn and net capital of at least $500m. Since the broker-dealer may take smaller deductions for market and credit risk, then the company must notify the Commission if its tentative net capital falls below $5bn, although in some cases the SEC may exempt the firm from this requirement.

In applying for permission to use the alternative method of computing net capital, a broker-dealer has to provide a description of their internal risk control system and how the firm intends to use it for deductions of net capital. The broker-dealer may use a VaR model for calculating market risk, provided he uses the multiplication factor to help provide capital during periods of market stress. In a further concession, the SEC agreed that broker-dealers need not limit their VaR calculations to securities for which there is a 'ready market'. Broker-dealers were permitted to use internal calculations to determine counterparty credit risk weightings without any specific maturity adjustment factor, although Basel did specify a maturity adjustment. The Commission had proposed an additional charge for credit risk, if the broker-dealer's aggregate current exposure for all counterparties for unsecured exposures was greater than 15 per cent of its net capital, but when the industry objected, this suddenly turned into 50 per cent.

These examples have been set out in some detail as they illustrate the failings of this attempt by the Securities and Exchange Commission to regulate financial conglomerates. The above quotations from the Federal Register of Monday 21 June 2004, have been referenced partly because they reveal the extent to which the SEC modified the rules in response to pressures from the industry, and sometimes in an arbitrary fashion. The SEC's focus is entirely on changing the rules for broker-dealers, and do not appear to be concerned with the supervision and overall evaluation of a financial conglomerate, despite the reporting requirements. By contrast, the 2002 EU Directive's whole emphasis is on the need for group-wide supervision, having noted the accelerating pace of consolidation in the financial services industry and the intensification of links between the financial markets. Supervisors of different sectors of the financial services industry and of various member states should be able to establish a coordinated approach so that an overall prudential assessment can be made,

The EU Directive introduced a series of rules for the supplementary supervision of financial conglomerates, especially capital adequacy, intra-group transactions and management with a single co-ordinator selected from the relevant member state. The group's 'own funds' could be used more than once to provide capital adequacy for the parent company and also for a subsidiary. It was up to the regulatory authorities in each member state to make sure that at the level of the financial conglomerate that the capital adequacy requirements were properly met. The methodology to be used in calculating the appropriate level is set out in an Appendix to the Directive. However, the capital required at group level is not available to bail out one of the member companies. The US 'source of strength' doctrine, where the bank holding company and/or subsidiaries were expected to support an ailing deposit-taking subsidiary, is not part of the EU Directive.

By contrast, although the SEC recognizes that large broker-dealers are owned by holding companies which also own other entities involved in financial services worldwide, the emphasis does not seem to be on the supervision of the financial conglomerate as a whole. That is in spite of the requirement that the holding company must have a group-wide internal risk management system and would make periodic reports to the SEC, where the SEC's supervision would consist of analysing reports and records provided by the CSE of the broker-dealer. The CSE rules do not allow for the role of a co-ordinator to facilitate the supervision of other companies in different sectors of the financial services industry, nor would the SEC examine any functionally regulated affiliates of the broker dealer.

In evidence to the Committee on Financial Services on 22 May 2002, Annette Nazareth declared that the Commission and the EU approaches to 'group-wide supervision' were based on the same principles:

These principles focus on capital adequacy, regulatory scrutiny of the risk profile of the group, fit and proper or other qualification tests for the key personnel, and information-sharing among supervisors of a financial conglomerate. Although the Commission does not conduct consolidated supervision precisely as described in the Proposed Directive, the Commission does undertake group-wide supervision, that, like consolidated supervision, provides sufficient tools to identify the major risks of the entire enterprise.[22]

This suggests that the SEC had adequate tools and statutory backing for taking on the consolidated supervision of the Big Five investment banks, and would develop appropriate procedures when it published the final rules. That is why the voluntary CSE scheme is focused entirely on the effects of the actions of the holding company and its affiliates on the 'safety and soundness' of the broker-dealer. This was because

the Commission believed that it should only supervise on a consolidated basis those firms engaged primarily in the securities business, and not holding companies affiliated with a broker-dealer incidental to its primary business activity. As a result, the rule effectively requires that a principal broker-dealer have tentative net capital, measured as equity plus subordinated debt less illiquid assets of at least $5 billion.[23]

SEC Deputy Director Robert Colby then describes the liquidity standards the CSEs were required to meet:

Securities firms rely on a wide range of funding sources, notably repo and repo-like secured financing of assets ... CSE firms must conscientiously manage this liquidity risk using their own resources ... Generally, each CSE firm must have sufficient stand-alone liquidity and sufficient financial resources to meet its expected cash outflows in a stressed liquidity environment for a period of at least one year ... Each CSE has undertaken to maintain a liquidity pool of a specified size.

Later in the same presentation he added that 'the CSE regime is tailored to reflect the reliance of securities firms on mark-to-market accounting as a critical risk and governance control.' The supervisory regime consisted of regular monthly meetings with senior market and credit risk managers, including a 'granular system of limits', 'articulates to each business or desk the risk appetite of senior management'. These meetings also reviewed the performance of models and aggregation tools and the risk reporting and analytics prepared for senior management. SEC staff discussed the amount and nature of liquid assets held by the holding company with the CSE treasury managers and with the financial controllers to review the financial results. In particular, SEC staff examined the results of the firm's internal price testing procedures, intended to validate the marking-to-market of complex and illiquid products.

Colby's testimony paints a picture of efficient and thorough supervisory activities on behalf of Commission staff. However, further examination in the next chapter indicates that all was not as it seemed. The SEC's inability to carry out effective supervision was to be revealed all too soon.

The Largest Bankruptcy in American History

The Lehman Chapter 11 bankruptcy case represents the 'largest, most complex, multi-faceted and far-reaching bankruptcy case ever filed in the United States'.[1] As the parent corporation, Lehman Brothers Holding Incorporated (LBHI) managed and directed the affairs of the enterprise, which consisted of a global network of approximately 8,000 subsidiaries and affiliates, with offices in every major centre in the world engaged in the various business activities of Lehman, ranging from derivatives, commercial loans, underwriting, real estate, bank ownership and broker/dealer operations. LBHI managed the cash generated by the enterprise. All such cash was placed in cash concentration accounts at LBHI every night, and then LBHI disbursed the required cash to all its subsidiaries and affiliates.

The Examiner, Anton Valukas, was appointed by the Bankruptcy Court for the Southern District of New York on 16 January 2009 to report on the causes of the Lehman bankruptcy as directed by the Court.[2] He concluded that Lehman was unable to maintain confidence because it made a series of business decisions that left it with a heavy concentration of illiquid assets of deteriorating value in commercial and residential real estate. He found that the policies Lehman followed were in error, but that they fell within the 'business judgement rule'. However,

> the decision not to disclose the effects of those judgements does give rise to colorable claims against senior officers who oversaw and certified misleading financial statements – Richard Fuld and its Chief Financial Officers, Christopher O'Meara, Erin M Callan and Ian T Lowitt and against Lehman's external auditor Ernst & Young . . . for its failure to question and challenge improper or inadequate disclosures in those financial statements.

He defines a 'colorable claim' as one for which the Examiner has found that there is 'sufficient credible evidence to support a finding by a trier of fact' to determine whether the claims are valid. That applies to the use of Repo 105, since their sole purpose was balance sheet manipulation.[3] After the bankruptcy process was completed, there was no further investigation of the Examiner's conclusions about the 'colorable' claims. None of these have been investigated further by any court or by the regulators, and no action has been taken against any of the four named individuals. This chapter explores the main issues cited as the cause of the bankruptcy and the reasons why Lehman conducted its business in the way it did without any proper oversight.

The Examiner pointed out that Lehman's business model was not unique; all of the major investment banks at that time used a high-risk, high-leverage model, which depended on retaining the confidence of the counterparties. Lehman maintained about $700bn of assets and corresponding liabilities on capital of about $25bn. Lehman borrowed heavily to meet its cash needs, creating a high debt-to-equity ratio. The assets were generally long-term, whilst the liabilities were short-term; for example, Lehman financed most of its balance sheet in the short-term repo market to the tune of over $200m. per day in 2008. It relied on short-term secured financing to conduct its daily operations. Vast sums of money were borrowed each day so that the company could stay open for business. They had to be confident that Lehman was in a position to repay in order to roll over its daily funding. At that time, the other investment banks operated in the same way, but after the collapse of Lehman Brothers, it is not surprising that investment banks no longer use that business model.

As noted above, Lehman decided to adopt an 'aggressive growth strategy', take on more risks and increase its leverage. The company continued to invest in commercial and residential real estate, despite the growing problems in these markets, which it failed to take on board, in the belief that they would win in the end, as they had done in the late 1990s by surviving the Russian debt crisis. The Examiner quotes one of the board members, who reported that management advised that 'virtually all subprime originators have cut back on their operations or gone out of business', but that it was management's view that 'the current distressed environment provides substantial opportunities as it did in the late 1990s'.[4]

The use of Repo 105

The extent of such investments was deliberately concealed by the Repo 105 and Repo 108 devices. To hide the extent to which LBHI was leveraged, the company developed and used a version of Repo 105 and Repo 108 in 2001, but used the device much more extensively in 2007 and 2008, as analysts and rating agencies began to focus on the leverage ratios of investment banks.

At first sight, these appear to be the standard repurchase and resale (repo) transactions, which investment banks use to obtain short-term financing. Usually with a repo, one party sells an asset (usually fixed income securities) to another party at one price at the start of a transaction and is committed to repurchase the asset from the 'buyer' at a different price at a future date, usually overnight or within 30 days. Because of the commitment to repurchase, the buyer has only temporary use of those assets, and the seller only has temporary use of the cash proceeds of the sale. The difference between the price paid by the buyer at the start of the repo and the price he receives at the end is the return on the cash he is effectively lending to the seller. In the repo agreements, this return is quoted as the repo rate, a percentage per annum.

One of Lehman's former senior employees dismissed the 'obsession' the Examiner had with Repo 105 as simply that. In his view, the Examiner did not understand that it differed little from the UK 'bed and breakfasting', which applied to share transactions in which shares were sold one day and reacquired the following morning, but the term is now used more generally to cover arrangements whereby a person sells an asset only to buy it back again a short time later. The purpose in the UK was to create a disposal for the purposes of avoiding capital gains tax (CGT) but to regain ownership of the asset. The taxpayer established a loss at the date of the transaction. The rules have now changed and it is no longer possible to buy the same shares back in under 30 days if the taxpayer wishes to crystallize a capital gain. The new rules came into effect in April 2008.

Lehman used the same term Repo 105 to refer to both Repo 105 and 108, since the accounting treatment was the same, except one used fixed income securities with a minimum of 5 per cent over-collateralization (i.e a minimum of $105 value of securities for every $100 borrowed), and the other for equities a minimum of $108 value of equities for $100 cash borrowed. Lehman strayed from the standard use of repos by accounting for its repo transactions as 'sales' in order to reduce its publicly reported net leverage. Their quarterly reports did not disclose the cash borrowing from the Repo 105 transaction, that is, the company did not disclose either the cash borrowings or the obligations to repay the debt. According to the interview with Martin Kelly, former Global Financial Controller from December 2007 to September 2008, Repo 105 was used to pay off other business liabilities, thus reducing the leverage. A few days after the new quarter began, Lehman would have to borrow the necessary funds to repay the cash borrowings plus interest, buy the securities back and restore the assets to the balance sheet.

In its forms 10-K and 10-Q for the SEC, Lehman defined its 'net leverage ratio' as net assets divided by tangible equity capital. Net assets were defined as total assets, excluding cash and securities segregated and on deposit for regulatory and other purposes; securities received as collateral; securities purchased under agreement to resell; securities borrowed and identifiable intangible assets and goodwill. Tangible equity capital included shareholders' equity and junior subordinated notes. It calculated its leverage ratio by the standard method of dividing the total assets by shareholders' equity. The issue is the effect of the surge in the use of Repo 105 in 2007 and 2008, and the impact of these transactions on the firm's net leverage ratio. The Examiner placed considerable reliance on Martin Kelly, both for the extent of the use of this device and his view that 'a careful review of Lehman's Forms 10-K and 10-Q would not reveal Lehman's use of Repo 105 transactions', which Kelly considered had as their 'only purpose or motive for the transactions … a reduction in the balance sheet' and that 'there was no substance in the transactions'.[5] Other senior executives were aware of the use of Repo 105, but not the board. Neither its use nor its purpose was ever revealed to members of the board.

Lehman had began selling Repo 105 in 2001, but from mid-2007 onwards, selling its inventory positions without incurring substantial losses proved increasingly difficult. Such 'fire sales' would have led to a loss of market confidence in Lehman's valuations. Raising equity was also a problem since, although it would have improved its net leverage, it would not have solved the underlying problem of its leveraged loans and commercial and residential properties, which were falling in value by the day. Lehman turned increasingly to Repo 105. The Examiner highlights a document produced in February 2007, describing Repo 105 as a 'low cost way to offset the balance sheet and leverage impact of the current market conditions', since 'exiting large CMBS position in real estate and subprime mortgages before quarter end would incur large losses due to the steep discounts required to sell them … As a Repo 105 would help to avoid this without negatively impacting our leverage ratios'. Lehman used the cash borrowing in Repo 105 to pay various short-term liabilities, real liabilities to unrelated third parties, thereby reducing the total assets and liabilities, and thus its reported leverage ratios. The firm temporarily reduced its net balance sheet by $38.6bn in the fourth quarter of 2007, by $49.1bn in the first quarter of 2008 and by $50.38bn in the second quarter of 2008.[6] Lehman's publicly reported net leverage ratio for 30 November 2007 (fourth quarter 2007), 29 February 2008 (first quarter 2008) and 30 May 2008 (second quarter 2008) was 16.1×, 15.4× and 12.1×, respectively. Without the balance sheet benefit of Repo 105 transactions, Lehman's net average ratios for the same quarterly returns would have been 17.8×, 17.3× and 13.9×, respectively.[7]

When Lehman first introduced its Repo 105 programme around 2001, it was unable to find an American law firm which would provide it with an opinion letter, allowing the true sale accounting treatment under US law, so Lehman conducted the programme under the auspices of an opinion letter provided by Linklaters in London. The letter was provided for Lehman's European broker-dealer firm there on 31 May 2006.[8] The Repo 105 transactions allowed Lehman to maintain its level of earning assets while reducing the size of the balance sheet. The letter analyses the implications of the Global Master Repurchase Agreement (GMRA) which Lehman Brothers International (Europe) intended to use for Repos. The letter advised that the transfer of the purchased securities to the buyer for the purchase price might, under English law, be classified as a sale involving the disposition of the seller's entire proprietary interest, as opposed to a charge. It states that 'this opinion is limited to English law as applied by the English courts and is given on the basis that it will be governed and construed in accordance with English law'. One of the assumptions in the letter was that the 'purchased securities consist of liquid securities, so that the buyer could easily dispose of purchased securities and acquire equivalent securities if it wished'. This assumption was more honoured in the breach than the observance in 2007 and 2008 by Lehman.

Finally, the opinion was described as solely being for the benefit of LBIE, although a 'copy of this opinion may be provided by Lehman Brothers to its auditors for the purpose of preparing the firm's balance sheets.' The existence and use of this letter explains why the Repo 105 transactions were conducted through LBIE.

The Repo 105 transactions were structurally and substantively identical to ordinary repo transactions, using the same documentation and with the same collateral and counterparties, making them more difficult to detect. They were also supposed to consist of liquid assets. Lehman also used US-based securities, such as assets held in US trading books for Repo 105s, a procedure which rapidly increased from late 2007 through to 2008. These were usually 'agencies, bullets[9], Fannie and Freddie'. Another email, dated 20 February 2008, stated that 'we are likely to use more agency product as collateral and might even use some TIPS (Treasury Inflation Protected Securities) and discount notes'.[10] The method used was booking Repo 105 transactions through LBIE using inter-company repo transactions. These amounted to $8.3036bn in November 2007, $14.889bn in February 2008, and $13.6307bn in June 2008. The liquidity requirements were well known throughout the company, but were not always observed.

In January 2008, Richard Fuld made a strategic decision that Lehman would embark on a firm-wide effort to reduce its balance sheet and lower the firm-wide net leverage ratio by selling assets. But by then many of Lehman's assets, especially mortgages and real estate securities, had become difficult to sell without incurring substantial losses. In addition, investors and the rating agencies had become much more focused on leverage ratios, and Lehman was anxious not to lose its rating. The extensive use of Repo 105 was then the only way to reduce its leverage ratio. The Examiner, Anton Valukas, amassed considerable evidence, especially from internal emails, showing that Lehman had never disclosed its Repo 105 practice, but that the firm's disclosures of its cash holdings at each quarter-end further strengthens the witness statements and other evidence that Lehman used the Repo 105 for other business purposes, such as paying off short-term liabilities. This was confirmed by Martin Kelly and also Edward Grieb, former financial controller at Lehman.[11]

Awareness of the use of Repo 105 was widespread throughout the firm and at every level. An email addressed to Bart McDade from Hyung Lee said: 'I am not sure you are familiar with Repo 105 but it is used to reduce net balance sheet in our government businesses around the world.' To which Bart replied (as head of equities in April 2008, but shortly to become President and Chief Operating Officer in June 2008): ' I am very aware . . . it's another drug we're on'.[12] Valukas states that several additional emails sum up the reasons for Lehman's Repo 105. 'The firm has a function called repo 105 whereby you can repo a position for a week and it is regarded as a true sale to get rid of the next balance sheet', and 'we have been using Repo 105 in the past to reduce balance sheet at the quarter-end.'[13]

Use and misuse of Repo 105

First of all, Dick Fuld denied any knowledge of the use of Repo 105 as described by the Examiner in his testimony under oath before the House Committee on Financial Services on 20 April 2010. He stated that 'another piece of misinformation was that Repo 105 transactions were used to hide Lehman's assets. That is also not true. Repo 105 transactions were sales as mandated by the accounting rule, FAS 140.' He also stated that the 'Examiner himself acknowledged that Repo 105 transactions were not inherently improper and that Lehman appropriately accounted for those transactions with its outside auditor [Ernst & Young] ... and that E&Y reviewed that policy and supported the firm's application of the relevant rule, FAS 140.' Chairman Bernanke in his statement to the same committee pointed out that the Federal Reserve was 'not aware that Lehman was using so-called Repo 105 transactions to manage its balance sheet.'

In her evidence to the House Committee on Financial Services on 20 April 2010, Mary Shapiro, Chairman of the SEC, pointed out that

> Lehman did indeed fund itself in large part through short-term repurchase transactions, borrowing tens of billions of dollars on a daily basis. . . . Accounting standards establish guidance for whether a repurchase transaction should be reported as a financing transaction (debt) or a sale, which depends in part on whether the reporting entity has surrendered control over the asset. Typically, repos are accounted for as financings (debt) as control over the assets is not fully surrendered.

Owing to the loss of confidence about Lehman's leverage in 2007 and 2008, Lehman increasingly relied on Repo 105s, which, 'unlike typical repo transactions' were 'treated as sales for accounting purposes.' Lehman temporarily removed billions of dollars of assets from its balance sheet, using the cash to pay down liabilities as a means of reducing its reported leverage, but did not disclose the fact that it treated these transactions as sales but accounted for them as transactions. She added that regulators, including the SEC, rating agencies and the Lehman board, were unaware of Lehman's use of Repo 105. It is interesting to note the differences between Shapiro's account of Repo 105 and accounting rules with Dick Fuld's statement, which seems to slide over the explanation of the complexity of FAS 140.

In fact, the arrangements made by Lehman were more complex than Fuld's statement suggests. The rationale for counting the Repo 105 transactions as sales was that the securities were 'significantly over-collateralized' (although they were probably over-valued):

> Since the lenders held collateral worth 105 per cent of the amount advanced . . . for debt securities, the lenders might not necessarily enforce Lehman's obligation to repurchase the inventory, since they could liquidate the collateral profitably. (Repurchases collateralized by equity securities were nominally 8 per cent over-collateralized, and called 108 per cent inside Lehman).[14]

Even if the valuations were true, this would not change the fundamental nature of the secured borrowing. That part of its inventory used as collateral was removed from the books and replaced by cash, but no debt was recorded. Using the borrowed funds to pay down other obligations, slimming down the balance sheet but improving the debt/equity leveraging, even if only by a small amount, is legitimate. But the 'two step process engaged in by Lehman would seemingly be an attempt to conceal its holdings of risky, perhaps value-impaired inventory, its large debt obligations for repurchasing that inventory and its high debt/equity leverage ratio.'[15] It took some time for the Financial Accounting Standards Board to close the loophole, whereby Fuld was able to present repurchases as sales. The new rule replaced the 98 to 102 per cent which enabled Lehman to count the Repo transactions as sales because the lenders' held collateral worth 105 per cent of the amount advanced. Under the new rules, Repos will not count as sales unless it is a real transfer of the risk and reward of the asset. If that does not happen, then it is a loan and the assets remain on the borrowers' balance sheet. The full details of the new rules were not agreed until June 2014.[16]

Fair value accounting

Lehman adopted fair value accounting under GAAP in the first quarter of 2007 in order to maintain the value of its assets in the eyes of its investors and competitors. Early adoption was recommended by the Financial Accounting Standards Board, and Lehman announced that they had done so in their Form 10-Q for the first quarter of 2007. If there is no market, or a declining market, for its assets, then SFAS 157 (statement of financial accounting standards) allows a company to use its judgement to determine fair value, taking into account its view as to the assumptions that market participants would use in pricing the assets. Fair value is defined as the 'price that would be received to sell or buy an asset or paid to transfer a liability in an orderly transaction between market participants at the measurement date'. It allows for 'usual and customary' transactions and does not apply to forced sales. These constitute Level 1 valuations, according to the hierarchy of values created by SFAS 157.

Level 2 valuations are those requiring other inputs besides the market price, which may not always be available. Such inputs could include quoted prices for similar assets or liabilities in active markets. More importantly, given the markets in which Lehman Brothers was operating, Level 2 includes quoted prices for identical or similar assets or liabilities in markets that are not active, that is, markets in which there are few transactions for the asset or liability, the prices are not current, or price quotations vary substantially either over time or among market makers, or in which little information is released to the public. These adjustments will depend on various factors relating to the asset or liability, such as its condition or location. Level 3 refers to situations where there is little, if any, market activity. Valuing these assets and reporting on them is based on the company's own views about the assumptions that market participants would use in pricing the asset or liability. Such assets or liabilities would be marked to model using discounted cash flow models or hypothetical hedge portfolios, based on knowledgeable market participants' views and assessments. The market in RMBSs and commercial real estate declined sharply throughout 2007 and 2008, when it virtually collapsed. That meant it was not possible to mark-to-market for an increasing proportion of its assets, so that Lehman had to rely on its judgement in terms of Level 2 and Level 3 in order to assess the fair value of its assets.

Lehman, according to the Valuation and Control Report–Fixed Income Division indicated the extent to which the company went in order to try and value assets during that period. Lehman reported an increasing proportion of Level 2 and Level 3 assets in its financial statements from the fourth quarter of its 2007 fiscal year to the end of the first quarter of 2008. By the end of the second quarter of 2008, Level 1 assets had decreased substantially, and at the same time Level 2 and Level 3 assets had increased as a proportion of the firm's total assets. Lehman reported that during fiscal year 2007, its Level 3 assets increased, ending the year at 13 per cent of financial instruments and other inventory positions owned. By the end of the second quarter of 2008 the aggregate amount of Lehman's financial inventory considered Level 2 or Level 3 had decreased on a quarter-by-quarter basis, the majority of this decrease having occurred in the Level 2 category, and there was an even more substantial decrease in the amount of Level 1 assets over the same period, so that the proportion of Level 2 and Level 3 assets increased on a quarter-by-quarter basis. Perhaps Lehman was aware of the advantages of using Level 2 and especially Level 3 as the value of assets declined owing to market developments. The Level 3 valuations gave Lehman the scope to produce its own valuation of the assets.

During the earnings call on 16 June 2008, when Lehman sought to present losses of \$2.8bn for the quarter in the best possible light, Fuld explained that Ian Lowitt, the new Chief Financial Officer replacing Erin Callan, would describe the valuation process. Lowitt summarized their asset valuation and controls, describing the work of the 'independent' Product Control Group (PCG) of approximately 500 finance professionals dedicated to the production, analysis and reconciliation of daily profit and loss results. With that group was a smaller unit of about 100 staff globally who verified pricing by reviewing recent sales activity for that or similar assets, making comparison with prices provided by external data providers, broker quotes, index levels and industry research reports. With regard to residential mortgages, Lowitt noted that the company had sold $11bn and bought about $6bn, across the capital structure and loan types including Alt-A and subprime, 'giving us a good transparency in our pricing'.[17]

But the analysts representing their competitors were not impressed by Lehman's valuation procedures, although they appeared to accept Lehman's replies. Prashant Bhatia, Citi analyst, mentioned the $54bn of residential and commercial mortgage exposure, asking: 'in rough numbers, what do you think the intrinsic value of the $54bn is', and was assured that it was on a mark-to-market basis, with 'a lot of transparency, as a result of all the sales'. Bhatia also asked about the non-performing loans balances broken down by residential, commercial and real estate investment related, but the CFO replied that he did not have those figures to hand. Bill Tanona, from Goldman Sachs, pointed out that where assets were marked was 'obviously a big concern in the market-place' especially with Level 3 assets being about $38bn for the quarter. He wanted to know what percentage of these assets were mortgage-related, and why a large proportion of the European market had moved from Level 2 to Level 3. Once again, the answer from Ian Lowitt was incomplete: it was too early in the process to say where mortgage and asset-backed securities were likely to be. They valued the decline in European mortgages at a 28 per cent fall in house prices, although what they saw was a decline of 7 per cent. Lehman insisted that the marks they had given were conservative. The earnings call and the responses to analysts' questions were hardly inspiring, leading Einhorn to conclude that

> there is good reason to question Lehman's fair value calculations … Lehman could have taken many billions more in write downs than it did. Lehman had large exposure to commercial real estate … Lehman does not provide enough transparency for us to even hazard a guess as to how they have accounted for these items.[18]

He had taken the unusual step of announcing that he was shorting Lehman's stock on 8 April, in his presentation at Grant Spring Investment Conference. But perhaps that was not so surprising after all. If others started to short the stocks, then his profits would increase. But as the *New York Magazine* put it, Einhorn 'sees no conflict between his public moralism and the fact that he stands to profit from it.'[19]

Valukas points out that the lack of confidence in Lehman's valuations was also shown in the demands for collateral by Lehman's clearing banks throughout 2008 to cover the risks they assumed in connection with clearing and settling Lehman's tri-party and currency trades and other extensions of credit. Without this access, Lehman would be unable to carry out day-to-day operations, so Lehman sought to pledge its structured instruments, such as collateralized loan obligations to JP Morgan and Citigroup, two of its principal settlement banks. Citigroup refused to accept these assets, which they regarded as being illiquid, and found impossible to value. JP Morgan accepted Lehman's structured instruments, but insisted on additional collateral in cash. Their own analyses showed that these instruments did not have the value Lehman assigned to them.

Lehman's methodology for the valuation of its assets

The Examiner's first step was to evaluate the reasonableness of Lehman's mark-to-market valuations, in two distinct but related contexts. The first was to consider whether there was enough evidence to show that Lehman's valuations were 'unreasonable' for a particular asset class, such that 'the court could adjust, or even disregard, such valuations in determining the solvency of these debtors.' The second was to determine that there was sufficient evidence that the valuations were so unreasonable, and, if so, were these the product of actions of a Lehman officer, so that there was a 'colorable claim of a breach of fiduciary duty'.[20] The Examiner noted that the courts have assessed the reasonableness of a debtor's valuation or projection of future cash flows in the light of information available at the time the valuation was undertaken, and that the valuation of illiquid assets requires considerable judgement.

In the Bankruptcy Report, Valukas examines the valuation procedures for Lehman's commercial real estate portfolio, which included commercial mortgage loans and commercial mortgage-backed securities, backed by real estate properties generating cash flow. Lehman's intention was to syndicate, securitize and/or sell these assets to investors shortly after their origination or acquisition. Lehman's assets included highly leveraged debt or equity investments in real estate assets that Lehman intended to hold for its own account while a developer improved or developed the underlying asset. The investment would then be sold, along with a sale of a real asset after the development or improvement was completed. Lehman would provide bridge equity, as well as debt financing to a real estate company, enabling it to acquire particular properties of another company through a leveraged buy-out. On 31 May 2008, Lehman's Global Real Estate Group (GREG) valued its global portfolio at $49.3bn, consisting of $28.0bn in the United States, $12.5bn in Europe and $8.9bn in Asia. Given that the Examiner's focus was on US assets, the commercial real estate figures were: commercial $15.1bn; Principal Transactions Group (PTG) $8.5bn; and bridge equity $3.1bn. Then virtually all in the commercial group were classified as Level 2 and the PTG and bridge equity positions were classified as Level 3. By 31 August 2008, GREG valued its commercial portfolio in the United States as $23.4bn with Level 1 at $15bn, Level 2 at $20.1bn and Level 3 at $12.5bn. The Examiner also reclassified $0.6bn of SunCal positions from PTG into the 'other' category.

Each commercial real estate business unit was responsible for valuing its assets, based on their knowledge of the development of the real estate asset. Other commercial positions were valued by those working in that section based on their understanding of how debt was trading in the applicable market. The process involved referring the valuations to the product controllers, whose role was to conduct price verification for the CRE assets. They tested the positions by inputting position-specific information into spreadsheet models, which produced an 'output' value based on calculations and formulas selected by Lehman price-testing tools. They then considered whether the variances exceeded a certain threshold. The variances were discussed with the business unit in question, and if no agreement could be reached, then the matter was referred to more senior staff and ultimately to the CFO.

The bankruptcy report notes that Mark Walsh was clear that senior management never changed the 'marks' he deemed appropriate. He found that management played an active role in resolving disputes between Lehman's trading desks and the Product Control Group as to proper valuations in late 2007 and 2008. During that time, it became more difficult for him to resolve disagreements as to a position's value, and Walsh was more inclined to "'kick it upstairs" for resolution by McDade, Kirk or Lowitt'.[21] He also stated that there never was a time when a write-down that GREG proposed was overruled or modified, or when senior officers predetermined the amount of write-downs that would be taken for a quarter, or limited the amount of write-downs GREG was allowed to take. On the basis of both Walsh's evidence and that of others, the Examiner found no evidence that 'senior management involvement [had] led to unreasonable valuations during the whole period'. He noted that senior management became concerned with 'late breaking news' about proposed CRE write-downs more particularly in the third quarter of 2008. But even during this period, Valukas concluded that

> evidence is in great conflict as to whether senior management tried to impose artificial limits on write-downs or whether more junior managers saw a management 'push-back' as management interference. The write-downs were never published, and anyway would only have amounted to $200m., small by comparison with the losses of $3.9bn.

Indeed at a time when markets were collapsing, it is only to be expected that senior management would scrutinize the valuations of their assets, since they would need to be sure of the extent of the problems they faced.

The difficulties Lehman faced in valuing its commercial real estate positions arose from the changes in its strategy in 2006, when the company turned to the historically profitable commercial real estate (CRE) business, reporting at the end of 2007 that CRE assets had risen to $55.2bn at the end of its 2007 fiscal year, up from $28.9bn at the end of 2006. During July and August 2007, Lehman realized that the market for securities backed by CRE assets was 'virtually closed', although they were already committed, largely by the activities of Mark Walsh. Lehman stopped originating new loans until the end of the third quarter of 2007. However, it had already agreed to finance several large CRE deals, including Archstone, which were completed in October and November 2007. Mark Walsh was head of GREG, who reported to the head of Lehman's Fixed Income Division (FID). He and the two managers serving under him, the head of US originations, and the head of Credit Distribution served on GREG's Global Credit Committee and were responsible for approving the origination of CRE deals.

Walsh had already acquired a reputation in Wall Street as the

> most brilliant real estate financier on Wall Street ... a lot of Wall Street firms tried to duplicate Lehman's commercial real estate strategy ... [Walsh] had generated more than 20 per cent of Lehman's $4bn in profits at the peak of the real estate boom of 2006. He introduced 'bridge equity' deals for large acquisitions such as Archstone.[22]

By quickly committing to fund required debt and equity, Lehman was able to obtain deals with large profits as positions were securitized and longer-term equity capital was raised. But that left large balance sheet positions when market conditions changed.

> Bridge equity became one of Lehman's signature products, which Mr Walsh's group deployed in dozens of deals, including Tishman Speyer's $1.7bn purchase of the MetLife Building on Park Avenue in 2005 and Beacon Capital Partners' acquisition of the News Corporation's headquarters on the Avenue of the Americas for more than $1.5bn in 2006.[23]

He was regarded as easily the most aggressive lender of bridge equity, the short-term loans of equity that helped deals to complete quickly with the expectation that Lehman would replace the loan with new equity partners after the deal closed and receive the fees.

According to interviews with Mark Walsh conducted by the Examiner, he knew that it was necessary to reduce the balance sheet during the fall of 2007 with a target of $25bn in the USA, $10bn in Europe and $10bn in Asia. But by the end of the first quarter of 2008, only 13 positions had been sold in the USA, for $350.5m., none in Europe, and one in Asia, for $33.1m.[24] Over the course of 2008, Lehman wrote down its CRE positions by more than $3bn. It had recognized in January 2008 that its CRE portfolio was at risk due to market conditions with the 'continuance of the capital markets meltdown', CMBS spreads had 'widened to all-time highs and investors [were] staying on the sidelines'. The consequences then were that Lehman was unable to hedge its floating rate book and the mezzanine[25] classes of their fixed rate loans continued to result in losses. GREG carried out a valuation review of their entire portfolio, taking into account among other issues, the lack of liquidity in the market place.[26]

Disruptions in the market and valuation

Geithner remarked in a speech to the Economic Club in New York that

> the funding and balance sheet pressures on banks were intensified by the rapid breakdown of securitization and structured finance markets. Banks lost the capacity to move riskier assets off their balance sheets, at the same time they had to fund, or prepare to fund, a range of contingent commitments over an uncertain time horizon.[27]

That obviously created difficulties for Lehman's valuation of its commercial real estate assets. These were typically backed by assets already constructed, operating and generating cash flow. Lehman had expected to syndicate, securitize and/or sell them within a few months. But the market conditions forced the company to retain the assets on its books. Its exit strategy for these assets disappeared and inevitably the value of its assets fell with $195m. in write-downs in the second quarter of 2008, with a further write-downs of $306m. in the third quarter of 2008.

Lehman was able to sell some of its assets and was able to use that data in determining the value of the assets but that may have given a false picture of the value of the remaining assets, since the valuations of the remaining assets suggested a higher yield and lower values than is reflected by the actual sales during the quarter. This data was Lehman's own up-to-date information, whereas the theoretical models in use at the time relied on data from third parties which was often stale.

The procedures used by the Product Control Group (PCG) have already been set out. The Group used a variety of methodologies, depending on the kind of asset and available information to verify the pricing information provided by the business desk. The PCG had to abandon its usual method of using a mock securitization model based on the latest Lehman deal. But that market ceased to operate in early 2008, so the Principal Transactions Group (PTG) had to consider other methods.

The PCG based this on an examination of the PTG's own price testing analysis, in which the PCG identified a $70m. net negative variance, equal to about 0.5 per cent of Lehman's $15bn commercial portfolio, but Lehman's marks for the assets tested were higher than the test prices, suggesting an over-valuation. Furthermore, for the second quarter, Lehman produced an analysis of the sales data with the carrying values of assets remaining on the balance sheet. It concluded that the average selling yield was lower than the average carrying yield of the remaining assets, so that the prices which Lehman achieved on actual sales were higher than the assets on its balance sheet. But the Examiner noted that there was great variation on positions even in the single asset category, so that there would have to be a position-specific analysis to determine the exact value. However, his analyses suggested that the PCG had sufficient sales data to price the commercial book during the second quarter of 2008. Indeed the available sales data indicate that Lehman's marks for these assets were conservative. He added that, assuming the assets sold were 'comparable to the remaining assets, the Commercial Book as of May 31, 2008 was undervalued in the light of the second quarter available. Lehman relied on sales data to support the valuation of Commercial assets at the quarter end.'[28]

The bankruptcy filing took place just fifteen days after the third quarter ended, so less information was available. The process used by PCG was similar, with reliance on sales data where that was available, and using the Large Loan and Junior Note pricing models in the absence of such data. Even in that quarter, sales took place in each asset class, including large loans (floating and fixed rate), mezzanine (fixed and floating rates), B-notes and securities, totalling $2,468m. The review of these models shows that for the Large Loan Floating Rate model, there was a $45m. positive variance, or a 0.7 per cent potential undervaluation of $6.3bn worth of positions. For the Junior Note price testing model, there was an $87m. net negative variance, or a potential 3.5 per cent over-valuation of $2.5bn worth of positions. Taking actual sales into account, the pricing models on average predicted a higher spread than the average selling spread, indicating that the positions were marked at lower prices than similar positions sold during the third quarter. The Examiner therefore concluded that 'there is insufficient evidence' to show that 'the Commercial Book valuations as of the third quarter of 2008 were unreasonable'.[29]

However, it appears that there were greater difficulties in valuing the debt and equity investments in real estate projects, which were intended to be held while the underlying real estate was developed and improved. This work was carried out by the PTG. These assets were not for sale and were relatively illiquid even when the commercial real estate market was booming. They were apparently valued through a combination of financial projections and 'gut feeling', owing to the fact that each asset was unique, compounded by the lack of sales data for the debt and equity positions. There was, the Examiner records, considerable disagreement about the necessity of valuing these assets at a price they could be sold to a third-party investor in 2007 and 2008. Instead the valuation of these assets depended on whether the development was proceeding according to the project's business plan. Even so, this methodology did result in an approximate write-down of $1.1bn out of $8.6bn PTG portfolio at the end of 2007.

This was partly because TriMont, Lehman's real estate adviser, had to provide models with an internal rate of return (IRR) for each development. These were designed to assess the value of the real estate by discounting the projected cash flows of the completed project to a present value. The model was not completed until July 2008. Even when it was developed, it used a yield which did not necessarily match the investors' required rate of return (market-based interest rates) as at the particular measurement date. The application of this model led to the decision that it would be appropriate to write down PTG assets by $714m. for the third quarter of 2008, although Jonathan Cohen believed that there was a

$500m. limit on write-downs for the third quarter, but he did not advise anyone senior to him, apart from Gerard Reilly, Global Head of Risk Management, that he and Anthony Barsanti, PTG Senior Vice President responsible for marking the PTG positions, had calculated write-downs beyond $500m. so about another $214m. of write-downs were not taken.

Here the Examiner concluded that 'there is sufficient evidence to support a finding, for purposes of solvency analysis, that certain of Lehman's PTG valuations as of May 31, 2008 and August 31, 2008 were unreasonable'. He stated that his 'analysis of these assets does not present an opinion as to the fair value of these assets as of May or August 2008, but simply investigates the assumptions and practices Lehman used in valuing the selected PTG assets and reaches a conclusion as to the reasonableness of those assumptions and practices'.[30]

The Examiner also provides an overview of Lehman's Principal Transactions. These were primarily debt or equity investments in real estate development and improvement projects. These had no cash flow, as the land was due to be developed, or less cash flow than was projected to be generated on development, such as the conversion of rental apartments to condominiums. The plan was to exit from these positions when the project was completed and produce a cash flow through leasing or sales. Development projects were usually completed between two to five years after Lehman provided the funding, after which the underlying property was usually sold. Its main relationships were with developers with a proven track record of successfully completing projects.

Lehman was aware that these were higher risk/higher return projects, due to the lack of stabilized cash flows and the risk that the development might not be completed according to the business plan. This portfolio increased in size, and the average position became riskier during 2006 and 2007. The levels of risk also increased because of the increased focus of land development projects; the focus on California and other boom markets and a greater proportion of equity investments. Investment in development of land for residential purposes brought higher returns than, for example, office upgrades. The company's risk exposure increased as it took equity stakes in developments, up from 26 per cent in 2004 to 34 per cent in 2005 and 2006. During 2007, noticing that the market was 'dropping like a stone', as one executive put it, approvals for new deals were not given and originators stopped submitting deals where Lehman was not sufficiently senior in the debt structure.

Lehman originated fewer positions during the last quarter of 2007, a trend that continued into 2008, and also wrote down the value of PTG investments by $137m. in the fourth quarter of 2007, by $271m. in the first quarter of 2008, and by \$302m. in the second quarter of 2008. At that time, the company held 741 positions in the PTG portfolio, and Lehman valued these positions at \$8.5bn, with an average position of \$11m. Approximately 33 per cent of the overall portfolio (210 positions) was in land for development, with condos and conversions at 21.7 per cent. The size of this portfolio decreased slightly between the second and third quarters of 2008, to 690 positions valued at \$7.8bn as a result of a further write-down in the third quarter. Although Lehman slowed down the pace of new originations, the company still held a large number of relatively risky positions originated between 2004 and 2007.

Conclusions as to the reasonableness of Lehman's valuation of the PTG portfolio

The Examiner found sufficient evidence to support his view that 'Lehman did not appropriately consider market-based yield when valuing PTG assets in the second and third quarters of 2008.' The company did not introduce a methodology that used market-place yields quickly enough, and even when it did implement such a methodology (IRR models), the yields in the IRR models reflected the weighted average of the contractual interest rate for debt at origination and Lehman's expected rate of return rather than market-based rates.

The Examiner set out the 'conflicting statements' as to whether 'PTG assets were valued at the price at which the asset should be sold, and, in particular, whether the valuation took into account the market-based yield that would be required by an investor in the light of the then-current market conditions'. Despite that, he concluded that Lehman's assets were not so marked in the second and third quarters of 2008. One of his interviewees, Anthony Barsanti, the person who was primarily responsible for determining PTG marks, said that 'he did not know whether PTG assets could be sold at the price at which they were marked, and stated that *he had not really thought about it*'.[31] Other senior staff, such as Jonathan Cohen, involved in valuing Lehman's assets, took the view that PTG was not required to mark assets at 'fire sale' prices, pointing out that a significant number of positions were carried at 90 per cent par value and stated that a 'willing buyer was not going to pay that'.[32] Over 90 per cent of Lehman's third quarter write-downs were based on credit impairment, with only 7 per cent related to yield. However, both Jonathan and Kenneth Cohen stated that the valuation for credit impairment would take into account yield impairment. The switch to IRR models in the third quarter of 2008 led to a large drop in the value of the assets, showing that they had been overvalued in the second quarter. The valuations or 'marks' in that second quarter were not 'reasonable assessments of fair value' for the purposes of a solvency analysis. Kenneth Cohen and Jonathan Cohen regarded the PTG marks as representing fair value, because they had concluded that PTG 'was not required to mark these illiquid assets, backed by non-stabilized real estate, at prices they could sell for during a sharp market downturn'. The logic behind this was that Lehman had a 'policy against valuing assets based on distressed sales'.[33] This, however, misses the point entirely. The requirement to mark assets at fair value for the purposes of solvency or SFAS 157 is not overridden by Lehman's plans for the sale of the asset.

Archstone and SunCal

These were two major commercial real estate investments made by Lehman. In 2003, Mark Walsh introduced a set of 'bridge equity' deals in which the bank held on to the equity until it sold its equity stake, which had to be as soon as possible; otherwise the bank risked being left 'holding the baby'. Lehman was able to charge 4 per cent for its equity investments, above the going market rate of 1.5 per cent. Walsh pursued and gained an exclusive partnership with the SunCal Companies of Irvine, California. The company bought land, mainly in its home state, sought approval for residential development, prepared the land (infrastructure, services and communications) and then sold it to residential construction companies at a profit.

Walsh wanted an exclusive partnership with SunCal, although other investment banks wanted to be part of the deal. Walsh lent SunCal $2bn on the SunCal Bakersfield site, a projected community development project, that was 10 per cent of the entire capital then, based only on the developer's blueprint and, not surprisingly, formed a close relationship with its founder, Boris Elieff. The site was never developed. On another occasion, in May 2006, land prices in California took a further hike, at the conclusion of the sale of a piece of land between Century City and Beverly Hills, for which SunCal paid $110.2m., outbidding Donald Trump's offer of $100m. Loans to the company were difficult to syndicate, owing to the difficulty of estimating future income streams. At one stage in 2006, Walsh invested about $140m. from funds into SunCal deals, and then, realizing that investors wished to withdraw the cash from the funds, he arranged for those investors to withdraw their funds. Even though that exercise made a profit, Lehman was left with even more risky assets on its balance sheet.

It is worth noting that Lehman was not the only investment bank using bridge equity. In October 2006, Wachovia and Merrill Lynch pledged $1.5bn for Tishman Speyer's $5.4bn acquisition of Stuyvesant Town, a vast apartment complex in Manhattan. In February 2007, Goldman Sachs, Morgan Stanley and Bear Stearns put up $3.5bn into the Blackstone Group's $32bn deal to buy Equity Office Properties Trust. JP Morgan were also involved in equity bridge loans, as was Citibank, often acting jointly with other banks, such as Morgan Stanley and Citigroup. JP Morgan offered a $1bn equity bridge in an LBO offer for a Texas Utility, TXU Corp. Lehman also owned part of the Rockefeller Foundation and the Chrysler Building, together with Bank of America's Strategic Ventures and Barclays Capital. The only difference between Lehman and the other investment banks was the size of their commitments to commercial real estate. Lehman ended up with $29bn commercial real estate exposure on its books in the second quarter of 2008, 30 per cent more than Deutsche Bank and Morgan Stanley, and 70 per cent more than Goldman Sachs.

Equity bridge financing has been available for many years, but it became fashionable again between 2000 and 2006, when the size and frequency of the deals rang warning bells amongst some bankers and officials at the Federal Reserve. The Office of the Comptroller of the Currency (OCC) described the increased risks associated with equity bridges as 'a heavy responsibility on sponsors to sell equity to limited partners and other investors, potential contractual limits on sales rights, a limited secondary private equity market and the questionable ability to place the equity if the deal sponsor has tried and failed.'[34] Almost a year before that, in response to a question from a banker in the audience at the conference, Chairman Bernanke had stated that 'there are some significant risks associated with private equity including bridge loans. We are looking at that.'[35] Not very hard, one might conclude from the fact that little action was taken, at least as far as investment banks were concerned. Perhaps the fact that the Federal Banking Agencies had already issued the 'Final Guidance on Concentrations in Commercial Real Estate Handling' in December 2006 might have been regarded as sufficient.[36]

The focus of the Guidelines was on the degree of concentration and less on the method of acquiring the assets. It was 'guidance' as well, designed to influence bank behaviour in a more flexible and timely way than is possible with official rule-making. It was unusual guidance, in that it set very specific threshold limits describing the concentration levels at which increased supervisory attention to a bank's risk management procedures for its CRE lending would receive much closer attention from bank supervisors. That might lead to a downgrade of the bank's official supervisory ratings, together with a greater involvement of supervisors in a bank's decision-making processes. This, however, only applied to state member banks and bank holding companies and their non-bank subsidiaries. That still left the investment banks and private equity companies beyond the ambit of such guidance. Even then, the guidance does not seem to have come fully into force until 4 January 2007, according to the Federal Reserve Bank's supervisory notice.

Mark Walsh continued to make deals in the commercial real estate market. He was described by a former Lehman employee as 'holding the keys to the kingdom'; as another real estate financier who had worked with Lehman put it, Walsh had 'extraordinary authority to commit capital as he saw fit'.[37] Lehman's partnership with SunCal continued, but by September 2008, Lehman was left with $2.2bn in exposure to SunCal on its books. Gone were the days when others were clamouring for a piece of SunCal and when Lehman was able to syndicate $320m. in loans on several SunCal projects in California.

The Examiner focused on Archstone, the largest investment. SunCal together with Lehman had invested through its complex company structure in California and many sites had either not been developed or were left with only part of the agreed work with the local authority undertaken by 2008. Following the collapse of Lehman a number of SunCal companies became insolvent or filed for Chapter 11 in November 2008.

Lehman, together with Tishman Speyer, agreed to acquire Archstone, a publicly traded Real Estate Investment Trust (REIT) on 29 May 2007, and the deal was finalized on 5 October 2007. Its portfolio of properties included expensive apartment buildings in metropolitan areas such as New York, Washington DC, San Francisco, Seattle and Boston. On 31 December 2007, Archstone owned 154 apartment communities, composed of 46,566 units, some of which were still under construction. Just before the sale, it was the second largest publicly traded apartment REIT in the USA, measured by market capitalization and enterprise value.

Lehman funded the approximately $5.4bn purchase price. Archstone was its largest commercial real estate investment. Tishman put up only $250m. of its own equity. The Examiner records that Lehman brought Bank of America to the acquisition, and on the Commitment Date each institution agreed to provide half of the debt financing and to purchase half of the bridge equity, although Bank of America did not purchase a permanent equity position. On 11 June 2007, Barclays agreed to purchase 15 per cent of the debt and 15 per cent of the bridge equity, and on 2 July 2007, agreed to increase its participation to

25 per cent. Barclays' commitments came out of Bank of America's share, and did not affect Lehman's potential exposure to Archstone. As of 2 July 2007, commitments for debt (excluding mortgage and assumed debt) and bridge debt were: Lehman: 47 per cent, BofA: 28 per cent and Barclays: 25 per cent. It was a difficult deal to complete, given that the institutional market for investments backed by commercial real estate was 'virtually closed'. William Hughes, Managing Director of Loan Syndication, added that, 'We will have to devise a strategy to syndicate this risk to bankers. That said, many of the logical candidates on the bank side are wounded from the current sell-off. This is clearly a deal we shall all have to watch carefully.'[38]

However, when the deal was closed, on 5 October 2007, the asset-level debt was secured by mortgages on Archstone's properties and comprised of $9.5bn of first lien mortgage debt, $1.1bn of mezzanine mortgage debt and $1.4bn of existing mortgage debt. Archstone had $4.6bn bridge equity and $500m. of permanent equity. As part of the closing, $1.4bn of properties from Archstone's portfolio were sold and the proceeds used to repay acquisition debt. This reduced Archstone's value from $23.6bn to $22.2bn at closing. In September 2007, Freddie Mac agreed to purchase approximately $1bn of Archstone mortgage debt and Fannie Mae committed to purchase $7.1bn of Archstone's mortgage debt. In an interview with the Examiner, Mark Walsh and Lisa Beeson, then Head of Real Estate Mergers and Acquisitions in Lehman's Investment Banking Division, said that 'these decisions confirmed the underlying soundness of the acquisition', an astonishing statement, given the extent of Fannie Mae's and Freddie Mac's failures, which even then were coming to light.[39] At the closing, Lehman, BoA and Barclays had syndicated only $71m. of bridge equity, that is, 1.5 per cent of the aggregate $4.6bn bridge equity commitment. After closing, the three banks did not syndicate any bridge equity and only syndicated $43m. of term loans. At the closing date, most of Lehman's positions (86 per cent) were term loans (42 per cent) and bridge/permanent equity (44 per cent). That meant that 86 per cent of Lehman's investment was subordinated to over half (55 per cent) of Archstone's capital structure. This put Lehman in a vulnerable position, since it meant that, especially with regard to its equity positions, it was exposed to the risk of significant losses, if the Archstone investment fell over time (or gains) if its value increased.

The three banks had agreed a 'side letter' in October 2007, setting out the terms and conditions of 'price flex'. This is a way of facilitating a sale or syndication of a loan by the initial lender without incurring a loss. The side letter in this case allowed the Archstone lenders, after 24 March 2008, to require Archstone to alter the pricing of the applicable loans (spreads, margins or fees) in order to achieve a successful syndication of such loans. The Bank of America held an escrow account, originally funded with $39m. to equal any losses suffered based on the market price of unsold Archstone debt. It had to be marked to market by BoA at the beginning of every month, and if it was too small, then Archstone had to put additional funds into the account. The only deposit before Lehman collapsed was $33m. on 28 February 2008, so the account had a balance of about $74m. at the beginning of August 2008. The Examiner commented that he did not find sufficient evidence to support a determination that Lehman's valuation of Archstone debt options covered by price flex was unreasonable.[40]

After the Archstone closing, Lehman held $5.4bn in Archstone positions: $3.0bn of debt and $2.4bn of equity, designated as Lehman's 'funded exposure', because they constitute the amount of debt that Lehman invested, net of any repayments of debt by Archstone. After that, Lehman took three valuation-related write-downs on its Archstone positions. At the end of March 2008, Lehman took a $200m. write-down on the bridge equity and $50m. on permanent equity. In May 2008, the company took a $90m. write-down on bridge equity and a $10m. write-down on permanent equity. Finally in August 2008, Lehman took a $110m. write-down on bridge equity and a $15m. write-down on permanent equity. However, the Examiner points out that a review of the weighted average is better than a mark on any specific position, because Lehman was determined to value all its Archstone holdings in aggregate; for example, because an assessment of Lehman's bridge equity on its own would not separate the change in value due to the price flex mechanism, which meant that the equity absorbed any loss of value in debt.

However, the Examiner did not find any evidence that Lehman was engaged in an effort to systematically value its Archstone commitments before that date.[41] This was true even at the end of their financial year at 30 November 2007. The trigger for a careful valuation was an article in *Barron's*, 'Apartment House Blues' on 21 January 2008, in which the author, Andrew Bary, argued that the Archstone transaction could be 'disastrous for Wall Street firms and other equity investors ... as rent increases will slow even in relatively strong markets, and that the value of Archstone equity could be zero'. Bary also pointed out that

> Archstone is a classic example of a good company with a bad balance sheet. It has more than $16bn of debt, and its interest expense is running at more than $1bn annually. Cash flows from its properties was running at just a $700m. rate

in the second quarter of 2007, meaning that the company is burning cash. The LBO sponsors told potential lenders in September that Archstone was actually covering its interest expense, but that was only because of a pre-funded $500m interest reserve.

It is odd that none of this seems to have entered into the discussions about the issue of debt or the interest expenses due, although even after due diligence was conducted, the size of the total debt remained at $6.6bn against the total enterprise value of $20.2bn without any reference to interest expenses.

Not surprisingly, the article was a wake-up call for Lehman, leading to plans to ramp up the disposition programme in 2008. Meetings took place between BoA, Barclays, Lehman and Tishman Speyer. The latter proposed allocating more capital to developments with higher returns whilst selling its core portfolio apartment complexes, which would be difficult to achieve at that time. The collapse of Bear Stearns in March, meant that 'all of the large deals we were trying to put together earlier this year have been unsuccessful to date', as Tishman Speyer advised in another memo.

The March 2008 valuation reflected Lehman's view that the risks associated with Archstone's generation of its projected cash flows had increased. There was an additional $100m. write-down in May 2008. Ian Lowitt in the earnings call set out the methodology, emphasizing comparisons with AvalonBay, another similar company to which an independent research company ascribed a higher capitalization than Archstone's. Barclays and Bank of America complained that the reduction in the valuation of Archstone's equity positions was lower than the mark they were using. The write-downs for the third quarter were, as already stated, $110m. for bridge equity and $15m. in permanent equity. With regard to the valuations during 2008, the Examiner found that in each quarter, 'for the purposes of a solvency analysis that Lehman's valuations for its Archstone bridge and permanent equity investments were unreasonable', but that there was no 'intent to produce incorrect values or to conduct the valuation process in a reckless manner.'

The Destruction of Value

The process of bankruptcy destroyed value

Under its dramatic headline, 'Lehman's chaotic bankruptcy filing destroyed billions in value', the *Wall Street Journal* proclaimed that a 'less hurried Chapter 11 bankruptcy filing would have preserved tens of billions of dollars of value'. A study carried out by the advisory firm Alvarez & Marsal argued that 'an orderly filing would have enabled Lehman to sell some of its assets outside the federal court bankruptcy protections and would have given it time to unwind its derivatives portfolio in a way that might have preserved value.'[1]

Alvarez & Marsal's co-founder and co-CEO, Bryan Marsal, was appointed CEO of Lehman Brothers, overseeing the largest bankruptcy in America history, at about 10.30 pm on Sunday 14 September 2008, just hours before Lehman actually filed for bankruptcy. He arrived at 8.30 am the following morning and saw everyone leaving with boxes. In December 2008, he estimated that the total value destruction would be between $50 and $75bn, once losses from derivatives trades and asset impairment were combined. Lehman had 1.2 million derivative contracts, with a notional value of $39 trillion. 'That is what the Fed and Treasury did not understand – the worldwide implications of the derivative book.' In an interview he gave in July 2013, he said that 'in the Lehman matter, the creditors lost $150bn. That's a $150bn of value out of pension funds and savings.'[2]

International derivative contracts were not the only problem. Lehman had over 7,000 legal entities in over 40 countries, of which 209 were registered subsidiaries, in twenty-one countries. Its collapse resulted in over 75 separate and distinct bankruptcy proceedings immediately, and affected thousands of financial market participants through its wide range of contracts. These included mortgage banks for whole residential mortgage loans; other banks/dealers for market making, firm finance, OTC derivatives; hedge funds for prime brokerage, custody, trade finance, OTC derivatives, secondary trading and MBSs and

CMBSs; sovereign and municipal debt issuers for credit and interest rate derivatives and the primary dealer; money market funds for commercial paper; insurance companies for debt and equity securities, commercial paper, OTC derivatives and MBSs and CMBSs; and finally corporate issuers for debt, equity and OTC derivatives. Many clients and counterparties found themselves exposed to multiple Lehman Brothers entities in various legal jurisdictions, with different bankruptcy and insolvency laws and contractual protections and remedies.

Lehman Brothers International (Europe) based in London also suffered from the nightly sweep. Like so many global corporations, Lehman Brothers in New York swept the cash from its regional operations back to New York, and released funds the next day. The Friday sweep on 12 September 2008 had taken $8bn out of the London-based company. Without cash, the business would not be able to meet its financial obligations on Monday morning, 15 September. An apparently thriving business of over 5,000 staff and investments worth billions of dollars was broke. But the bank's European team were ahead of their American holding company. On Friday 12 September 2008, Lehman's shares closed at $4.22 – down more than 75 per cent from the beginning of the week. Everyone knew about the meetings taking place in New York, but 'the bank's European team felt they ought to develop a just-in-case plan should their US counterparts be unable to pull off a deal', so Tony Lomas, head of PwC's restructuring and insolvency practice, bringing a small team with him, was invited to attend the firm's office in Canary Wharf. He did not leave until Tuesday, when the team took over the European part of the bankruptcy. They had learnt about the cash sweep on Sunday evening, and they needed to get the administration orders that would appoint them as administrators before the London markets opened at 8.00 am on the Monday. They succeeded with four minutes to spare. The Financial Services Authority was on hand when the judge signed the administration orders, since the bank was responsible for 12 per cent of all the trades on the London Stock Exchange. Its prime brokerage business, serving the hedge funds, was one of the largest in London, holding $40bn of client assets.

The sudden announcement of the bankruptcy, however much the markets might have anticipated it, meant that the previous three days' trades had not been finally settled or completely recorded in the bank's systems. The volume of trades had rapidly increased, since no one wanted to be caught holding them. This meant that the stock exchanges began to work through the deals to reach settlement, and securities traded by Lehman were simply left alone.

Then there were the cancellations, when counterparties such as banks or hedge funds with whom Lehman had traded rushed to trigger legal clauses to extricate themselves from some deals. Thousands of e-mail cancellations hit the bank. Either for itself or its clients, Lehman held securities such as stocks, currencies, commodities, bonds and various derivatives ... Monday brought the realisation that the broken deals meant that many hedges were no longer in place.[3]

There were both winners and losers in those frantic days. Lehman won in some instances, as the bank had some long positions when the market went up, and had some short positions, when the market went down. 'For some positions that we moved', according to PwC, 'we made gains that exceeded the entire earnings of one of the divisions last year'.[4] The markets were extremely volatile in the days following Lehman's bankruptcy.

If winding up Lehman Europe created chaos, the US bankruptcy was even worse. There is an interesting and important difference between the board of Lehman Brothers (Europe), whose board met on the Sunday and called in PwC in preparation for a possible bankruptcy so that they were prepared before the markets opened on Monday 15 September, whereas the board of Lehman Brothers Holding Company had to be told, in effect, to commence bankruptcy proceedings. These turned out to be even more chaotic than those in London.

Harvey Miller, whose firm had represented Lehman on various legal matters since 1984, was summoned to the New York Federal Reserve late on Sunday afternoon, 14 September with other Lehman executives and officials from the Federal Reserve, the Treasury and the SEC to hear Tom Baxter, general counsel for the FRBNY announce that since the Barclays deal had failed, Lehman had to file for bankruptcy by midnight. Miller argued: 'You don't realize what you're saying. It's going to have a disabling effect on the markets and destroy confidence in the credit markets. If Lehman goes down, it will be Armageddon.'[5] He was right. Later in the course of the bankruptcy proceedings, he stated that he believed that the regulators could have stepped in, not necessarily to save Lehman, but to head off the meltdown that followed: 'They totally missed it.' He added: 'When companies rushed to terminate contracts with Lehman, investor confidence plummeted in just about everything – securities and the markets they trade on, corporate debts and the assets backing them ... demand for corporate debt utterly evaporated.' In the hearing in mid-September, he said that 'events moved with a velocity that almost defies comprehension', adding that in one 24-hour period, Lehman lost \$1.6bn when the Chicago Mercantile Exchange closed out all Lehman's positions.[6]

In his evidence to the Financial Crisis Inquiry Commission, Miller provided more of the background to 'Armageddon'. On 15 September 2008, Lehman was party to over 10,000 derivatives contracts relating to about 1.7 million transactions, and a major participant in hundreds of substantial real estate and loan transactions. To a limited extent, Barclays' purchase of Lehman's North American Capital Markets business to BarCap for \$1.75bn plus \$250m. in cash for its trading assets valued at \$72bn and trading liabilities worth \$68bn, within five days of the beginning of bankruptcy proceedings, helped. Miller described the sale as being 'of enormous benefit to the nation. We saved a business that would have put 10,000 people out of work if it hadn't been sold.'[7] Miller argues that

> A government sponsored plan to support an orderly wind-down of Lehman's business over a reasonable period of time might have negated or substantially eliminated the risks to the financial system and the public that were actually encountered. It has been estimated by some commentators that a government sponsored wind-down with limited guarantees, might have cost \$40 to \$50bn. That cost would have been far less than the initial \$700bn of value that disappeared during the first week of Lehman's Chapter 11 bankruptcy case and the additional costs to the economy that followed in subsequent weeks.[8]

In his testimony to the House of Representatives Committee on the Judiciary, Miller pointed out that the whole point of the Chapter 11 bankruptcy is to provide an automatic stay so that the debtor and its creditors can try to preserve the value of the debtor's assets and possibly increase their value, which would benefit all stakeholders. The problem was not only the lack of time for any preparation for filing for bankruptcy, but also the fact that most of the relief that is typically available to debtors was not available to Lehman, for two reasons. This is because, Miller argued, the most serious liquidity needs were with its broker-dealer, Lehman Brothers Inc. (LBI), an entity which could not be a debtor under Chapter 11. On the other hand, LBI, together with Lehman's fixed income division, were among the company's most valuable assets. However, 'its value depended on Lehman's ability to assure its clients and customers of its financial and operational integrity', which it was 'unable to do in the circumstances surrounding its bankruptcy'.[9]

Lehman also engaged in derivatives trading with some of the largest counterparties in the world, contracts representing another substantial asset for Lehman. Most of these contracts did not benefit from the protection of automatic stay.

> Non-debtor counterparties to such contracts are allowed to exercise certain contractual rights triggered by the Chapter 11 case or financial condition. They have the right to terminate the contract and take advantage of positions in their favour and to leave in place contracts in which they owe money to the debtor. This caused a massive destruction of value for Lehman.[10]

On 15 September, the bankruptcy date, Lehman's derivative counterparties totalled about 930,000, of which about 733,000 sought to terminate their contracts.

That was only part of the problem. Miller describes further practical issues, to which little attention was paid in the crisis-ridden days of September 2008. As more and more subsidiaries ran out of cash, and administrators, receivers and liquidators took over, each subsidiary was cut off from the others and Lehman Brothers Holdings Inc. (LBHI), the parent company, by the various jurisdictions. It was not possible to generate information and liquidate assets efficiently and identify ways to maximize value.

> All the accumulated information in Lehman's systems totals 2,000 terabytes of data, an amount that would completely fill 20,000 computers to the maximum. This vast sea of information spreads across 2,700 software systems applications and is dispersed throughout ledger accounts in the numerous subsidiaries ... The financial information must be retrieved ... and collated and cross-referenced for accuracy and consistency.[11]

Regulators had not by that stage addressed this problem. It was only after the financial crisis that regulators addressed the issues of recovery and resolution procedures through the Financial Stability Board, the Basel Committee for Banking Supervision and the European Union. Amongst the lessons for the authorities which emerged from the collapse of Lehman, was the necessity for access to temporary liquidity. The provision of temporary liquidity for Lehman's broker-dealer, Lehman Brothers Inc., enabled an orderly transition to its acquisition by Barclays Capital.

After the financial crisis, international monetary institutions and regulatory authorities did address the problems involved in the failure of an internationally systemic financial institution by establishing agreed recovery and resolution procedures with particular reference to the removal of legal barriers to cooperation arising from the existence of different jurisdictions.[12] The practical problems of the magnitude Miller describes remain.

Did unwinding derivatives really destroy value?

One of the key issues was whether or not a collapse of the magnitude of Lehman's and its role in the derivatives market caused disruptions and volatility in derivatives trading. The Bank for International Settlements (BIS) published a detailed report as part of its semi-annual reports tracking derivatives market data. The report for the second half of 2008 states that the

> financial crisis in the second half of 2008 resulted in the first ever decline in the total notional amounts of OTC derivatives since data collection began in 1998. Notional amounts of all types of OTC contracts stood at around $592.0 trillion at the end of December 2008, 13.4 per cent lower than their total of $683 trillion six months before.
>
> Against a background of severely strained credit markets and increased multilateral netting of offsetting contracts the volume of outstanding credit default swaps (CDS) contracts fell by 27.0 per cent to $41.9 trillion. However, despite the lower outstanding volumes, the gross market value for CDS contracts increased by 78.2 per cent to $5.7 trillion as a result of the credit market turmoil.[13]

The notional amount of foreign exchange derivatives decreased by 21.0 per cent to $49.8 trillion. Volumes of forward and forex swaps, which account for almost half of the total OTC FX derivatives in terms of notional amounts, declined by 23.1 per cent, while options volumes fell by 28.8 per cent. Currency swaps only contracted by 9.7 per cent, with the dollar and the euro remaining the most important currencies, followed by the yen and sterling. Commodity derivative markets also declined by two-thirds. These figures give some idea of the scale of the impact. Equity derivatives also fell sharply, in a sharp change from the first half of 2008, when they had risen by 20.1 per cent. OTC equity derivatives decreased by 36.2 per cent to $6.5 trillion.

The figures paint a dramatic picture of the impact of the Lehman Brothers bankruptcy, as it 'triggered a confidence crisis ... one of the biggest credit events in history'.[14] The fall-out from the Lehman bankruptcy in the $57.3 trillion CDS market was the most immediate concern, where Lehman had a central role as a major counterparty and reference entity. The bankruptcy would trigger default clauses in CDS contracts referencing Lehman and terminate contracts that the firm had entered into as a counterparty. This was why the special trading session was organized on Sunday 14 September, before the filing, which allowed the main CDS dealers to net out counterparty positions involving Lehman and to rebalance their books through the replacement of trades. Later, following ISDA (the International Swaps and Derivatives Association) procedures, an auction was conducted on 10 October to determine the recovery rate to be used in the cash settlement of CDS contracts, referencing Lehman and the net amount exchanged between parties. BIS notes that this set the recovery value at 8.625 per cent, based on quotes submitted by fourteen dealers. This bond price was only slightly lower than the bond price immediately before the auction.

Lehman's major source of funding was its issuance of commercial paper, to which money market funds were attracted because of their high credit ratings and yield premiums relative to US government paper. As noted previously, one of the funds, the public money market fund, Reserve Primary, 'broke the buck' by falling below $1 per share. The fund was liquidated and distributions made to investors as cash accumulated either through the maturing of portfolio holdings or their sale. This prompted massive runs on the other funds, leading to about $172bn worth of redemptions from the sector, which was worth $3.5 trillion. The run stopped on 19 September 2008, when the US government introduced a temporary programme of insurance for money market investors. Even so, most funds reduced their holdings in commercial paper, as it was then deemed risky. A month later, the total value of outstanding commercial paper fell to $1.4 trillion from $1.76 trillion. The Federal Reserve began purchasing commercial paper on 26 October for the first time, which stabilized the market. By January 2009, the Federal Reserve held paper worth $357bn, 22.4 per cent of the market, which it gradually reduced during that year.

The BIS Review provides another illustration of the legal problems in such a complex bankruptcy with filings in so many different jurisdictions. Lehman provided prime brokerage services to a large number of hedge funds, as a result of which hedge funds placed investment assets with Lehman's broker-dealer units in various jurisdictions. These assets were used as collateral for funding activities and were then reused by Lehman to meet its own obligations (re-hypothecation). The bankruptcy meant that many of Lehman's clients could not access their collateral assets during the whole process, whilst their assets changed value and they waited for the completion of differing legal processes.

This would alter the size and location of hedge fund activities with their prime brokers, which together with attempts to reduce risk exposures, added to pressures in the funding and securities lending markets. On Sunday 21 September, as a result of the continuing concerns about counterparty risk and the unrelenting funding squeeze, Goldman Sachs and Morgan Stanley obtained permission from the US authorities to convert themselves into bank holding companies. This was designed to stop the transfers of counterparty positions and client funds to third parties, with CDS spreads for both credits tightening as a result. The BIS account of the immediate impact of Lehman's bankruptcy makes it even more astonishing that neither Chairman Bernanke nor Hank Paulson, who were in a position to understand the complex and interrelated effects such a sudden collapse would have, appeared to have any understanding of what was about to happen. It is true that some appropriate actions were taken immediately, but an immense amount of damage was inflicted both on America and the rest of the world, when a much smaller price might have mitigated the worst effects, even if it only took the form of temporary measures.

It is also important to disentangle the effects of the process of bankruptcies in New York and so many other jurisdictions from the bankruptcy itself. Here it is important to focus on the procedures set out by ISDA and to consider what contribution the Master Agreements were able to make to sorting out the enormous number and the wide range of derivatives, running into trillions of dollars.

Did ISDA's Master Agreements help to avert yet further catastrophe?

For over twenty years, the over-the-counter swaps and other derivative contracts have been documented using the standard terms of the Master Agreements developed by ISDA. The first version was published in 1992 and the other in 2002.[15] The 1992 version was the first to be designed in a form which applied to derivatives other than swaps and to allow for both financially and physically settled transactions. The 2002 version was revised as lessons were learned in the markets, and to reflect changes in the markets. New categories of transactions, such as credit derivatives and repos, were included in the definition of a 'specified transaction' for the purposes of default under a 'Specified Transaction Event of Default'. The term 'default' was also widened to cover a default under any credit support arrangement for the particular derivatives transaction. The 'Bankruptcy

Event of Default' was modified to restrict the circumstances in which a grace period will apply and to reduce the grace period where it does apply. The market quotation and loss valuation methods were replaced by the close-out amount as a single valuation measure. The set-off clause was introduced to enable the non-defaulting party to set off any early termination amount against amounts owing to or from the defaulting party, whether or not arising from the ISDA Master Agreement. These are largely changes to events of default and termination events and changes to the mechanism for calculating termination payments after an early termination date and including a detailed set-off provision. The rules for interest on defaulted and deferred payments and compensation for interest on early termination and unpaid amounts were also then changed.

The ways in which the Master Agreements are applied in American and English law differ and make a difference to the settlement provisions for derivatives under the bankruptcy laws of each country. The underlying principle underpinning the US Bankruptcy Code is that the debtor's assets must be distributed in a fair and equitable way amongst the creditors. The policy is enforced by the 'automatic stay', that is the creditors of a bankrupt company cannot enforce their contractual rights against the debtor without the Bankruptcy Court's authorization, or unless there is a specific statutory exception. A series of amendments to the Bankruptcy Code from 1982 onwards allows for just such exceptions. These apply to securities contracts, commodities contracts, forward contracts, swaps agreements, repurchase agreements and master netting agreements, called 'qualified financial contracts' (QFCs). This was because these financial instruments, such as swaps, raise unique systemic issues. The automatic right of stay could mean that the non-defaulting counterparties were exposed to rapid changes in market conditions and interest rates over which they had no control and could lead to a series of settlement failures. ISDA had successfully argued over the years that a solvent counterparty's inability to immediately terminate its contract could interfere with its efforts to hedge and even jeopardize the counterparty's solvency. The reason for limiting the right of stay to such instruments was to preserve the stability of the financial system overall.

The principle underlying English solvency law is 'anti-deprivation'. This rule is based on the premise that the parties to an agreement cannot contract out of the mandatory provisions of legislation governing the distribution of an insolvent debtor's assets. These principles affected the way in which the bankruptcy was handled and the valuation of the derivative contracts.

The procedures, where one or other party defaults, require the termination of all contracts, which triggers the unwinding of all open contracts governed by the

Master Agreement. Then the value of all contracts must be determined. The amounts owing or owed on individual transactions should be netted off to arrive at an aggregate sum, which one party owes the other – 'close-out netting' under the 2002 Master Agreement. Any net amount has to be paid. In the case of the bankrupt party, the amount is paid to the bankruptcy trustee or administrator. If an amount is owed by the bankrupt party, then that is a debt, which will have to be paid out of recoveries. This assumes that the non-defaulting party can close out its positions at market rates, and can then enter new positions to establish replacement hedges to avoid the risk of losses from changes in prices or rates.

What actually happened once Lehman Brothers Holdings Inc. filed for bankruptcy was that its status as guarantor for LBSF's derivative transactions meant that non-defaulting parties were able to elect to terminate their transactions, even though LBSF did not file for bankruptcy until 3 October 2008. Approximately 80 per cent of the derivatives counterparties to LBSF terminated their contracts under the ISDA Master Agreement within five weeks of bankruptcy. What happened then was that where the non-defaulting party owed LBSF money, that was paid, and if LBSF owed money to the non-defaulting party, that was not paid. Kimberley Summe, former Managing Director at Lehman Brothers Inc/Barclays Capital, reports that the Lehman estate was able to advance from its cash position of $7m. on 14 September 2008, to $15bn by 1 February 2011.[16] In other words, the Lehman bankruptcy did not have the disastrous effects that some had envisaged. Summe also quotes Daniel Ehrman, a managing director at Alvarez & Marsal, who said, 'we discovered that out of all the claims against the Lehman estate, those in the derivatives subset were the most inflated'.

It is not easy to apply this methodology to more complex derivatives, where valuation will inevitably depend on factors such as the exact timing in a volatile market. It will also depend on the calculation agent and the calculation statement. The agreement allows the agent, often the dealer, to calculate the loss 'in good faith', taking into account all the relevant facts. If the dealer is the defaulting party, as in the case of Lehman, then conflicts and disagreements are very likely to occur, as indeed they did. The process, however, depends on the normal functioning of the market, allowing the non-defaulting party to re-hedge positions and to establish valuations with reasonable accuracy. Those with swaps found that they were unable to replace hedges in a reasonable time period and the large differences between the costs incurred and termination values under the ISDA procedures led to significant losses for the counterparties. At the time of its filing, Lehman had around 1.2 million derivative contracts open, with a notional face value of $39 trillion.[17] In September 2009, the court imposed a deadline for the settlement of about 6,000 derivative claims worth some $60bn payable by Lehman on the Lehman estate, including claims from forty of the largest US banks. There were operational issues as well. Market participants which had dealt with various Lehman entities had multiple ISDA Master Agreements in place, with different transactions recorded under each contract. Many of the counterparties' information systems had inaccurately grouped contracts together for netting and assessing net exposure, which made it difficult to determine the risks and the required hedging strategies.

The focus here is on the bankruptcy proceedings in the US and the way in which the automatic right of stay was suspended for derivatives. The safe harbour provisions of bankruptcy law can create perverse incentives for counterparties to jettison their contracts, when a debtor files for bankruptcy. This can create a run on the debtor's assets, as many counterparties terminate their contracts and seize any collateral securing those contracts. These incentives contribute to the systemic implications of a firm's failure, creating a stampede for exits, according to some analysts. Ayotte and Skeel, who argued for the removal of the blanket reversal of the automatic right of stay in the case of derivatives, pointed out that 'if the debtor is one of the handful of major derivative counterparties, the debtor's failure to could itself cause market-wide damage, since the glut of terminated contracts may overwhelm the market's ability to provide replacements.'[18]

They point out that when Lehman filed for bankruptcy, the counterparties cancelled over 700,000 of the 930,000 derivative contracts, which threatened to create chaos, but the potential disruption was 'diminished somewhat by netting and the inability of many counterparties to retrieve assets to satisfy their claims.'[19] Some counterparties whose claims were collateralized could end their contract and use the collateral to meet Lehman's obligations. Counterparties without collateral were able to close out the contract, but they were free to take further steps to collect what they were owed. If they had been able to close out their contracts and to insist on immediate payment, then Lehman would have been forced to liquidate many of its assets. This would have further complicated the orderly resolution of the bankruptcy. Those without collateral can arrange to purchase an alternative hedge, but the principal cost is uncertainty as to the amount and timing of the payment in the debtor's bankruptcy case. If the contract is large, the costs of re-hedging could be prohibitive, but in many cases this was not the real problem. There were also standard procedures for determining their losses, and these were applied successfully in many cases. Some counterparties can terminate their contracts, but they will be vulnerable if they do not have collateral. That vulnerability gives counterparties a strong incentive to ensure that they are fully collaterized.

Ayotte and Skeel argue that the solution is to remove the exemption of derivatives from automatic stay which 'would strengthen counterparties' incentives to both carefully monitor the debtor and to avoid overexposing themselves to a single counterparty'. The costs of the automatic stay could also be reduced by setting deadlines on the debtor's decision on whether or not to retain the contract.[20] In fact, it is not clear that the process of unwinding derivatives requires the removal of the automatic stay which some, including Ayotte and Skeel, have proposed. To understand that, it is necessary to see what actually happened to derivatives in the process.

It appears that the settlement of derivatives went ahead smoothly due to the use of the Master Agreements and exemption from automatic stay. Kimberley Summe stated that at the time of filing for bankruptcy, the Lehman estate reported that it was counterparty to 906,000 derivative transactions documented under 6,120 ISDA Master Agreements. The whole portfolio represented about 5 per cent of the global derivatives transactions at that time. In her article she states that 'approximately 80% of Lehman's derivatives counterparties terminated their transactions within five weeks of bankruptcy'. Furthermore, none of Lehman's counterparties filed for bankruptcy nor did

> the derivatives market grind to a halt after Lehman's bankruptcy filing … In addition, while it was widely estimated in the lead-up to October 10, 2008 credit default swap auction for bonds referencing Lehman Brothers that close to $400bn could be required in payments to settle outstanding contracts, in fact only $6bn in net settlement payments were ultimately needed.[21]

A more detailed analysis was published in the *Economic Policy Review* in March 2014.[22] The advantage of this report is that the bankruptcy process is over and the results of most aspects of the process are known, since Lehman emerged from bankruptcy on 6 March 2012, although various legal cases were still pending then.

Some have argued that 70 per cent of the derivatives receivables worth $48bn were lost that could otherwise have been unwound. The alternative view is that the Lehman estate did not suffer any substantial loss on its derivative positions since the LBHI's counterparties initially overstated some of their claims, which were later overturned by the bankruptcy court.[23] Duffie, Li and Lubke also pointed out that the use of novations enables counterparties to exit their positions by assigning them to other dealers, which depleted LBHI's cash reserves and therefore those of LBI since they were the main source of LBI's funding. This was the result of Lehman's original dealer counterparty, through novation, transferring its position to another dealer. As a result Lehman lost the associated 'independent amount' of collateral. This was not replaced because the initial margins were not posted as dealer-to-dealer trades.[24]

The OTC derivatives market was highly concentrated then, as shown by the fact that of the outstanding contracts in January 2011, the share of the thirty big bank counterparties was 85 per cent of the number of trades and 48 per cent of the derivative contracts by dollar value, but only 5 per cent of the number of contracts. Lehman and its counterparties had to negotiate an appropriate method for settling the remaining contracts. These banks, all affiliates of thirteen major institutions, were Bank of America, Barclays, BNP Paribas, Credit Suisse, Deutsche Bank, Goldman Sachs, JPM Chase, Merrill Lynch, Morgan Stanley, RBS, Societe Generale and UBS. The Lehman estate argued that the bank counterparties had submitted inflated claims, centring on the time and date of valuation; the method of valuation, for example, the use of the bid or ask price, as well as including additional amounts to the mid-market price; and set-off. The valuation of claims was made more difficult because of the 'replacement cost' methodology required by the Master Agreement, and the wide bid-offer spreads prevailing at the time. The progress of settling the claims was slow. A derivatives claims settlement framework was included in Lehman's January 2011 liquidation plan, but even that meant that Lehman had only settled with eight of the major financial firms at that time. Even by the beginning of 2013, about 1,000 derivatives contracts were still not settled. The Lehman estate argued that the need to carry out due diligence on numerous, complex claims on an individual basis was the chief cause of delay.

Problems occurred with some of the large contracts, such as Metavante and Nomura. The former had entered into a $600m. interest rate swap with Lehman Brothers Special Financing (LBSF), which required the company to pay 3.865 per cent p.a. to LBSF and receive three-month LIBOR in return. Metavante could have terminated the contract immediately after the Chapter 11 filing, but did not, refusing to make the required payments. The company was obliged to pay LBSF the difference between 3.865 per cent and the lower three-month LIBOR. If Metavante had ended the contract, it would have owed Lehman $6m., hoping that interest rates would rise, lowering the cost of ending the swap. The court ruled against Metavante and the issue was finally settled through mutual agreement. Other companies bringing cases against valuations included Nomura

International, Nomura Securities and Nomura Global Financial Products. Finally, Lehman brought a case against Nomura in April 2010. Lehman finally abandoned its case against Nomura's claim for $720m. in January 2012, and a settlement was reached out of court.

Various reasons for the delays in settlement have been put forward, but, echoing Harvey Miller's description of the structure of the company,

> Lehman's organisational complexity resulted in delays. In many instances Lehman and its counterparties were uncertain of the identity of the specific Lehman entity against which creditors had claims ... Lehman's interconnectedness (in particular, guarantees by the holding company to affiliates) led to delays as holding company creditors argued in the hope of greater share of recovery than under strict priority rules.[25]

Further challenges followed, even with the well-defined and well-used process set out in the Master Agreements for assessing the value of terminated transactions. The process involves reconciling and reviewing counterparty valuations and then agreeing on a settlement. It is extremely demanding, owing to the duty of care imposed on the trustee, who has to review the methods by which each non-defaulting party reached its early termination amount for each derivative trade. With over 6,000 counterparties and about a million transactions to be considered, it is not surprising it took two years to settle 45.6 per cent of the claims.

Miller's point about the identity of Lehman's counterparties no doubt contributed to the problems of the bankruptcy, but the identification issues were becoming increasingly clear after the launch of the Depository Trust and Clearing Corporation's Trade Information Warehouse in November 2007, the repository of all derivatives trading details. Lehman was one of the participants in the launch, along with 200 other financial institutions, followed within a few months by a further 700 participants. All that information was available to regulators and others. It was also available during the bankruptcy proceedings, but the cause of the delays had more to do with valuation, and other practical and legal challenges. As Lehman's Financial Statements of November 2009 note:

Recoveries in respect of derivatives receivables are complicated by:

(i.) Whether counterparties have validly declared termination dates in respect of derivatives and lack of clarity as to the exact times and dates when counterparties ascribed values to their derivative contracts;

ii.   Abnormally wide bid-offer spreads and extreme liquidity adjustments resulting from market conditions as of the time when the vast majority of the company's derivatives transactions were terminated and whether such market conditions provide the company with a basis for invalidating counterparty valuations;

    iii. Counterparty credit worthiness which can be reflected both in reduced actual cash collections from counterparties and in reduced valuations ascribed by the market to such counterparties' derivatives transactions and whether, in the latter circumstance, such reduced valuations are legally valid deductions from the fair value of derivatives receivables; and

    iv. Legal provisions in derivatives contracts that purport to penalize the defaulting party by way of close-out mechanics, suspended payments, structural subordination in relation to transactions with certain special purpose vehicles, deductions for financial advisory and legal fees that the company believes are excessive and expansive set-off provisions.

Some of the non-defaulting counterparties who were out-of-the-money, and would have owed large sums to Lehman, if they had been in a position to pay, chose not to send in a termination notice. Some of these were municipalities and non-profits. They had issued floating rate bonds and entered into interest rate swaps where they paid a fixed rate and received a floating rate. Some of the swap counterparties were out-of-the-money to Lehman as the fixed rate was higher than the floating rate before Lehman's bankruptcy. Naturally Lehman wanted to settle these potentially valuable contracts, and considered that market movements might reduce the amount owed. Lehman and its counterparties failed to agree on valuations, partly because the markets were illiquid. These claims are determined by replacement costs, which diverged from fair market value because of the large bid-offer spreads at that time. Lehman asked the court to approve procedures to allow the valuation of non-terminated contracts by assigning them to third parties with the consent of unsecured creditors and the counterparty. The effect of this was to encourage the use of already established dispute resolution procedures. By January 2009, there were 2,667 out of over 6,000 contracts of this kind at the time of the bankruptcy. By 17 June 2009, only 17 per cent of the contracts and less than 1 per cent of the trades were not terminated.

Despite these complications, and special pleading on the part of the large banks, while the valuation of derivatives and the settlement of claims took time, they did not cause the disruption to the markets that many had feared. The settlement of claims took time for different reasons for the varying groups of contracts outstanding at the time. The Lehman estate took steps to speed up the process. On 25 January 2011, Lehman amended its liquidation plan and proposed to reallocate payments owed to derivative counterparties to creditors of the parent company. As a result, LBSF transferred $7.35bn in cash and investments, to add to LBHI's $2bn. This proposal coincided with the estate's decision that the defaulting party should rely on a standardized methodology to value remaining derivative claims. This was approved on 6 December 2011. The first distributions to creditors were made on 17 April 2012. Summe concludes that the 'allegations that derivatives destroyed value is flatly at odds with the fact that derivatives were the biggest contributor to boosting recoveries for Lehman's creditors'.[26]

The adoption of the Joint Chapter Plan on 6 December 2011 did not entirely resolve the issue of derivative claims by the large banks, but the claims and counterclaims had more to do with the activities of the parties to the disputes than with the actual nature of the contracts. Summe's detailed analysis does not support the view that the process itself caused the destruction of value. Nor does that proffered by Fleming and Sarkar. Summe notes that 'Lehman's organisational complexity resulted in delays. For example, in many instances, Lehman and its counterparties were uncertain of the identity of the specific Lehman subsidiary against which creditors had claims.'[27] All that means is that a preplanning phase would have taken longer anyway. The authors conclude that the 'predictability of Lehman's claims and settlement procedures were hindered by the novelty of the business and financial structure', and by the fact, that, although existing case law provided a useful starting point for Lehman's resolution, the court provided new interpretations of the Bankruptcy Code (for example, regarding some aspects of the safe harbour provisions for derivatives). This reflected the 'prominence of complex financial scenarios that the bankruptcy court had to analyse perhaps for the first time.'[28]

The above analyses were not taken into account by regulators, policymakers or lawmakers alike. It was argued that the Bankruptcy Court was too slow and expensive as a means of dealing with the bankruptcy of a major financial institution. The Orderly Liquidation Authority (OLA) was introduced as Title II of the Dodd-Frank Act. The new authority requires the Secretary of the Treasury to obtain the consent of the board in order to act, and if he fails to get their consent, he has to obtain the approval of the court, for which a period of twenty-four hours is allowed. Financial institutions have to provide 'living wills' designed to prepare for handling a distressed company, which would then have the ability to borrow from the Federal Reserve for debtor-in-possession funding. The OLA would also be authorized to draw on the Federal Reserve to finance a bridge financial company, one of the purposes of which would be to support the collateral of the failed company's derivatives. Title II, however, only allows for a one-day stay on ipso facto clauses after which a derivatives contract terminates and can be closed out. Title II gives the government considerable power and discretion to intervene, take over and liquidate financial companies without any time allowed for judicial review or analysis, and puts the power to handle the process in the hands of the Federal Deposit Insurance Corporation. In the eyes of many, the FDIC lacks the ability to run such a liquidation process in a predictable rule-like manner. If Title II had been in place for any failed 'systemically important' financial company, it is unlikely that the OLA would have resulted in any substantial change in the way in which derivative trades are handled post-bankruptcy. Together with the requirement that derivative contracts are placed at clearing houses, the risk is that the clearing house would have to be bailed out by the government as well. The issue of who bears the losses in the event of failure: the clearing houses, their member banks, investors or governments, is one which is now occupying the minds of all the players. The OLA has, of course, yet to be tested, but its necessity has not been proved by the handling of derivatives in the Lehman bankruptcy process.

Nor did the fault lie with derivatives themselves, but rather with the fact that the derivatives were *derived from* the subprime mortgages, and that is where the destruction of value was to be found. Derivatives traded between 'sophisticated parties' were not regulated, except as part of the general 'safety and soundness' overseen by the regulators of banks and securities firms.[29] Alan Greenspan, giving testimony at a Senate hearing in 2000, quoted with approval the report of the President's Working Group of which he had been a member, stating that

> regulating financial over-the-counter derivatives, involving professional counterparties was unnecessary ... as financial derivatives are not readily subject to manipulation and because professional counterparties can protect themselves against fraud and unfair practices.[30]

The Act effectively removed a wide range of derivatives, including credit default swaps, futures, options, mortgage-backed securities and collateral default obligations, from regulation. In effect, it meant that the OTC market was exempt from capital adequacy requirements, reporting and disclosure, opening the way for excessive speculation.

Too big to manage?

Inevitably, in the aftermath of the financial crisis, regulators turned their attention to capital, liquidity and supervision, in order to prevent the failures of what then became known as 'systemically important financial institutions' (SIFIs). This resulted in new capital and liquidity requirements and an increased regulatory focus on macro-prudential surveillance and the development of specific tools to address the build-up of systemic risk in the financial system. Individual large banks are now required by the regulators to produce recovery and resolution plans outlining detailed plans for the way in which they would regain viability if they were under severe financial stress. The plans, often called 'living wills', require extremely detailed information from the banks, which has to be updated regularly. The full details are not released publicly, since this would indeed defeat the object if they were released before or during a financial crisis. It is, however, unlikely that such plans would ensure the orderly wind-down that regulators envisaged, given the difficulty of identifying and predicting risk, problems of confidentiality with the additional possibility of loss of experienced and skilled staff if they knew that, in a crisis, their business unit would be one of the ones to be sacrificed. That is linked to market reactions to the immediate prospect of an orderly winding down of a particular bank. In other words, it would not prevent the kind of 'bank run' which is part of the explanation of what happened to Lehman. If the market is strong, then the possibility of rescuing an individual bank is higher, but living wills cannot resolve systemic problems that affect all SIFIs market-wide, such as a sudden sharp rise in interest rates or sovereign defaults.

However, even if recovery and resolution plans do not serve the purpose for which they were intended in the next crisis, they may play a part in fending off another crisis. The issue which has been neglected too often in the focus on 'too big to fail' is the issue of 'too big to manage' or better, 'too complex to manage'. The analysis of the Lehman bankruptcy proceedings revealed the complexity and hence the lack of transparency in the bank's structure which impeded progress and may also have led to a lack of fairness in the way in which creditors were repaid.

> In 2008, when Lehman Brothers collapsed, regulators found it next to impossible to identify all the counterparties that were exposed to the bank and, in turn, to each other. Senior policymakers had to hold their collective breath when that and other major Wall Street events took place, because they had no reliable way of determining who would be affected and in what way.[31]

Too many others experienced the same difficulties at that time.

The OCC recognizes that

> one potential obstacle to risk management and corporate governance is the multiplicity of legal entities within banking organizations ... [These] add greatly to the complexity of the company and measurably increases the difficulty of managing it.[32]

As a result, banks are reducing the number of legal entities within their organizations, which will benefit the banks in terms of reducing legal, accounting and other costs, and provide other benefits in terms of system integration.

This goes part-way towards the recognition that the informational requirements for living wills are likely to be much more useful for regulatory supervision and management of the whole enterprise by the banks. The extensive detailed information as set out, for example, by the UK Prudential Regulatory Authority (PRA) and the Bank of England, should provide the basis for banks to design an appropriate management and management information structure as the basis for risk management procedures. The bankruptcy proceedings served to highlight both the complexity of Lehman and the lack of management information systems, enabling one part of the bank to communicate with another. At times, the suspicion arises that the holding company in New York simply received the cash at the end of the business day, without knowing enough about the circumstances in which the money was earned. At the very least, the complexity adds to the difficulty of management.

The role of large banks in the financial crisis prompted many to argue that there is an optimal size of banks or that the range of activities of banks should be restricted (the Volcker rule).[33] The argument is that market-based activities and organizational complexity increase systemic risk but not the individual bank risk. This implies that it is not possible to look at any one bank in isolation but that the connections between them may well increase systemic risk. It is quite clear that the connections between both the 'big five' investment banks and banks throughout the world and Lehman Brothers were not understood either by the regulators or by Hank Paulson, although he was formerly the chief executive of Goldman Sachs, and others, during that fateful summer of 2008. When large banks fail, 'they are more likely to fail together precisely because they are more interconnected through asset and short-term lending'.[34] However, the study fails to recognize the significant risks to the ability to manage posed by over-complex banks.

Size and complexity are not always a disadvantage; indeed, there may be value in having multiple business units and operating on a global scale. However, managing a complex business by simplifying the organization's business structure is essential. Making sure that the accountability lines are clear and deciding to withdraw from certain markets, dropping unprofitable business lines or those which require the investment of too much time, money and effort are the routes to success. Charles Taylor of the OCC observed that 'banks going through the legal entity simplification process are the ones making noticeable progress in meeting our heightened expectations around risk management and governance'.[35] Large and complex banks can only be well-managed if the role and responsibilities of senior management are clear and the board oversight is both competent and independent. The role of the board in risk management and in retaining value is considered in Chapter 9.

Lehman's Valuation of Its Assets

The purpose of this chapter is to examine the whole issue of valuing Lehman's assets. This is a more complex subject than it may first appear. The way in which Lehman valued its assets has to be set in the context of the way in which assets were or should have been valued at the time. The reasons for the market's lack of confidence in Lehman's valuations are explained in this chapter. The kind of regulations governing valuation in force between 1994 and 2007 are set out here. None of these applied to the Big Five investment banks, only to banks regulated by the agencies: the Office of the Comptroller of the Currency (OCC), the Federal Reserve, the Federal Deposit Insurance Corporation (FDIC) and the Office of Thrift Supervision (OTS). That left another regulatory gap. The SEC did not examine the real estate risks Lehman ran, lacking a mandate and regulations to do so. In other words, it was not the process of bankruptcy that destroyed value. Lehman's real estate assets did not have the value the company had attached to them. Ultimately, the value of the derivatives depended on the value of the underlying assets, and the fall in their value reflected the fall in real estate prices from mid-2006 onwards.

Lehman's estimates of the valuation of Archstone and SunCal

Lehman, in its Earnings conference call, referred to its two large positions: SunCal and Archstone. The former was one of the largest privately held developers of master planned communities in the Western United States. Lehman's exposure to SunCal was primarily in Southern California, consisting of 23 separate residential developments and one luxury high-level residential development.

These positions, approximately 90% of which were originated as senior debt, have an aggregate carrying value of $1.6bn, are marked in the mid-70s ... The portfolio is marked to where an investor could achieve a 15% unleveraged return over a five-year hold period.

With regard to Archstone, Lehman pointed out that

> Archstone also has an extensive land development platform and land inventory which do not generate current cash flow but have substantial value and are often overlooked in evaluating its worth ... in recognition of the change in real estate valuation metrics, we have taken a significant markdown on the position. Our equity exposure in Archstone is currently carried at 75 for a value of less that $1.8bn.[1]

Lehman claimed that the valuations were fair, but that was on the basis of their own valuations with the assistance of their real estate adviser, TriMont. The valuations were Lehman's own, and were presented as being marked to market.

Risk management and valuations are inevitably closely linked, especially as Lehman used pricing models to 'value, aggregate and hedge risk positions'. These 'pricing models produce valuations and risk-factor sensitivities ... which are fed into the risk models used by the Global Risk Management Division'.[2] Lehman's Principal Transactions Group (PTG) was responsible for valuing the company's investments in real estate development or improvement projects, generally lasting two to five years, after which the property would be sold. These positions were illiquid until completion, and were not put up for sale before that, which meant that PTG could not rely on any sales data. The Examiner records that Anthony Barsanti, the PTG Senior Vice President responsible for marking the PTG positions, told him that Lehman valued these investments through a combination of financial projections and 'gut feeling' due to the unique nature of each asset and the lack of sales data regarding comparable debt and equity positions.[3] The 'gut feelings' included judgement based on 'experience, the collateral's performance with respect to the development's business plan, and other market data related to the collateral's geographic region or property type that was not always accounted for in their models'.

The PTG's 'portfolio was supposed to represent Lehman's judgement as to the price at which each position could be sold to a third party as of a particular measurement date, as required by SFAS 157'.[4] As noted earlier, the Examiner records that 'Barsanti, whom Kenneth Cohen identified as the person principally responsible for determining PTG marks, stated that he did not know whether PTG assets could be sold for the price at which they were marked and stated that *he had not thought about it*'.[5] The valuation was 'based on whether the development was proceeding according to the project's business plan and not the price the buyer would pay for the asset'.[6] The assets, which were valued at about $9.6bn at the end of the fiscal year 2007, were written down by $1.1bn over the first three quarters of 2008.

The Examiner also describes the ways in which TriMont operated, and the contempt with which Lehman's employees viewed the company. Aristide Koutouvides, Vice President of PTG, for example, 'considered the stabilised value reported by TriMont to be useless', because their asset managers were relying too heavily on developers' assurances that a particular project would be successful, rather than looking at the deteriorating market conditions. Barsanti did not share Koutouvides' belief that TriMont provided high valuations, but he agreed that PTG often had to instruct TriMont to correct the data.[7]

These are the key points arising from the Examiner's analysis of Lehman's approach to valuation. The purpose of this chapter is to detail the regulations covering appraisals and valuations of real estate, applicable at the time and to consider Lehman's approach in the light of these regulations.

Interagency Appraisal and Valuation Guidelines

These are the guidelines which applied before 2008. They include Title XI of the Financial Institutions Reform, Recovery and Enforcement Act 1989, which required the agencies to provide guidelines for the appraisal and valuation of both residential and commercial real estate. These were set out by each of the agencies separately in 1992.[8]

The 1994 Guidelines

The first set of interagency guidelines was issued in 1994. These were designed to promote sound practice in the banks' appraisal and evaluation programmes, including independent appraisals and valuations. The 1994 Guidelines emphasize the need for the independence of the appraiser, as well as the requirement for the appraiser to have the necessary qualifications, as set out in the state regulations. The Guidelines state that

> because the appraisal and the evaluation process is an integral component of the credit underwriting process, it should be isolated from influence by the institution's loan production process. An appraiser and an individual providing evaluation services should be independent of the loan and collection functions

of the institution and have no interest, financial or otherwise, in the property or the transaction.[9]

The Guidelines also placed the responsibility for reviewing and adopting policies and procedures that establish an effective real estate appraisal programme on the institution's board of directors. These Guidelines typically provide detailed procedures for appraisals and valuations.

The 2003 Guidelines

The 1994 Guidelines were followed by another interagency set of guidelines for the independent appraisal and evaluation functions, on 27 October 2003. These laid down stricter rules for the selection of individuals to carry out appraisals or evaluations, including independence, competence, qualifications and experience. The 2003 Guidelines expressly forbid the use of a 'borrower ordered' appraisal or a 'readdressed appraisal'. The lender must directly engage the appraiser. The 2003 Guidelines included effective internal controls and compliance reviews. The company had to be able to confirm that appraisals and evaluations were reviewed by qualified and trained staff, not involved in the process of granting loans. Banking supervision included checks on the appraisals.

The 2006 Guidelines

Further guidelines were issued in December 2006, with the focus this time on concentrations in commercial real estate lending and on sound risk management practices in particular.[10] The regulators had observed the increased concentration and that this added 'a dimension of risk that compounds the risk inherent in individual loans, making the institutions more vulnerable to cyclical CRE markets'.[11] There should be a risk management framework to identify, monitor and control CRE concentration risks.

The responsibilities of the board of directors are clearly set out. These included establishing policy guidelines, making sure that management implemented procedures and controls. It was management's responsibility to identify and quantify the nature and level of the risk, and review the CRE risk exposure limits, reducing them when necessary.

Management was expected to monitor concentration levels of loan participation, whole loan sale, securitization and selling CRE loans. If the contingency plan included the latter, then management should assess the marketability of the portfolio. Management had to be sure of its ability to access the secondary market and that its underwriting standards matched those in the secondary market. The regulators were clearly becoming concerned about the mortgage market and the commercial real estate market. But the publication of their new Guidelines at the end of 2006 was almost too late. Much of the damage had already been done.

The purpose of the 2006 Guidelines

The focus of the 2006 Guidelines was on the risks of concentration in CRE lending at banking institutions. These were defined as follows:

- Loans for construction, land and land development (CLD) represented 100 per cent or more of a bank's total risk-based capital and total CRE non-owner-occupied represented 300 per cent or more of the bank's total risk-based capital.
- The growth in total CRE lending had increased by 50 per cent or more during the previous 36 months.
- The guidance stated that such banks should have in place enhanced credit risk controls, including stress testing of the CRE portfolios.
- These banks would require further supervisory examination.

Irrelevance of the 2006 Guidelines

An analysis completed in 2013 found that 31 per cent of all commercial banks in 2006 exceeded at least one of the supervisory criteria. In 2006, these banks held $378bn in outstanding CRE loans, almost 40 per cent of all outstanding CRE loans. These exposures began to decline in 2007. Not surprisingly, these banks were more likely to fail and in fact, 23 per cent did during the years between 2008 and 2010. Banks exceeding the construction criterion limits accounted for about 80 per cent of the losses to the FDIC between 2007 and 2011. In addition, the banks that had exceeded the CRE construction levels were more likely to reduce the size of their portfolios between 2008 and 2011, especially in construction.[12]

The regulators took no further action if banks failed to keep to the guidelines. The expectation was that banks would set up appropriate risk management strategies. It was possible to exceed the limits, but without any external checks on the effectiveness of their controls. The agencies did not set any caps. Banks with concentration levels above the limits in 2011 were also above the limit in 2006.

The 2006 Guidance clearly was not very successful in ensuring that the banks would reduce the level of concentration and the risks involved.

November 2008 proposed Interagency Appraisal and Evaluation Guidelines

These were intended to replace all previous guidelines. They would include revisions to the Uniform Standards of Professional Appraisal Practice (USPAP) and developments in collateral valuation practices since 1994 and would reflect improvements to the supervision of banks' appraisal and valuation programmes since 1994. The new guidelines were published in the Federal Register on 10 December 2010, when the worst of the financial crisis was over. Reference is made to the new Guidelines because it shows how slowly the agencies react to market developments, posing real risks to the viability of banks.

It is true that Lehman was not bound by the guidance. Even though the agencies were largely ineffective, at least some standards were available as a yardstick by which to judge the risks a bank was taking. For Lehman and other investment banks, there was nothing. Despite the lack of regulation, it would have made sense for Lehman to select one of the international property companies operating in the USA, experienced in providing valuations for large-scale development projects, such as SunCal. Such firms would have carried valuations at regular intervals to take account of all the changing circumstances, including changes in macroeconomic conditions.

Valuation methodologies and mark-to-market

Lehman used various approaches to valuation from 2006 onwards for its commercial-principal transactions group's portfolio (PTG). They used both mark-to-credit and mark-to-yield. The first recognizes any changed collateral value due to any change in the business plan, which also changes the amount and/or timing of future expected cash flows from the collateral, which were the properties underlying the PTG's positions. Marking to yield takes account of the changes in the market generally, even if the condition of the particular asset have not changed. Yield, or the rate of return or discount rate, is the rate used to determine the present value of future expected cash flows, taking account of the fact that the asset may not perform as expected. These approaches are essential for marking to market, which is integral to the concept of fair value. Both marking to yield and marking to credit involve changing the value of the property, due to changed circumstances or in recognition of the changed risk that the asset will not perform as expected.

Lehman increasingly relied on TriMont for loan servicing and asset management, and by May 2008, TriMont serviced over 90 per cent of Lehman's PTG assets. It provided other services such as handling insurance issues, administration for construction, and it dealt with local developers for Lehman. Its range of services also included asset management, asset servicing, bond financial services, underwriting, defeasance consulting and information management. It did not provide valuation and appraisal services. Had Lehman hired a firm providing valuation and appraisal services, then it would have been able to point to its independent valuations.

Its reliance on TriMont provided Lehman with property-level data and information about the overall value of a development and status of the project, upon which Lehman's staff relied. TriMont also provided the collateral value eight months after Lehman had made its investment, and annually thereafter, using two broad approaches: historical cost-based valuation and market-based methods applying that method to 228 positions in the second quarter of 2008 and market-based methods for about 245 positions. The Examiner notes that several Lehman employees stated that TriMont's data very often contained errors.

Late in 2007, Lehman decided to abandon its Cap*105 capitalization method and to move to the discounted cash flow method, leading to IRR (internal rate of return) models to provide the discount rate. When the discount rate is applied to all future expected income and capital flows, it equates the price with the present value of those discounted income flows. However, because there were so many delays in rolling out the IRR models, staff had to rely on collateral values based on Cap*105, and when real estate values began to fall in 2007, this led to the over-valuation of assets.[13] Because the method simply calculated current capitalization and added a 5 per cent premium, it could never capture the fall in value, when property values throughout the market began to decline.

The IRR models were the preferred model for the PTG, because it meant that collateral could be valued under a discounted cash flow method. The delays meant that, by the third quarter of 2008, the discounted cash flow method did not apply to *all* of Lehman's PTG book, but only to a substantial part of it. The method had been introduced on a rolling basis. When applied, it had resulted in lower estimates of collateral values and showed that material write-downs were appropriate for a significant number of PTG assets.[14]

The Uniform Standards of Professional Appraisal Practice (USPAP) reported in its 2008–9 edition that the discounted cash flow method (DCF) was an accepted analytical tool, which had become more widely employed when appraisers were able to automate the process. However because it is profit-orientated and dependent on the analysis of uncertain future events, USPAP warns that 'it is vulnerable to misuse', and sets out various requirements to prevent that from happening. USPAP points out that the DCF method was useful for the valuation or analysis of proposed construction, land development condominium development or conversion, rehabilitation and income-producing real estate of all kinds. By early 2008, USPAP could report that DCF was becoming the required method for, amongst others, asset managers, portfolio managers and underwriters, all the skills and services that TriMont purported to offer.

TriMont eventually provided details of its revised valuation methodologies in January 2008, but throughout 2007 and 2008, TriMont made 'substantial and extensive errors' and had 'weak controls' for valuing land development. The firm's staff were apparently unable to learn from their mistakes, which they repeated month after month. TriMont asset managers varied widely in ability, and 'some had become too close to the developers, such that asset managers were not reporting on deteriorating developments, preferring to rely on the developer's assurances that the project would be a success.'[15]

The IRR approach was being rolled out. It was applied to SunCal in 2007. There were many delays, and the company missed several deadlines in 2007 and 2008. Inadequate or erroneous data continued to be a serious problem. As late as March 2008, a PTG consultant emailed TriMont to point out that the Cap*105 method was 'worthless'.[16] The Examiner found that by the second quarter of 2008 about one-third of the total PTG portfolio still relied on the Cap*105 method.

Yet, if the DCF method was being widely used by asset and portfolio managers, as well as appraisers, TriMont should not have had so much difficulty in developing it. The company should have been able to identify and record the right data. Historical cost-based valuation methods were used for about 30 per cent of the positions in the PTG portfolio in the second quarter of 2008. Even as late as July 2008, many positions were valued relying on Cap*105 (or Cap*100), which meant that they were overvalued. The Examiner concluded that

> there is sufficient evidence to support a finding that the PTG business desk used its judgement to conclude that it should not use many of the values produced by TriMont when it was replacing Cap* 105 with IRR models ... In August 2008, Lehman's collateral values were $1.7bn higher than TriMont's collateral values.

The Archstone purchase, completed on 5 October 2007, is covered in Chapter 4, but it is important to recap some of the details. With regard to the acquisition of Archstone with Tishman Speyer, Lehman's plan was that the two companies would each contribute $327m. of permanent equity. Lehman would then commit the remainder of the capital, consisting of $3.7bn of bridge equity and $17.2bn of debt. Lehman expected to sell $9.2bn of properties at closing, and Archstone would use these funds to repay a portion of the acquisition financing which Lehman and its partner banks would provide.

Lehman also expected to sell an additional $9–11bn of debt before closing. In general, its expectations of selling debt and those regarding the income streams from apartments were over-optimistic, at the very least. Nevertheless, when the purchase was closed, the transaction was valued at $22.2bn, which was partly financed with debt and equity capital provided by Bank of America Strategic Ventures Inc, Barclays Capital and their respective affiliates. This meant that the Bank of America and Barclays were aware of the way in which they valued their investments at the time, which may well explain why both banks did not accept Lehman's valuations.

Two other familiar figures also played a part. Fannie Mae purchased a $7.1bn credit facility, secured by 105 multi-family properties. Freddie Mac executed a $1.8bn structured transaction that provided new financing for 32 multi-family properties across the country. David Worley, senior manager of risk management at Fannie Mae stated that 'Fannie Mae is pleased to serve as a constant and reliable source of liquidity in today's ever-changing capital markets'. Freddie Mac added that it was a great example of 'Freddie Mac's capacity to effectively and quickly serve as a reliable source of funding in all market environments'.[17] Just under a year later, Fannie Mae and Freddie Mac would collapse, followed within a few days by Lehman.

What is interesting about this array of partners is that before closing, they must have known that Lehman's original expectations for the sale of properties by Archstone and the expected profits would not be realized. Despite that, by July 2007, the commitments for debt and bridge equity were 28 per cent for Bank of America and 25 per cent for Barclays. Fannie Mae and Freddie Mac's involvement 'confirmed the underlying soundness of the acquisition.'[18] All of this indicates that Barclays and Bank of America, and no doubt others in Wall Street as well, were aware that Lehman's valuations were unreliable, and that this meant that none of them were inclined to buy Lehman in September 2008. They already knew, or at the very least strongly suspected, that Lehman had over-valued Archstone, as indeed Barclays and Bank of America may have done as well. At the time of its collapse Lehman had a 47 per cent stake in Archstone and the two banks had a combined 53 per cent stake, which presumably they did not seek to sell in a market in which multi-family real estate prices had also collapsed. After court cases, which prevented the sale to Equity Residential, they sold their stakes to Lehman for $1.58bn in an improving market in May 2012.

Fair Value Measurements Standard

The Financial Accounting Standards Board (FASB) issued its Fair Value Measurements Standard (SFAS 157) in September 2006, which Lehman adopted in the first quarter of 2007. The Standard itself was adopted to deal with the limited guidance previously available for applying fair value measurements. The definition of 'fair value' retains the concept of 'exchange price' found in the earlier definitions, but clarifies it. 'The exchange price is the price that an orderly transaction between market participants to sell the assets or transfer the liability in the market in which the reporting entity would transact for the asset or the liability, that is, the principal or the most advantageous market for the asset or liability.'[19] Fair value is a market-based measurement, which should be assessed based on the assumptions that market participants would use in pricing the asset or liability. It refers to the 'exit price', not the 'entry price', which is the price that would be paid to acquire an asset or received to assume a liability.

Further, according to the revised standard, the fair value measurement should be determined based on the assumptions the market participant would use. It favours the risk-averse, sceptical buyer, as opposed to the optimistic asset owner. The market-based assumptions must include assumptions about risk and the adjustments for risk, as well as 'assumptions about the effect of a restriction on the sale or use of an asset, as well as the risk that the asset will turn out to be non-performing'.

The definition of fair value for accounting is straightforward enough: it is the 'price that would be received to sell an asset or paid to transfer a liability in an orderly transaction between market participants at the measurement date'. It applies to a particular asset or liability and so the measurement of fair value has to take into account the specific asset or liability and of its sale in the principal market or the most advantageous market. SFAS 157 sets out three levels of information and techniques to measure fair value. Level 1 refers to active markets in which the transactions for the asset or liability occur frequently and in sufficient volume to provide pricing information regularly. The problems arise when the principal market is inactive or when there are no purchasers for the asset or liability.

In the event that Level 1 information is not available, then SFAS 157 requires that the models use observable inputs, to develop Level 2 information. A wide range of information should be used to estimate the value, including quoted prices for similar assets or liabilities in other markets. This may include markets that are less active, or other information such as credit risks, default rates, volatilities, interest rates and yield curves observed over time. Many other factors may be taken into account, such as the asset's condition or location, its similarity to other assets or liabilities, and the volume and level of activity in the markets.

Level 3 is much more difficult, as it is the attempt to value an asset or a liability for which there is no market and thus no observable inputs. In this situation, the company must use all the information available, including assumptions made by market participants, and the company's own valuation models. This approach can lead to 'highly variable results', which means that almost every estimate of fair value requires significant judgement'.[20] When Level 2 inputs have to be used, fair value accounting offers some discretion to management, although observable inputs are objectively verifiable. However, with Level 3, management has considerable discretion and the ability to use its own models, and objective verification becomes very difficult, if not impossible. Nonetheless, there should be sufficient information provided with the models used to be able to assess their quality.

Not surprisingly, the Financial Accounting Standards Board (FASB) received requests for further guidance on the valuation of assets in a market that formerly had been active but no longer is so. Once again, the FASB accepted that this required the use of 'significant judgement' based on the reporting company's 'own assumptions about future cash flows and appropriately adjusted discount rates is acceptable, including risk adjustments that market participants would make for non-performance and liquidity risks'. Broker or pricing services might also be an appropriate input. This guidance was issued by the FASB on 10 October 2008. It was too late to be of any assistance to Lehman. It was followed by further guidance at the behest of Congress and as a result of an extremely detailed critique by the SEC.

Mark-to-market and the collapse of Lehman Brothers and other banks

The Emergency Economic Stabilization Act (EESA) was signed into law on 3 October 2008, almost three weeks after the collapse of Lehman. Section 133 of the Act required the Securities and Exchange Commission to carry out a study of mark-to-market accounting standards set by the Financial Accounting Standards Board (FASB), in SFAS No 157, Fair Value Measurement.[21] The study was especially important, since claims were being made, not only in America, but in Europe as well, that mark-to-market accounting led to increased volatility in the markets. It was also claimed that it led to inappropriate write-downs of assets held by banks and other financial institutions, mostly because these write-downs were the result of inactive, illiquid or irrational markets. The values identified arguably did not reflect the underlying economics of securities. Not only the financial institutions were making such claims, but they were also voiced by politicians as well, pressing for the suspension or even the abandonment of such rules. The sternest critic of fair value accounting at that time was William Isaac, former director of the FDIC, who when addressing a conference on 29 October 2008, stated: 'I gotta tell you that I can't come up with any other answer than that the accounting system is destroying too much capital and therefore diminishing bank lending capacity by some $5 trillion. It's down to the accounting system and I can't come up with any other explanation.'[22]

On the other hand, the SEC reports that market participants including investors valued the transparency of the financial information for the public provided by mark-to-market accounting. Removing it would weaken investor confidence, which would lead not only to instability in the markets, but could freeze the markets. By 2008, many had woken up to the fact that the root causes of the crisis lay in poor lending decisions and incompetent risk management. The SEC study analyses the possible linkages between fair value accounting and bank failures which occurred during 2008. The SEC staff selected 30 issuers, including banks, insurance companies and broker-dealers, which covered

75 per cent of the financial institution assets, totalling over $135bn for the first quarter of 2008.

The aim was to examine the effects of fair value accounting and SFAS 157 on their financial statements, comparing financial information at the end of 2006 (when SFAS 157 and 159 did not apply) and at the end of the first quarter, 2008 to show the progression and changes in fair value over time, as applied to assets, liabilities, equities, income statements and recognized impairments. The study had a particular focus on Level 2 and Level 3 assets and liabilities. The exhaustive study was extended to include the causes of decline in net income for the financial institutions, showing that this was not due to the impact of mark-to-market, since its application was only relevant to a relatively limited part of the income statements studied. The SEC staff concluded that 'the net income for banking, credit institutions and the Government Sponsored Enterprises (GSEs) was most significantly impacted by the increase in the charge for provision for loan losses', a historical cost concept, as the provision for loan losses is based on 'incurred' losses. 'Losses stemming from the lending activities of banks had a profound effect on all financial institutions in 2007–2008' and the losses captured in the fair value rules flowed from that.[23]

Others have supported the SEC's argument, emphasizing what others may have been unwilling to stress. The crisis started when house prices declined and delinquency and default rates increased. Starting in 2007, declining house prices, defaults by subprime borrowers, foreclosures, cases of mortgage fraud and rating downgrades created major problems for mortgage-backed securities, and especially for complex mortgage-based structured instruments. Banks and investors knew that the housing bubble had burst and what the implications might be for the assets they held. Inevitably, investors were nervous about the value of the banks' assets, just as the banks were nervous about each other's. Uncertainty and information asymmetry dried up the refinancing and repo markets, which were crucial for investment funds, investment banks and some large bank holding companies. Since the business model of investment funds and investment banks is based on market values, fair value accounting is a necessity. Even if it were not, investors would not have been impressed with historical cost accounting, the main alternative, either.

However, the authors of the SEC report and others, such as Christian Laux and Christian Leuz, argue that fair value accounting did not contribute to the financial crisis, because its application to banks' financial statements was limited. Laux and Leuz point out that 'many banks with substantial real-estate exposure and large trading portfolios used cash-flow models to value their mortgage-related securities by the third or fourth quarter of 2007'.[24] Hedge funds and 'special investment vehicles' saw a huge outflow of capital in mid-2007. As a consequence, Bear Stearns, BNP Paribas and others stopped withdrawals and refused redemptions of their investment funds, arguing that it was impossible to value the assets in these funds, as there were 'just no prices' for some of these securities. These actions were also taken because the funds had been largely financed with short-term debt and with falling asset prices, withdrawals created the threat of insolvency. Bailing out investment funds by providing guarantees and secured loans did not save them, as was the case with Bear Stearns. Investors were anxious about the value of investment banks' assets, and that would have been the case even if the assets had been recorded at historical cost.

Laux and Leuz point out that the complaint about fair value accounting would have to be that it forced the investment banks to report losses that were unrealistically large and driven by short-term uncertainty and lack of liquidity in the market. But the evidence suggests that asset values reported by three investment banks were too high relative to the price they could obtain if they sold them. That created the lack of trust which was the root cause of illiquid markets. Merrill Lynch sold $30.6bn of collateralized debt obligations backed by mortgages for 22 cents on the dollar, with a consequent pre-tax loss of $4.4bn. David Einhorn, Lehman's fiercest critic, pointed out that the company wrote down its $339bn commercial real estate mortgage-backed securities by only 3 per cent, when the commercial mortgage index of AAA commercial mortgage-backed bonds fell by 10 per cent in the first quarter of 2008. The causes of the financial difficulties had much more to do with the quality and timing of their investments, use of short-term debt financing, high leverage and the declining value of the underlying assets, than to aggressive write-downs due to mark-to-market accounting.

Laux and Leuz point out that for the 31 bank holding companies that failed and were seized by US bank regulators between January 2007 and July 2009, loans accounted for 75 per cent of their balance sheets, and trading assets had an extremely limited role. Fair value accounting on either the balance sheet or the income statement does not apply to loans held for investment or loans held to maturity. As far as the available-for-sale securities are concerned, these are subject to fair value accounting but changes in value are only reported in 'other comprehensive income', if the bank can claim that it has the intent and ability to hold the assets until prices recover, so that the losses can be classed as temporary and the effects of fair value losses for income and regulatory capital can be avoided. The trading book, the only one all regard as being appropriate for fair value, is also the only one for which large write-downs might have been too aggressive, at least as later seen with the benefit of hindsight. It is a difficult issue to settle but a comparison between investment grade risk and the equity markets suggest that prices in the former were not distorted, but that rests on the assumption that the equity market was not distorted either.

Mortgage-related assets were central to the financial crisis, but they were rarely classified by the banks as Level 1 assets, generally being classified as Level 2 or 3 assets, which gave the banks much more discretion in identifying their 'fair values'. JPMorgan reported that in the fourth quarter of 2008 the 'majority of collateralized mortgage and debt obligations, high-yield securities and asset-backed securities (were) classified as Level 3'. The 'problem' assets were largely marked to models, not to market. JP Morgan's position as a clearing bank for tri-party repos certainly put it in a strong position to see the way in which such securities were valued.

However, in response to the illiquid markets, pressure from Congress and the political fall-out both in the USA and in Europe, on 30 September 2008 the standard setters issued new guidance, designed to address the most immediately urgent fair value measurement questions. The guidance confirmed that management's internal assumptions regarding, for example, expected cash flows, could be used, in appropriate circumstances, to measure fair value when the relevant market does not exist. Multiple inputs from various sources might also provide the best evidence for fair value. Broker quotes may be an input, but are not enough if there is no active market and if the quotes do not result from market transactions.

Distressed or disorderly sales do not represent fair value, which only takes orderly transactions into account in assessing fair value. Whether or not a market is inactive is an issue that requires judgement, taking into account the number of bidders and the gap between the asking price and the bidding price. A similar exercise of judgement is required in determining if an investment is other than temporarily impaired, requiring details of the specific facts and circumstances of each investment, and the nature of the underlying investment, whether the security is debt, equity or a hybrid. Since fair value measurements and the assessment of impairment may require significant judgements, clear and transparent disclosures are critical to enable investors to make their own assessments of management's judgements. The FASB provided extensive discussion of the factors to be taken into account.

A few months later, the FASB issued further guidance for fair value measurements and impairments, called 'Determining Whether a Market is Not

Active and a Transaction is Not Distressed'. After an intensive programme of consultation with 'virtually all of the investors expressing the need for greater transparency by banks,' the FASB set out its requirements for significantly expanded and enhanced disclosures.[25] The new guidance issued in April 2009, FAS 157-4, covers transactions which are not 'orderly' and seeks to clarify the way in which fair value can be assessed when the formerly active market for that debt obligation has become inactive. Once that has been decided, the company will have to do more work. The company must see if observed prices or broker quotes obtained represent 'distressed transactions'. Other techniques such as discounted cash flow analysis may be used, as long as they meet the objective of estimating the orderly selling price of the asset in the current market.

FAS FSP 115-2 and FAS FSP 124-2 deal with the recognition and presentation of other-than-temporary impairments (OTTI) in order to address the different factors impacting the market value of certain securities. The fair value guidance has to be modified prospectively by the OTTI guidance, which may be applied to both existing and new investments held by a company at the beginning of the interim period in which the OTTI guidance is adopted. What the revised guidance requires the company to do is to determine from all the available evidence whether or not the market price is a forced liquidation or distressed sale, and, if so, the company does not have to use the market price to set fair value. That, however, only applies when the company can demonstrate that the market is not operating normally by demonstrating that various factors do not apply. These factors include the volume and level of activity in the market, price quotations not based on current information, no or hardly any new issuances and abnormally wide bid-ask spread or significant widening of the bid-ask spread, amongst others. Once an OTTI is determined for a debt security, the portion of an asset write-down attributed to credit losses may flow through earnings and the remaining portion will be reported in other comprehensive income.

The guidance sets out further factors to be taken into account, including the fact that the seller was in or near bankruptcy, or that it was a forced sale because of regulatory or legal requirements, or that the transaction price was out of line with other similar assets or liabilities. The OTTI guidance no longer required the company to state that it intended to hold the debt or security to maturity, but would only have to recognize the credit losses in earnings as other than temporarily impaired. Once again, there are many factors that the company would have to take into account, designed to show whether or not a credit loss existed, including, for example, adverse conditions specifically related to the security, such as the industry or industries within which the issuer operates, or local conditions in a particular area of the country. Many did not think the guidance went far enough, and wanted to see further changes. Economic losses could not be reversed through earnings. With market losses booked against other comprehensive income, the company's capital would still be depleted. In the immediate aftermath of the financial crisis, further changes were not made.

The point, however, is that the proposed changes in mark-to-market accounting had to be accompanied by complete transparency. The model used should ideally be described in detail, and the factors taken into account should be spelt out. Such an approach is often described as 'subjective'. That in turn suggests that the choice of the factors taken into account is arbitrary. But it is not arbitrary if such transparency makes it possible for others to assess the model and the assumptions on which the model is based. It is then possible to judge whether or not the values assigned to the assets or the debts were reasonable or not. Transparency is essential to that process of assessment, but was clearly lacking at the time, so that it was not possible to assess the assumptions or the information on which a bank based its valuations. It was that lack of information that undermined confidence and increased volatility.

Lehman's risk management processes

Lehman could have avoided so many problems if it had had proper risk mitigation and appropriate risk management techniques, had those been understood and applied consistently throughout the company. The company should have measured, monitored and managed liquidity risk and had accurate daily views of positions, values and liquidity measurement in place. Lehman would then have been able to value its assets even where difficult judgement was required in a way which the market would have accepted. It was, after all, perfectly clear that the value of both residential and commercial real estate was falling rapidly. As noted earlier, Lehman adopted a more aggressive business strategy in 2006, by committing its own capital to investments in commercial real estate, leveraged lending and private equity type investments, despite the fact that the first signs of the subprime mortgage crisis appeared in late 2006, and persisted even when the crisis became more obvious in late 2007. These investments such as SunCal and Archstone were long-term investments, but ones in which Lehman planned to recover at least part of its original investment in the near term. Lehman, in common with others in the market, and government officials (including Chairman Bernanke), did not believe that the subprime mortgage crisis would spread. Dick Fuld, in particular, did not believe that commercial real estate investments would fall in price, but would continue to rise. Even when he recognized that prices were falling, he thought he would be able to weather the storm and come out on top, just as he had done in the past.

The Examiner pointed out that Lehman had 'sophisticated policies, procedures, and metrics in place to estimate the risk that the firm could assume without jeopardizing its ability to achieve a target rate of return, and to apprise management and the board whether Lehman was within various risk limits.'[26] Madelyn Antoncic was Chief Risk Officer for Lehman Brothers until September 2007, when Lehman announced that from 1 December 2007 she would be replaced by Christopher O'Meara, who was then Chief Finance Officer. Antoncic moved to a new position as Head of Financial Market Policy Relations. Valukas reports that several Lehman employees did not believe that O'Meara had either the necessary technical proficiency or background in risk management, but the board and regulators considered that he had good managerial skills and Fuld considered him to be 'more practical' than Antoncic, which may be translated as meaning that he was unlikely to oppose taking on greater risks. Valukas's interview with Antoncic revealed that she considered that she was being marginalized from early 2007, and did not participate in major decisions such as Archstone.[27]

Shortly before her transfer, Antoncic gave a presentation, 'Where Vision Gets Built', outlining Lehman Brothers' approach to risk management.[28] In her introduction, she described risk management as being 'at the very core of Lehman's business model, with a conservative risk philosophy, and effective risk governance being the unwavering focus of the Executive Committee'. She added that 'all risk metrics [are] within established limits'. The presentation details a complex structure in which market, credit and quantitative risk are integrated, and risk is minimized through geographical, industry, asset class and customer diversification.

She listed twenty committees overseeing risk-taking activities, grouped as management oversight committees, firm-wide transaction approval committees and business level transaction approval committees. The risk management function was independent from trading, with the reporting line being from the CRO to the Executive Committee to the Head of Strategic Partnerships, Principal Investing and Risk, who reports to the Chairman and CEO. The Global Risk Management Division consisted of several departments covering every aspect of risk, from market risk to risk control and analysis. The Department employed 398 professionals, with 228 risk managers and 162 technologists. The breakdown of the staff showed that it included many highly qualified and experienced individuals, including former regulators. Antoncic described it as an integrated framework, taking into account the firm's financial targets, its risk appetite (how much the firm was prepared to lose in a year from market, event and counterparty risk), risk equity (the economic capital the firm required to protect it against various risks augmented by capital requirements due to external constraints) and risk limits. The presentation then set out the familiar techniques used to assess risks and losses, such as value-at-risk (VaR), a measure of market risk, which is expressed as the 'maximum amount that can be expected to be lost with a certain degree of certainty over a given time horizon'.[29] Other risks that were carefully considered included event risk, in which Lehman claimed to measure stress, and 'gap risks' which go beyond potential market risk losses. These 'were measured using statistically measurable stress analyses which capture losses associated with, for example, defaults for sub-prime mortgage loans and property value losses on real estate'. The presentation provided more details of the way in which the company tackled a wide range of risks, including counterparty credit risks, derivatives exposure, its stress testing and its controls for hedge fund risk.

The key issue was Lehman's attitude to risk limits. Lehman described its risk appetite framework as its primary expression of 'risk tolerance', designed to express the maximum amount of risk that Lehman could take, and the amount of money it was prepared to lose due to market, event and counterparty credit risk. Between 2007 and 2008, Lehman discussed the firm's risk appetite figures with members of the board and reviewed its risk appetite calculations with the SEC on a monthly basis. This, according to Valukas, greatly impressed the SEC, which believed that 'unlike its peer firms, [Lehman was able to manage its] market and credit risk . . . in an integrated fashion through their aggregation into a single measure called risk appetite in its Credit Risk Review, 2005'.[30]

Lehman's market risk management limit policy involved the 'establishment and maintenance of a sound system of integrated market risk limits', which was fundamental to Lehman's risk management function. The policy was described as one of zero tolerance for ignoring those risk limits, with disciplinary action, including dismissal, being taken against individuals. Antoncic stated that the

> risk appetite limit is recommended by the Chief Risk Officer and approved by the Executive Committee and the board on an annual basis and is reviewed quarterly . . . limits are cascaded down to divisions, businesses and regions.

Trading desk heads further allocate limits to individual desks. Limits are monitored daily.

The most important and difficult limit was the overall firm-wide risk appetite limit, which was set by the Finance and the Executive Committee, later the Risk Committee. It was unclear whether any changes required the approval of the board or not, and what course of action would be taken by the Executive Committee if this limit was breached. In fact, the board was not informed about the changes in the overall risk limits or the way in which these changes were achieved. At the end of 2006, Lehman 'dramatically increased its risk appetite limits for 2007 from \$2.3bn to \$3.3bn and subsidiary limits also increased significantly.'[31] Antoncic, as CRO, objected, but was overruled.

The Examiner notes that to justify the increased limit, Lehman changed the way it calculated the limit. If the same method had been used, the 2007 limit would have been several hundred million dollars lower. The full amount of the 2007 limit was used quickly and then exceeded. Lehman also abandoned the single transaction limit in 2006, because the firm considered it had lost significant opportunities, largely because the limit was lower than that of its competitors. It did not in any case apply to its commercial real estate deals.

Lehman conducted stress tests against a portfolio of risks designed to measure 'tail risk', a one-in-ten-year-type event, as required by the SEC. The requirement, however, seems to have been more honoured in the breach than the observance. Lehman's senior management decided what should and what should not be included in the stress test. Furthermore, both Lehman's Finance and Risk Committee and the board were not informed that many of the firm's commercial real estate and private equity investments were excluded from its stress tests. Valukas records that the 'omission was noted on January 29, 2008, when the Finance and Risk Committee received materials stating that real estate owned and private equity were excluded from stress testing',[32] and although the board received the revised disclosure, its significance was not drawn to the attention of the board. The board was not told that Lehman's management had decided not to apply the single transaction limit to its leveraged loans, an important omission. The board had agreed the growth strategy but without the relaxation of the risk limits in order to facilitate the strategy being revealed to them; indeed, they were deliberately concealed.

Interestingly enough, the SEC confirmed that when Lehman informed them that the firm was in excess of its risk limits, their main concern was making sure that the limit excesses were settled in accordance with the firm's own procedures.

The SEC did not believe that its role was to replace Lehman's business judgement with its own. Lehman and the other CSEs were required to provide information to the SEC about the holding company and its affiliates, including information about its risk reporting policies and procedures, risk appetite and equity framework and limit monitoring. The SEC relied on Lehman to provide it with all the information it needed to assess the efficacy and accuracy of Lehman's risk measurements and risk management, but the SEC did not carry out an independent audit of the company's risk management framework and make sure it functioned effectively. The CSE programme also required Lehman to develop and maintain a market-based stress testing programme under which the portfolio were to be tested against hypothetical and historical stress test scenarios.

The impressive array of stress tests was in place to ascertain the potential financial consequences of an economic shock to its portfolio of assets and investments. It appears that the SEC 'monitoring' team looked at what was in place, but did not ask the key question: what happened if a proposed purchase or deal failed one or more stress tests? Was the proposed investment or business strategy abandoned if it was not going to be worth the risk? If not, why not? In fact, the purpose of such tests was not to impose a legal requirement on management not to exceed the limits, but simply to ensure that management considered the risks. Even so, the approach should have been seriously questioned by the SEC.

Lehman's risk management integrated framework looked very impressive, and apparently fulfilled the SEC's requirements for fully functioning risk management processes and stress testing. Every aspect of risk appeared to be covered. Large teams of well-qualified staff were employed. They were capable of using all the then relevant models to identify all the risks to which the firm was or could be exposed. It was well regarded in the industry as being one of the best systems, designed to 'proactively identify, evaluate, monitor, control the firm's market, credit and operational risks and develop risk-related policies, procedures, models and limits'.

Did Lehman's risk management work in practice?

The first issue to be considered here is: did Lehman actually make use of the complex risk management structure it had put in place?

The value-at-risk models were widely used and well-regarded at that time. The inadequacies of these models were revealed by the financial crisis. Not only did banks apply their internal models in different ways, but the models themselves did not capture the full extent of losses a bank might face in times of significant financial stress.

Furthermore, the market risk framework the regulators required was based on the assumption that trading book positions were all liquid, that is, banks could exit or hedge these positions over a ten-day horizon. 'The crisis showed all too vividly that such an assumption was false. During 2008 and 2009, banks were forced to hold risk positions for much longer than expected, and incurred large losses from changes in values.'[33]

The second reason was that regulators in the UK and USA were increasingly concerned that banks were misusing their internal risk models when they calculated the risk weightings for risky assets. Banks could easily manipulate the models to assign low risk weightings for risky assets in order to reduce capital requirements. However, these are concerns that also applied to many other banks besides Lehman, although Lehman did manipulate its risk measurements so that the value of its assets was increased. It is Lehman's use of, or failure to use, its risk management procedures, which is the central question here.

Valukas sets out in detail the evidence that he obtained of the extent to which senior management disregarded its risk managers, risk policies and its risk limits, including removing Antoncic and Michael Gelband, head of the Fixed Income Division, because of their opposition to the management's growing accumulation of risky and illiquid investments.

Even the Office of Thrift Supervision, a notoriously weak regulator, had questioned Lehman's risk management and its commercial real estate investments:

> Lehman's commercial and real estate investment portfolio is very diverse with large holdings in the USA and Asia. As its largest single asset class, totalling $50.4 bn at May 31st 2008, the portfolio represents very substantial credit and market risk and is a major source of continuing concern among regulators and investors. Total real estate related exposure would reach nearly $60bn by including $9.5bn of corporate debt and equity and other real estate assets managed by GREG. Taking an outsized bet on real estate, the Firm's exposure to the commercial real estate market is larger than its competitors despite its smaller size and may likely precipitate major management and board decisions regarding additional capital raises, sales of strategic business or the ultimate sale of the firm ... fair value price discovery has been difficult for the company's real estate commitments, given that Level 3 commercial loans and securities totalled

$13bn or 63.1% of the $20.6bn total mortgage and asset-backed securities ...
At $22.7 bn real estate held for sale, an illiquid asset class, but not one which
is fair valued by SFAS 157, exceeds mortgage loans and securities by a wide
margin.[34]

The OTS also noted that there were major failings in the risk management
process, with senior management deciding to make major real estate loans and
investments and in 2007, significantly breaching established limits by making a
very large commitment to the Archstone-Smith transaction. A cover note to the
Executive Committee, by not referring to 'a material breach of risk limits, implies
that profit considerations trumped sound risk management practices.' The OTS
did not take any further action following this report, although as one of the
supervisors of Lehman Brothers, it was entitled to do so.

The SEC did not question the application and use of the impressive array of
stress tests, either. The Examiner reports that management regularly chose to
disregard or overrule the firm's risk controls, but that this was not a 'colorable'
offence under Delaware company law. They were self-imposed limits.

Lehman decided to regard the risk appetite limit as a 'soft' guideline. As
Valukas points out, the company decided to override 'concentration limits', even
'single transaction limits' on its leveraged loan and commercial real estate
businesses, designed to ensure diversification by business line and counterparty.
Because these limits were ignored, they were exceeded by margins of 70 per cent
in commercial real estate and by 100 per cent with regard to its leveraged loans.
Stress tests were carried out every month and presented to the regulators and the
board, but its commercial real estate and private equity investments were left out,
as were leveraged loans for a time.

The inclusion of Archstone and other commercial real estate from regular
stress tests in the first half of 2007 might have led to a rejection of the $22bn
Archstone deal; for example, one experimental stress test predicted losses of
$7.4bn on the real estate and private equity positions that had been excluded,
and only $2bn on previously included trading positions ($9.4bn in all), and
another predicted losses of $10.9bn plus $2.5bn on positions already included.
The stress tests were conducted long after the assets had been acquired. According
to the Examiner's report of his interviews with Mark Weber and Christopher
O'Meara, the results of the tests were never shared with senior managers,
although the tests had been carried out on 30 June 2008.

Once again, it appears that the regulators did not ask which items were
included in the stress tests. Management did not have a regular and systematic

means of analysing the catastrophic losses that the firm could suffer from increasingly large and illiquid investments. Nor did Lehman stick to its balance sheet limits, designed to contain the overall risk of the firm and maintain the leverage ratio required by the rating agencies. That was concealed by the use of Repo 105, which took these assets off the balance sheet for a temporary period.[35]

The result was that Lehman was able to raise its risk appetite limit (RA) from $2.3bn to $3.3bn in December 2006: in September 2007, the RA was raised again, to $3.5bn, because Lehman recognized that 'it had been exceeding the firm-wide risk appetite on a persistent basis for some time', but it quickly exceeded that limit by $769m., so its RA was $4.27bn then, but it did not take any steps to correct that until January 2008, when the RA was increased to $4.0bn, backdated to December 2007.[36] All this was in spite of the fact that Lehman advised both the SEC and the board that the risk appetite limit was intended to constrain its risk-taking. Clearly, Lehman did not take its RA seriously.

Between May and August 2007, Lehman removed some of its largest risks from its calculations of its risk exposures, in particular, probably its greatest risk, the $2.3bn bridge equity position in Archstone. Even when it was included in the company's RA, Lehman continued to exceed its own limit for several months. Lehman did not attempt to reduce its balance sheet, which would have been an almost impossible task at that time, and instead raised its risk limit further. The Examiner's assessment was that, given past success, senior management decided to go for profits, rather than restricting the risks they were taking to the risk levels their risk management team laid down. 'They were confident making business judgements based on their understanding of the markets and did not feel constrained by the quantitative metrics generated by Lehman's risk management system. These decisions raise questions about the role of risk management in a complex financial institution.'[37] Once again, under Delaware company law, these would be classed as business decisions, however ill-founded, as they did not breach any fiduciary duties.

Lehman's management informed the board clearly and on more than one occasion that the aim was to take on more risk in order to grow the firm, that this would result in taking on higher levels of risk, and that market conditions after July 2007 were hampering the firm's liquidity. This information was sufficient to keep the board informed without misleading them. They did not have a legal duty to inform the board about the risk limits and the breaching of them, as these were only intended to guide management's business decisions.

Consequently, the board was not failing in its duty to monitor the company's risk-taking activities.

Lehman's corporate charter and Delaware company law protected the directors from personal liability based on their business decisions, since neither breached the duty of loyalty or good faith. Delaware law allows the board to rely on management reports, and they are protected by law when they do so. Dick Fuld and his management team considered that they would be able to deal with the changing market and the unfolding subprime crisis by pursuing a 'countercyclical growth strategy'.[38] They hoped to overcome adverse market conditions as they had done before, and emerge triumphant.

Measuring Value

Previous chapters have set out the ways in which Lehman Brothers sought to value its assets and to hide its losses. Professional standards for the valuation of commercial and residential real estate existed at that time, but as the bankruptcy Examiner Valukas demonstrates in his report, Lehman showed little interest in conforming to them or hiring those who knew how to apply them.

Against that background it can be seen that the bankruptcy process did not itself cause the destruction of value, although it added to it. The filing itself and the lengthy processes involved confirmed the anxieties which already existed in the market about Lehman. The destruction of value had already taken place before Lehman filed for bankruptcy. Before the end came, frantic attempts were made to restore value and, when that failed, to conceal the losses. The outcome of the bankruptcy proceedings raises the question of how and why value can disappear, and then return after a few years, at least when measured in terms of price. Examining the reasons for the fluctuations in price may cast light on whether or not price is the only measure of value, or if value remains when the price fluctuates. The purpose of this chapter is to set out the difficulties of valuing both complex financial instruments and real estate, and especially commercial real estate and development land. These are issues which economists do not take into account in developing theories of value. Such theories may also be detached from developments in financial instruments and the markets themselves. The chapter describes the methodologies used to value commercial real estate and complex financial instruments. It is already clear that Lehman either did not use the appropriate methodologies or applied them without making use of the relevant data, or did not use the correct verification procedures at all.

Lehman's assets fell into two broad categories: residential real estate and commercial real estate in particular, and derivatives. The latter are complex assets, especially when compared with more straightforward assets such as shares or bonds. Commercial real estate, especially development projects, are difficult to value, yet there are recognized procedures, which Lehman had not put in place, and even if they had, it is unlikely that they would have been followed. When Lehman filed for bankruptcy, it was holding $43bn in real estate loans and assets, of which SunCal was one. Lehman was SunCal's main financial backer, lending the developer over $2bn to buy land and add infrastructure, including roads, sewers and power lines, before selling it on to house builders for a profit. Lehman stopped funding construction work on SunCal's projects in 2008, so SunCal took more than 20 of these projects into bankruptcy protection.

Lehman should have used one of the large professional valuation firms in the USA to provide both the company and investors with the assurance of an independent valuation. Lehman's own methods of valuation left much to be desired. They selected TriMont, a property services company, to handle the commercial real estate portfolio, but this company did not offer valuations and clearly had difficulties in developing the appropriate models, according to the Examiner's Report. That was a mistake. It was hardly likely to inspire confidence in the valuation of their real estate assets, especially in 2007 and 2008, when prices in the real estate market were falling.

Recognized procedures have been developed by standard-setting bodies for valuation in the USA and in the UK. International standards are in the process of being established by the International Valuation Standards Council, a long-time partner of the Appraisal Foundation. This chapter draws on the procedures as set out by the Royal Institution of Chartered Surveyors in London, and the Appraisal Foundation, which sets the Uniform Standards of Professional Appraisal Practice (USPAP), the standards required by the Financial Institutions Reform, Recovery and Enforcement Act 1989.[1] It draws on the recommendations of both bodies in explaining the approach to the valuation of commercial real estate.

There are two approaches to valuing development land. These are comparison with the sale price of land for comparable development, or an assessment of the value of the scheme as completed. The latter, the residual method, requires a deduction of the costs of development, including the developer's profit, in order to assess the underlying land value. In practice, both methods would be used, but the residual method requires the valuer to make a number of assumptions. The valuer inevitably has to exercise judgement, but in making that judgement the valuer has to undertake all the necessary research to establish the facts and his assessment of them. It should then be possible for the valuer to show that his assessment is reasonable, taking all of these factors into account. Timing is important, as the valuation will depend on how far the development has advanced.

The nature of the site itself (such as any risk of flooding, landslides, or adverse geotechnical conditions, such as the nature of the soil or slope instability), establishing the legal ownership of the land, and any planning issues are amongst the first items on the valuation agenda. Since the real value of the land lies in its development potential, valuing the land will again depend on making an accurate assessment of the form and extent of the kind of development that can be accommodated on the land. The valuation may have to be undertaken with a team of professional project consultants, such as architects and quantity surveyors. The valuer then takes into account the time taken to develop the site, and the development programme. This will include all the issues involved in the pre-construction period, building contracts, preparing the site, actual buildings, completion to sales and letting out the completed development, and then possible liabilities.

An analysis of the market to establish the potential demand for the optimum alternative forms of development that may be possible should take all these factors into account. The decision of the nature of the development should also depend on the investors' requirements, the location, access and availability of transport routes, all the amenities attractive to tenants and/or buyers, the scale of the development in terms of sale or lettable packages, the form of the development, and market supply, including actual or proposed competing developments. When the land is going to be developed over a period of time, it is also important that the developed land is revalued at intervals, say, every six months to a year, since market and macroeconomic conditions may change.

The alternative method is one of comparison, but this only works if evidence of sales can be found and analysed on a common basis, such as site area, developable area or habitable rooms. Price comparisons are a useful check on the residual method. Many other factors have to be taken into account, including the condition of the site, site and construction costs, dates of sales, changes in planning laws, changes in price in a rapidly changing market, so that the date of a transaction is very important. The greater the number of variables and adjustments for assumptions, the less useful the comparison; and anyway, the comparison methodology is not appropriate once construction has begun.

If there are no useful comparisons to be made, then the valuer should turn to the residual method, which involves the input of a large amount of data, and small changes in any of these inputs can lead cumulatively to large differences in the estimate of land value. For example, the required rate of return may vary according to whether the client is a developer, a contractor, an owner occupier, an investor or a lender, as well as the time taken with the development and the risks involved. The residual method can be expressed in a simple equation:

(value of completed development) – (development costs + developers profit) =
land value.

The value of the completed development is the market value of the proposed development, assessed on the special assumption that the development is complete as at the date in the market conditions at that time. This is usually called the gross development value. Sometimes the value may be the total of the value of the individual properties, possibly on the assumption that the completed development is producing income, rather than being available for sale or letting. The net development value incorporates the transaction costs on the assumption that the completed development was sold on the date of valuation.

The planning, acquisition and site-related costs have already been outlined, to which should be added the costs of vacant possession, which might be offset by letting out advertising space, short-term tenancies or temporary car parking. Since large developments are phased over time, that is reflected in the developer's cash flows, and hence in the valuation of the property. This means that some of the costs can be deferred, as indeed receipts may be. Where the sales are residential properties or commercial retail units, they may begin before the development is completed, and may be phased in over a long period of time. The income then has to be recognized as cash flow and must be recognized at the appropriate time, as should relevant costs.

An accurate estimation of the building costs based on the gross internal area on the valuation date is a major component of the residual valuation. Clearly this method is very sensitive to variations in the estimated costs, and the degree to which the costs can be assessed accurately varies according to the specific site characteristics and the requirements for the development of the site. The valuer must also examine the exact contract made with the contractor, since even a fixed price contract may allow the contractor to amend the cost of the contract if there are any changes in the specification, or if unforeseen events occur.

The valuer has to take a wide range of costs into account, including fees and expenses, ranging from professional consultants, costs of legal advice, lettings and sales expenses, rent-free periods, raising development finance and prospective tenants or buyers incurring fees on monitoring the development. Other costs include interest on the costs of land and development, and opportunity costs, if it is a self-financing project. It is usual for interest to be regarded as a development cost up to the assumed letting date of the last unit, unless there is a forward sale agreement with different terms. In the case of a residential development, the units may be sold at different times, and various assumptions may be made regarding cash flow both inward and outward, and the rate of interest will reflect that.[2] The two most widely used rates of return for developing and constructing residential property refer both to profit and yield either on a static basis, which subtracts all the costs and expenses outlined above, or on a dynamic model in a discounted cash flow which projects sales revenues and costs over time. The latter method was used by Lehman for residential developments. Objective sources of data were available, and could have been used by Lehman as a justification for the firm's valuations of their commercial real estate: the National Association of Homebuilders' annual publication, *The Cost of Doing Business* and the 'PwC Real Estate Investor Survey' or the 'Developer Survey', published by RealtyRates.com.[3] All of these are reputable sources, but Lehman apparently did not refer to any of these.

In the previous chapter, the regulations which applied at the time in the USA were set out in detail, with the proviso that none of them applied to Lehman Brothers. Not only did Lehman not take any of the regulations into account, but also the company did not apply any reasonable measures of value to the development of residential or commercial plots of land. Lehman paid no attention whatsoever to any such considerations when investing in developments. Its approach was 'systemically flawed because Lehman primarily valued these assets on whether the development was proceeding according to the project's business plan and not the price a buyer would pay for the asset',[4] or just by reference to the project's capitalization.

Each Lehman banker within PTG who originated investments had relationships with certain developers with a proven track record in a particular real estate market. Lehman relied on the developer to successfully complete the project and the relationship between Lehman and the developer could be described as a 'marriage'.[5]

Completion of the project was necessary, as the underlying real estate was highly leveraged and the cash flow was not sufficient to repay the loan until it was completed. Lehman partnered with developers on the Principal Transactions Group. Not only Lehman's bankers were close to developers, but some of TriMont's asset managers were as well, according to the Examiner's Report, as they did not report on deteriorating market conditions but relied instead on the developers' assurances that the project would be a success. 'Appraisals should reflect what market participants actually do, not necessarily a particular client's desires ... Appraisers reflect the market; they do not set the market.'[6] Such appraisals would not have pleased Lehman Brothers.

The level of risk increased in these investments, as Lehman sought the required rate of return. The focus was on land development, especially in California, and equity stakes increased in the hope of gaining profits in a declining market. Lehman did not even consider the loan-to-value requirements set out in the Interagency FAQs. As for conducting the valuation, the criteria should have included the amount of future expected cash flows from the asset, and an investor's willingness to accept the risk that the asset would not produce them. Instead, 'the yields selected were based on Lehman's expected rate of return at origination, rather than the rate of return that a typical market investor would require.'[7] The approach to measuring value did not fulfil any of the standards of valuation or regulations which were generally accepted at the time. Nor did Lehman use the methodologies set out above for valuing commercial property and developments in particular. It is small wonder that when it came to the crunch, Lehman's valuations of its real estate portfolio were greeted with scepticism.

As noted above, the regulations for valuations for development did not apply to Lehman Brothers as they were not regulated by the Federal Reserve or the OCC. However, these were also the issues which the SEC should have addressed as part of its Consolidated Supervised Entities Programme. It was not until February 2008 that the SEC embarked on a special project to review the CSE's price verification processes for their CRE portfolio. The report was not completed before Lehman collapsed, but the Examiner provided the details of the informal analysis and comments the SEC provided during an interview. Apparently the SEC expressed its concerns to Lehman Brothers throughout its inspection, which took place during February, March, May, June and July, and Lehman apparently addressed some of the issues raised, including an overview of the CMBS business, an overview of the real estate risk process and the fixed income product control purpose. Later in the investigation, the SEC inspected verification procedures, price verification models and the valuation of particular positions. The aim was to determine if appropriate valuation controls had been designed and to test the price verification process to ensure that controls are operating as intended.

The SEC refused to share with the Examiner any of its formal conclusions, but only with an informal analysis and comments during an interview.

The SEC's requests for further information in July included questions about Lehman's internal rate of return models and information on credit spreads. Their requests for information continued until early August. The Examiner noted that the SEC considered that 'Lehman's price verification procedures were more pronounced than the other CSEs because the size of Lehman's balance sheet and the nature of its business'.[8] The SEC also recognized that Lehman's product control staff was insufficient to provide an independent check on the valuations provided by the business desk and the number of assets in the CRE portfolio. As the SEC was unable to complete its report, it is not clear what its conclusions were or what actions, if any, would have been taken. At least, the SEC should have been aware of the extent of the risky investments held by Lehman in 2008: Level 3 commercial mortgage loans and securities totalling $13bn, or 63.1 per cent of $20.6bn of total mortgage and asset-backed securities, and $22.7bn real estate held for sale, an illiquid asset class, but not one which is subject to the Fair Value rule, SFAS 157. In February 2008 Lehman provided a document to the SEC, entitled 'An Overview of the CMBS presentation to the SEC'. It largely describes Lehman's CMBS activities, but does not provide any substantial explanation of its methods of valuation of the portfolio.[9]

The Office of Thrift Supervision belatedly turned its attention to an examination of Lehman Brothers, starting in July 2008. (Lehman did own a small FDIC thrift, regulated by the OTS and was therefore subject to OTS inspections. The thrift was used as a conduit for mortgage securitization activities.)[10] The report, however, is simply that. It does not include any of the critical assessments of Lehman's procedures for valuing its commercial real estate later made by the Examiner. Its production at that time is unclear, since it does not refer to any courses of action to be taken by the OTS or by Lehman Brothers.

Collateralized debt obligations

The rest of this chapter examines some of the major derivatives in force when Lehman's collapsed, all of which depended on or were derived from assets such as loans on property. These include collateralized debt obligations (CDOs) and collateralized loan obligations (CLOs), as well as credit default swaps, which provide protection against credit loss on some other entity as the result of a specific credit event. The way in which these derivatives work will be explained further, as each type of derivative in considered. As a background to the discussion about derivatives, it should be noted that Lehman underwrote more mortgage-backed securities than any other firm, especially when the rate of delinquencies and foreclosures was rising in 2007: some $85bn, four times its shareholder equity in the fourth quarter of 2007. The valuation methodologies used by Lehman incorporated a variety of inputs, including prices observed from execution of trades in the marketplace as well as their own traders, ABX, CMBX and similar indices which track the performance of a series of credit default swaps and other market information, such as data on remittances received and cumulative loss data on underlying obligations. Their methodology was not quite as rigorous as might appear, since 'each trader had a different method for valuing the CDOs and there was no consistency from desk to desk'.[11]

The PCG analysed the traders' price valuations, paying closer attention to the marks towards the end of each quarter, but they lacked the skills and resources. The PCG did not have the 'same level of quantitative sophistication as many of the desk personnel who developed models to price the CDOs'. A former Vice President and Head of the Credit Valuation Group told the Examiner, 'We are not quants'.[12] The Group did, however, create a model using the Intex Cash Flow engine, or interest-only models, which depended on the underlying assets of the CDOs. However, the method was considered to be unreliable, so most members of the PCG tended to check their valuations against the desk traders' numbers. Even then they only checked 78 per cent of the CDOs valued by the desk traders. In many cases this was because 'the desk had already written down the position significantly'.[13] Using these methods, Lehman valued its derivative assets at $46.3bn and its derivative liabilities at a net value of $22.2bn. In other words, the valuation constituted almost a 100 per cent increase from the net value of $12.974bn reported on 30 November 2007.

A collateralized debt obligation (CDO) is a structured product, in which pools of cash-generating assets are packaged together into discrete tranches which can be sold to investors. They are called CDOs because the pooled assets, such as mortgages, bonds and loans, are debt obligations, which serve as collateral. Suppose a CDO consists of mortgages. The senior tranches are high-quality mortgages where the borrower is unlikely to default on the loan. The risks of such mortgages are much less than a subprime mortgage, where the borrower may well be unable to maintain repayments on the mortgage, and may default. The risks of the borrower defaulting on the loan are much higher than the loans in the senior tranches of mortgages. The senior tranches are safer investments as they will have first call on the collateral, in the event of a default. They have a higher credit rating than the junior tranches, so they offer lower coupon rates than the junior tranches, which offer higher coupon rates to compensate for the higher risk of default. CDOs are unusual in that they represent different types of debt and credit risk, with the different kinds of debt being described as 'tranches' or 'slices', each of which has a different maturity and risk associated with it. A CDO investor takes a position in an entity which has defined risks and rewards, not directly on the underlying assets. The investment is dependent on the quality of metrics for defining the risk and reward of the various tranches.

The process of constructing a CDO involves the establishment of a special purpose vehicle (SPV) to acquire a portfolio of fixed income assets, such as mortgage-backed securities. This allows the parent company to make highly leveraged or speculative investments without endangering the entire company. It will also serve as a counterparty for swaps and other derivative instruments. The investment bank is also the issuer of the CDO, but only through the SPV, earning a commission at the time of issue and a management fee during the life of the CDO. The order in which senior, junior and equity notes are entitled to the cash flows from the CDOs are set out as the 'Priority of Payments' in the transaction documents, with the senior tranches receiving payments from the principal first, with prepayments and payments until they are paid off. An investment in a CDO is therefore an investment in the cash flows of the assets, rather than a direct investment in the underlying collateral. The CDOs can take two forms: cash CDOs and synthetic CDOs, with the former paying interest and principal to the tranche-holders using the cash flows produced by the CDOs' assets. Ownership of the CDO lies with the SPV. Synthetic CDOs do not own cash assets. The investor has the exposure to risk and reward, but this exposure is realized through a credit derivative, a credit default swap (CDS). In this case, the underlying asset is a bond market instrument such as a high-yield bond index or mortgage index. This, of course, means that the relationship between the CDO and the ultimate assets is much more remote.

Having set up a CDO, the next step was to price the CDO, and that required a means of modelling the correlation between defaults of different assets, bonds or loans. A particular model, the Gaussian Copula Model, was widely used following its invention by David X Li in 1999. It used a so-called 'copula function', which was a way of 'coupling' a set of risks of default. The correlation in question was that between the equity tranche and other tranches including the most senior tranche. If the correlations were high, then even the holders of the most senior tranches would be at risk of losing their investment. Hence modelling the correlation was the most crucial element in valuing a CDO.[14] David X Li's approach was to use historical data, which indicates that default rates are higher in recessions than in periods of strong economic growth, implying some correlation between survival times. Based on the assumption that survival times are correlated, the joint distribution for survival times makes it possible to draw conclusions about the portfolio. A copula function is then calculated to obtain the joint distribution from the marginal distribution. It was designed to provide one number that gave the probability of all the defaults in a pool of securities or mortgages taking place at once. If the default correlation was low, as they were not related to or dependent on each other, then this resulted in a low figure, which was taken to mean that the risk of default was low. The calculation did not depend on an analysis of historical data on actual defaults but was based on indices of credit default swaps. However, with regard to the credit default swaps, the length of the data series was only some ten years by 2007–8, since CDSs were only introduced in 1997 by Blythe Masters and her team at JP Morgan.

Others pointed out serious flaws in the distribution models. They were 'overly simplistic' and an inadequate means of valuing tranches of CDOs and other structured products. As far back as July 2008, Jon Gregory, former head of Global Credit Quantitative Analytics at Barclays Capital, London, showed that applying the Gaussian model, a super senior tranche of a CDO referencing 125 investment-grade assets should theoretically be able to withstand 46 individual default events before the super senior tranche experienced any loss of principal:

> So the result is that the holder of one of these tranches, with spreads having blown out massively over the past twelve months, would be able to receive as much as 50 basis points for holding a CDO that, on this basis, apparently has no risk. That is opposed to the three or four basis points an investor would have received on this kind of structure in early 2007... we have to ask how losses are going to factor into the (super senior) tranche over a given period. Will losses accumulate in a linear fashion over time so that you're just as likely to lose money in the first year of the trade as the second year, or will defaults be back-loaded so that losses are unlikely in the first three years but more likely later on?[15]

MacKenzie and Taylor Spears point out the deficiencies in the model, as perceived by quantitative analysts (quants or analysts whose work is to design and implement complex models allowing investment banks to price and trade securities), many of whom were sceptical about the use of the copula model even before the crisis began.[16] They argue that the source of the problem lay with the use of the model by the rating agencies when this was applied to CDOs for which the underlying assets were mortgages rather than pools of corporate debt. The rating agencies made minor modifications to the models used for CDOs and corporate debt, and made matters worse by rating the CDOs and the mortgage-backed securities separately. For example in November 2001, when Standard & Poor introduced its new one-period Gaussian copula system, CDO Evaluator, the same value (0.3) was used for the correlation between ABSs from the same sector as was used for the correlation between corporations in the same industry.

However, the difficulty with applying the copula model to estimate expected collateral losses on ABS CDOs was that it relied on correlations among bonds in the CDOs. The probability of default and expected losses produced by these models is that they are very sensitive to model parameters based on the historic performance of the underlying bonds, which were very reliable before 2007. 'Crucially, these models were not designed to directly capture the sensitivity of the performance of the underlying assets to systemic changes in house prices or changes in attributes that affect the mortgage loan performance.'[17]

Standard & Poor announced the introduction of its new CDO Evaluator in November 2001, designed to refine CDO credit criteria and analysis.[18] It took into account the credit rating, size and maturity of each tranche of each asset combined in the CDO, along with the correlation between each pair of assets.[19] It was used to assess the credit risk of a portfolio of assets for cash flow and synthetic CDOs, with the range of the probability of default from 0 to 100 per cent, but with the most likely outcome being that some but not all of the assets default. Taking the correlation between the assets into account, S&P adopted the Monte Carlo approach to estimating the probability distribution of default rates, with a large number of independent trials to determine which asset has defaulted or not. S&P argued that its methodology is robust due to its ability to deal with complex relationships between variables and can handle the effects created by portfolios containing assets that are unequal in principal balance, credit rating and maturity. S&P boasted that this approach

> enables one to simulate the behaviour of a system as it is modelled and then simply observe the results ... The key to successfully using Monte Carlo simulation techniques is one of performing enough trials to capture long-term certainty ... 30 seconds for 15,000 trials on a portfolio of 100 assets and 2.5 minutes for 100,000 trials on the same portfolio.[20]

The speed was extremely important, as so many CDOs based on mortgages were being issued that a method of valuation which bypassed analysis of each CDO, yet allowed for a cash flow analysis, was essential. The method also had to enable analysts to verify that each CDO tranche can continue to pay the principal and interest in accordance with the terms, up to the scenario default rates on the underlying portfolio.

The rating agencies were competing against each other to grab as large a market share of the lucrative market for rating the CDOs as possible. The existence of that market was partly created by investor demand for credit ratings. CDOs contain hundreds of underlying assets and modelling the pay-offs from these securities requires sophisticated cash-flow models, so the credit ratings were a substitute for any due diligence on their part. There was little public information on how the ratings were calculated and how ratings in the CDO securities related to the underlying asset quality. At the same time, financial regulation in the USA at the time relied heavily on the ratings provided by the 'regulated' rating agencies. Minimum capital requirements for banks, insurance companies and broker-dealers depended on the credit ratings of the assets on their balance sheets, as do pension funds, creating an institutional demand for highly rated securities, although the supply of highly rated single name securities is inevitably somewhat limited. That regulatory demand is still there, even though the fees for the ratings provided were paid by the financial institution, which was either rated itself or whose products were rated by one or other of the agencies.[21]

But the financial crisis finally exposed the weaknesses in the model, especially the assumption that correlations between different assets were constant over time and could be expressed in one number. Convenient though that assumption may have been, it turned out not only to have been a mistake, but a disastrous one as well. Their model sought to estimate the actual probabilities of default, which required the use of historical records. With mortgage-backed securities, the postwar records in the USA included one relatively mild recession but a relatively stable housing market during that period. That all changed from the mid-1990s onwards. What followed was a period of rapidly increasing house prices, which too many believed would not fall, even when the rise in house prices began to falter in mid-2006. Overblown valuations persisted until 2008.

Indeed, as argued by Cordell and others above, 'the only way to correctly value a CDO was by digging deep into its collateral and valuing it using loan level data.'[22] Lehman was aware of the risks, at least at one stage in 2005. The firm conducted bond analysis on new subprime issuance in 2005 across different house price appreciation scenarios (HPA). Their conclusion? 'New issue BBB subordinates have downgrade risk if HPA slows by 5% by end-2005 ... BBB subordination appears to be sized to an intermediate scenario between a 5% and 8% HPA for life'. It is thought that one of the co-authors, Sihan Shu, went on to work for John Paulson, the hedge fund manager who made billions by shorting the subprime market.[23]

Apart from Lehman's losses, the inadequacy of the model and its application to CDOs based on mortgages led to major losses for the leading banks on their CDOs based on asset-backed securities. Citigroup lost $34bn, Merrill Lynch

$26 bn, UBS $22bn and AIG $33bn. Looking at the rising rate of delinquencies and foreclosures and falling house prices from 2006 onwards, instead of only using models, might have helped to avert such heavy losses. Too much faith was placed in the model and its ability to estimate default probabilities, and too little attention was paid to what was going on in the world around them.

Credit default swaps

As explained above, a credit default swap (CDS) is a kind of insurance against a credit risk. It is a privately negotiated contract, in which one party buys protection against losses from defaults, the failure to pay interest or capital according to schedule or a debt moratorium, for example, and another, who is willing to take on the risk and to sell that protection. That seems straightforward enough, but then this quasi-insurance product enables others to implement various investment strategies; for example, a fixed income investor might buy protection so that he can hedge the risk of default involved in a corporate bond. Then an insurance company might act as the counterparty to this deal and promise to pay potential default losses. The seller of protection might then speculate on the bond issuer remaining in existence, so he is exposed to the investment without having to actually buy the bond in the cash market. These are some examples of the more complicated forms of credit risk derivatives. They all share the basic features of credit default swaps. They are designed to enable credit trading to take place and for risk to be shared amongst various market participants. The significant default swaps were the ones offering protection against defaults on portfolios of subprime mortgages or on CDOs which contained subprime mortgages. They had a part to play in the financial crisis. The CDSs were hard to price when they were written to provide protection to the holders of CDOs, themselves hard to price. The CDOs consisted of tranches of mortgages and were given triple A ratings by the rating agencies, which no doubt gave confidence not only to the holders of CDOs (and the sellers) but to the purchasers of credit default swaps. These were written to provide protection to the holders of CDOs as well.

The notional amount of outstanding CDSs grew rapidly from the beginnings of the market in the mid-1990s to a peak of almost $69 trillion at the end of 2007, but then declined sharply to just over $30 trillion at the end of the first half of 2010.[24] Trading volumes were higher than in the first part of 2007, according to Markit, a leading financial information service company. The subsequent drop in the volume of outstanding CDSs was due to trade compression and the move to central counterparties in the CDS market. The main concerns in 2008 were focused on the fact that the major CDS dealers were important counterparties to one another, and the exposures were large in gross terms. In addition the value of these exposures grew rapidly as credit spread widened, making it appear that any agreement to net obligations across contracts might not be enforced if there was a default.

Partly as a result of the role of CDSs in the financial crisis, and partly to support the central clearing of trades, 8 April 2009 saw a global 'Big Bang' – a major change in the CDS market. Contracts are now standardized. The 'event determination' committee was introduced, as a central decision point and trigger for credit and succession events. This prevents differing conclusions or triggers for different contracts on the same entity. When there is a credit event, there is a binding and standard cash settlement price. Fixed coupons ensure that the payment amounts are standardized, thereby making it easier to offset contracts. To this was added the standardization of accruals, which makes the timing and amount of payments uniform in the first premium period and throughout the contract across all trades, thus making it easier to offset contracts. 'The goals of reducing outstanding trades by trillions of notional dollars, restructuring the way trades are processed so that trades can be matched on the same day and the creation of a central counterparty mechanism are ambitious', but that is the aim.[25] The proposed changes had been underway before the financial crisis, but were no doubt accelerated by it.

Credit default swaps are a form of insurance in which the 'reference entity' takes various forms, such as a loan, a bond or some other kind of liability. Prior to the Big Bang, the CDS market operated quite differently, without the advantages of central clearing and standard contracts. The buyer of the protection usually pays the premium at fixed intervals over a period of time, and, generally, the seller of the protection pays compensation to the buyer if a 'credit event' (a default, for example) occurs and the contract is terminated. The value of a default swap depends not only on the credit quality of the underlying 'reference entity' but also on the credit quality of the writer of the CDS or the counterparty, since if the counterparty defaults, then the buyer of the default swap will not receive any payment if a credit event occurs. The value of a CDS depends on the probability of a counterparty default, the probability of a 'reference entity' default and the correlation between them.

The most important element in a typical derivatives transaction is the use of collateral, and the amount of collateral insuring a counterparty's performance on a contract changes with the value of the contract. If a bank had derivative positions with Lehman, for example, which would cost $100m. to replace, and if it had $110m. of collateral from Lehman when it failed, the bank could use the collateral and make no loss from Lehman's failure. Collateral arrangements were quite usual, but they were not universal. ISDA's survey in 2007 showed that 6 per cent of derivative contracts were subject to these agreements then (compared with 30 per cent in 2003). There was still a possibility of contagion through derivative exposures, depending on whether or not counterparties chose to manage their exposures actively. The failure of a large financial institution can lead to substantial changes in CDS prices, as well as liquidity, so that the collateral held just before the failure may not be enough to cover losses if other counterparties default.

Credit default swaps exist for asset-backed securities (ABSs) as well. The corporate CDSs are relatively simple. They first appeared on the scene in 1993, and were widely used from the late 1990s onwards, especially after the introduction of the ISDA template in July 1999. The ABS CDSs, which are usually for residential mortgage-backed securities but also on CDOs and commercial mortgage-backed securities as well, are more complex. They first appeared on the market in 2005 after the introduction of the ISDA template in June of that year. These are inevitably more complex than corporate CDSs. Mortgages are placed in a pool, typically set up as a trust, and notes, often called tranches, differ in their priority in receiving payments, with the most senior tranche having the first claim on interest payments and mortgage profits, since they always have a triple A rating. When mortgages default, the lowest-rated tranches suffer first from the default losses;, as these increase, even the highest-rated securities may experience default losses as well. A bank holding that debt and wishing to insure it could do so through a credit default swap, but a tranche of subprime securitized debt may not lead directly to a default but only to a reduction in debt payments, due to a rising level of defaults in the underlying mortgages. If an investor holds a AAA tranche with a principal amount of $100m. and the other tranches of the securitization are wiped out, and that during the month another $1m. of mortgages default so that the principal balance falls from $100m. to $99m., the investor would be paid $1m. from the CDS. The CDS would still exist after that payment, and would make payments as further mortgages default until the maturing of the contract.

Settling corporate CDS contracts in a credit event results in a payment to the buyer from the protection seller and the termination of the contract, but if such an event does not occur before the contract matures in anything from two to ten years, then the seller does not make a payment to the buyer. For these CDSs the settlement process is also straightforward. It is a cash settlement after a credit event auction under ISDA rules to establish the value of the reference obligation. The auction sets a price for all market participants who choose to settle in cash.

What happened after Lehman declared bankruptcy is a good example of the way in which the auction works. It took place on 10 October 2008, and a price of 8.625 cents on the dollar for Lehman Brothers debt was agreed. This meant that the sellers of protection on Lehman CDSs had to pay 91.375 cents on the dollar to buyers to settle and terminate the contracts. Those who had bought Lehman bonds but had also taken out protection through a CDS contract received 91.375 cents on the dollar, which offset any losses resulting from the bankruptcy. It was estimated that between $6bn and $8bn changed hands during the cash settlement of the CDS auction. The auction ended with a net payment of $5.2bn. Of course, those who had bought the bonds would have expected to receive par 100 when the bonds matured. However, the CDS meant that Lehman bond holders with CDSs received much more than they would have received as the recovery value, some years after the bankruptcy procedures were completed in March 2012.

Settling CDSs which refer to asset-backed securities is much more complicated. These are very different 'insurance' instruments from the ones in the corporate credit market. The seller of protection provides the buyer with protection covering the failure to pay off the principal by the legal date of maturity of the 'reference obligation', interest shortfall, that is, the amount of interest is less than required. The buyer can terminate the contract, if there is a 'floating amount event'. This refers to a write-down, a failure to pay the principal or an interest shortfall. It can include a distressed ratings downgrade for the asset-backed security itself, which could be a downgrade to CCC/Caa2, or even the withdrawal of a rating. That kind of downgrade means that the asset is no longer of investment quality.

In 2005, ISDA produced templates for that process and revised them in 2006, to deal with 'payment events' where the asset-backed security fails to meet the obligations set out in the contract. There are three options for determining the size of the payment to the borrower: fixed cap, variable cap and no cap. The first one requires that the seller has to pay the buyer the fixed rate; the variable cap means that the seller has to make up any interest shortfall on the security up to LIBOR plus the fixed rate, and in the third case, the seller has to make up any shortfall in the interest on the security. The buyer also has the option of ending the contract.

The price of a credit default swap is quoted as an annual percentage of the contract's notional value, taking into account the likelihood of default, the recovery rate in the event of a default and the liquidity, regulatory and market views about the credit, that is, the corporate bond and the quality of the issuer. The value or price of the corporate bond depends both on the financial strength of the company issuing the bonds and the market in which the company operates. These are the ultimate features on which the value of the derivative depends. The value is also subject to the risks of systemic failures which affect all the companies trading in CDSs based on corporate bonds. Ultimately, though, the positions between two counterparties, the banks trading across various derivatives, tend to have offsetting exposures, since some have a positive market value to a given counterparty and others have a negative market value. These have a netting effect so that only a net amount of the market value is at risk in a default by one of the counterparties.

However, it is possible that, because of their built-in leverage, CDSs may have made it more likely for investors to take on more risks than they would have done otherwise. Because of the way in which banks' capital requirements were assessed, financial institutions were able to hold less regulatory capital if they packaged loans into securities and held them on their balance sheet, than if they just kept the loans on their balance sheets. Others took the view that it was to their advantage to hold senior tranches of securitizations on their books if they insured them with CDSs and regulators allowed financial institutions to set aside less capital if they had bought such protection. That alone was a major reason for the increased demand for credit default swaps.

In a market in which CDSs are often sold and resold amongst parties, there are risks. Buyers may not be as financially sound as they should be to cover the obligation when there is a credit event, especially without collateral. To take account of this, the New York Federal Bank advised counterparties to inform their trading partners when the contract has been assigned to others. Concerns were raised by regulators in the UK and the USA about the growing backlog of documentation covering confirmation of the initial transactions and then the transfer from one party to a third party. The Federal Reserve Bank of New York called fourteen derivatives dealers, including the Bank of America, Barclays, Bear Stearns and Lehman Brothers, to a meeting, as a result of which a five-point plan was agreed, as well as the ISDA Novation Protocol of September 2005. The Protocol includes an agreement not to accept any transfer of a credit derivative unless the transfer has been agreed with the remaining party, who must receive full details of the transaction, all using the Depository Trust and Clearing

Corporation. Presumably, all were relieved that they had agreed to this Protocol in September 2008. Risks remained in the market, such as counterparty concentration risk. That risk had to be tackled by government intervention with the failure of a major counterparty, AIG, which would have left many market participants un-hedged and exposed to losses, as well as worsening the loss of liquidity.

In 2006, the ABX indices on subprime securitizations were introduced, representing a basket of credit default swap contracts on securitization tranches. In 2007, they became a widely followed barometer of the collapsing valuations in the subprime mortgage market and were also used by banks and other investors as a tool for hedging and trading as well. These indices consist of a series of equally weighted, static portfolios of CDSs, based on twenty subprime mortgage-backed securities, and were introduced when the issuance of mortgage-backed securities was strong in 2005.

A new series is introduced every six months, based on twenty completely new subprime deals, issued during the previous six months. The prices reflect the willingness of investors to buy or sell default protection, given their current views on the risk of the underlying subprime loans.[26]

The authors, Fender and Schneider, then consider the ABX prices for default protection and conclude that declining risk appetite and rising concerns about market illiquidity were some of the main drivers of the collapse in ABX prices since the summer of 2007. Indications of changes in risk appetite with regard to subprime mortgage risk may help to explain any deviation between observed market prices for the ABX indices and the projection of default-related cash flow shortfalls in the underlying subprime MBSs. They add that 'observed ABX prices are unlikely to be good predictors of future default-related cash flow shortfalls on outstanding subprime MBSs . . . This is in part because coverage of the ABX indices extends only to a small fraction of the outstanding subprime MBS universe.'[27]

Another study analysing the use of the ABX.HE index of the CDS market points out that the focus of regulators on banks using the CDS market prices as the basis for marking their portfolios to market was mistaken. The authors find that the market prices for AAA ABX HE index CDS 'at the peak of the financial crisis in June 2009 [were] inconsistent with any reasonable assumption for future default rates.'[28] They added,

We find that percentage changes in CDS prices are only weakly correlated with the credit performance of the underlying losses but are strongly affected by changes in the short-sale imbalances in the equity markets of the publicly traded investment banks. Because the short-sale activity measure is a proxy for demand imbalance in the market for mortgage default insurance, the relative importance of its correlation with price dynamics suggests that the practice of using the AAA ABX.HE index CDS to value subprime mortgage portfolios is quite problematic.[29]

That must be somewhat of an understatement!

In the years before the financial crisis, the possibility of the triple A tranches of CDOs with substantial AAA tranches defaulting did not seem at all likely. The significant probability of default would only occur if there was a major downturn in the housing market throughout the USA, which appeared to be an extremely low probability, based on historical data. When the downturn happened, the value of the underlying assets fell sharply and the value of AIG's credit default swap liabilities became very large when marked-to-market.

By August 2008, AIG had a total of $26.2bn of unrealized losses on its CDSs, on top of other losses on its subprime and other fixed income securities. The company posted $16.5bn collateral. On 15 September, a buyer of $10m. of protection of debt for five years had to pay $2.5m. immediately plus a $500,000 annual premium. On 16 September, after its downgrade by S&P and Moody's, AIG had to post $14.5bn additional collateral. It could not provide the additional collateral without a bail-out.

AIG's credit default swap business began in earnest in 2002, when Joe Cassano became CEO of AIG Financial Products (AIGFP), based in London. By December 2007, AIG had written CDSs with a notional value of $527bn, of which multi-sector CDOs amounted to $78bn, which the firm had begun originating in 2003, when AIG was AAA-rated. Cassano stated in his testimony to the Financial Crisis Inquiry Commission, that

> we made a decision at the end of 2005 to stop writing new deals that contained subprime capital. Although we completed deals that were already in the pipeline, the portfolio grew comparatively little after 2006 ... In dollar terms, our business grew every year because the CDS contracts were multi-year: adding even one increased the notional size of the book.

AIGFP decided to stop writing CDS protection on CDOs with subprime exposure. 'We announced our decision to the marketplace in February 2006', he added.[30] That is borne out by the Federal Reserve data, showing that AIG had borrowed a total of $128bn by the end of 2008, of which $28bn was used to purchase the CDOs on which AIG had sold protection and $20bn was allotted to buy subprime mortgage-backed securities in which AIG had invested as part of its securities lending programme. The remaining $80bn was a loan to enable the company to continue operating, whilst it sold off its non-core assets and capital investment through the TARP programme.[31] ISDA's argument is that it was not the CDSs per se which gave rise to the losses, but to the 'failure to assess the risks of MBSs, CDOs and other mortgage exposures'.

That view is supported by others and indeed by Cassano's own testimony. He accepted the analysis provided in 2005 by Eugene Park, who had taken over as the company's liaison with Wall Street. Park stated in 2005:

> The subprime loans underlying many CDOs formed too large a part of the packaged debt, increasing the risk to unacceptable levels. Those loans could default at any time, anywhere across the country, because the underwriting processes had been so shoddy. The diversification was a myth – if the housing market went bust, the subprime would collapse like a house of cards.[32]

AIGFP was advised and used mathematical models provided by Professor G. Gorton, an expert in corporate finance and models. These did not include the possibility of AIG losing its triple-A rating, which it did, or the growth of risky subprime lending. The value of such derivatives depends ultimately on the assets from which they derive. Models which do not incorporate the risks implicit in the underlying assets will fail to provide the users with an understanding of the risks involved.

Monitoring Value

Corporate governance after 2002

The purpose of this chapter is to consider who should have been responsible for keeping an eye on the value of assets in which Lehman Brothers chose to invest heavily, and on its risk management procedures. Lehman's board, as any other board, would have been expected to monitor the company in accordance with corporate governance requirements. The first question therefore is: what exactly was the Lehman board expected, indeed, required to do. The other two questions are considered later in this chapter. They are: was the board capable of carrying out its duties? Did the board actually meet the corporate governance requirements?

As corporate governance in the USA (as in other countries) continues to evolve, this description of corporate governance refers only to what was in force at the time. This is not as simple a task as it might seem. The sources of corporate governance law and regulation are state corporate law (mainly Delaware, since over half of US publicly traded companies are incorporated there); the federal Securities Act 1933 and the Securities Exchange Act 1934, and regulations of the Securities and Exchange Commission under those Acts; stock exchange listing rules (mainly the New York Stock Exchange (NYSE) and the NASDAQ); the Federal Reserve and other federal and state agencies with respect to banks and other financial institutions and the Sarbanes-Oxley Act 2002, amongst others.

> Because of the federal system of US law, these different sources of law are not always harmonised and corporations are often subject to different obligations to federal and state governments, as well as regulators at each level of government. This mosaic of rules and regulations, and the various authorities and mechanisms by which they are implemented and enforced, make for an environment of frequent change and evolution.[1]

That is certainly an understatement. The patchwork leads to confusion. It is entirely unclear which set of rules takes precedence over the others, where they conflict or appear to conflict. To an outsider that is a key question, yet that is not necessarily the case in the USA, where they are accustomed to the existence of more than one regulator at federal level and regulation at state level.[2]

The scandals leading to the Sarbanes-Oxley Act

Reforms in corporate governance were introduced with the Sarbanes-Oxley Act, after the major accounting scandals involving Enron and WorldCom emerged. Enron's reported revenues grew from under $10bn in the early 1990s to $139bn in 2001. The firm had invested heavily in broadband at the peak of the dot.com boom, but falsified its accounts, so that the losses were apparently occurring to 'independent' firms called 'Raptor entities'. Raptor had apparently agreed to absorb Enron's losses. Raptor entities were simply accounting contrivances, created and controlled by management. Once all was revealed, 80 per cent of Enron's profits since 2000 vanished. The Enron scandal was quickly followed by another, WorldCom. The company announced that its recent financial statements would have to be revised, after accounting irregularities came to light on 25 June 2002. The company had discovered errors amounting to $3.8bn in its accounts, which meant that it had net losses for 2001 and for the first quarter of 2002. Other companies, such as Tyco and Adelphia, were found to be weaker than appeared at first sight, because their executives had indulged in self-dealing transactions or had taken too much out of the company. On 28 June 2002, the SEC called for the CEOs and CFOs to personally certify in writing and under oath the accuracy of their recent annual and quarterly financial statements, thus making them personally liable. The SEC's action applied to the 947 largest publicly listed companies in America. Congress responded to the public outrage, and the result was the Sarbanes-Oxley Act.

The Sarbanes-Oxley Act 2002, introduced a number of changes related to corporate governance, which formed the basis of corporate governance until further changes were introduced following the financial crisis. Many of these related to the appointment of auditors, the processes of auditing and the presentations of financial data. It was thought that audit firms might (or had) become too closely involved with the company they audited, so changes in the relationship between auditors and their clients were introduced.

Some provisions of the Act

For the first time, auditing firms were prohibited from providing non-audit services to their clients, apart from tax compliance. Audit firms were required to disclose information about their operations for the first time, such as names of clients, fees and quality controls.

The audit committee of the board, composed of independent directors, became responsible for the appointment, compensation and oversight of the external auditor, rather than management. The Act also required lead audit partner rotation every five years instead of seven. Firms must have a system of internal accounting controls, which management is required to fully disclose and which the external auditors are obliged to test and evaluate.

- The Act clearly defines and places the responsibility for a company's financial statements on the CEO and CFO.
- Companies must certify (amongst other items) that they have reviewed each annual and quarterly report.
- Based on their knowledge, the financial information is fairly presented and does not include any untrue statement of material fact, or omit a material fact that would make the financial reports misleading.
- Companies must acknowledge their responsibility for establishing and maintaining internal controls over financial reporting and other disclosures.
- Companies must have evaluated the effectiveness of these controls, presenting their conclusion as to their effectiveness, and disclosing any material changes in the company's controls.
- They are responsible for maintaining 'disclosure controls and procedures', to make sure that they have all the relevant information, especially during the time in which a quarterly or annual report is being prepared.

The Act established other important investor protections:

- Companies must provide enhanced disclosures in annual and quarterly reports regarding material off-balance sheet transactions, arrangements and obligations.
- Companies must report material changes in the financial condition operations of the company on a rapid and current basis.
- Board members of public companies, officers and investors who own more than 10 per cent of the shares must file reports specifying the number of shares bought or sold within two days of the transaction.

- Board members and executive officers of public companies are prohibited from trading shares during a specific 'blackout period' before and after earnings reports or when other material results are disclosed.

New York Stock Exchange listing rules

The Act led to the introduction of new rules for listed companies on the New York Stock Exchange. These include the requirement for boards to have a majority of independent directors on the board, with a stricter definition of 'independence'. NYSE's Corporate Governance rules[3] state that a director is not independent if he has been an employee of the company during the past three years, holds a senior position with a company which carries out a significant amount of business with the company concerned, or if he is involved with a charity which receives substantial sums from the company.

The board must establish three committees: an audit committee, a compensation committee and a nominating committee, composed of independent directors. All members of the audit committee must be financially literate, and must include at least one financial expert.[4] In addition, each committee must publish a charter setting out specific tasks and powers of the committee.[5]

The NYSE amplifies the duties of the audit committee. It should discuss critical accounting policies and practices, alternative treatments of financial information under GAAP, and any accounting disagreements and other relevant written agreements between the auditors and management with the auditor and senior management. The audit committee is also required to receive and deal with any complaints about accounting, internal control and audit, and also to provide any employee the chance to make confidential and anonymous submissions about accounting and audit matters. This followed the collapse of Enron in 2001, following the revelations made by Sherron Watkins, then a Vice President of Enron and head of internal audit. She also revealed the contents of anonymous complaints from other employees.[6] These events were the background to the rules concerning whistleblowers introduced as part of the Act.

The full board of directors delegates the financial oversight responsibility to the audit committee, but both have a duty of care to the company and its shareholders, which means that the board members must be duly diligent and must act in good faith. For audit committee members the duties are more onerous. They must be fully informed, have a thorough understanding of the company's business, its risks and critical accounting policies, attend regularly, and proactively engage in discussions with the management and independent auditors. They must make sure that the company has an adequate system of internal controls and be able to monitor red flags as well as overseeing the integrity of financial reporting. Section 301 of the Sarbanes-Oxley Act added a new section to the Exchange Act covering these issues, so that by 26 April 2003, the SEC had to, by rule, direct the national securities exchanges and NASDAQ to prohibit the listing of securities of any company, including foreign companies that did not meet these requirements.

The SEC welcomed the Act and had completed most of the rule-making within six months and all of it in under a year, so that by 2004, the largest companies were fully subject to all the new regulatory requirements of the Sarbanes-Oxley Act. It was especially welcomed by SEC as it strengthened the enforcement of federal securities laws. It added a number of new weapons to the Commission's enforcement arsenal, in particular section 1103, which enables the Commission to seek a temporary order to escrow extraordinary payments by an issuer to its directors, officers, partner, controlling persons, agents or employees, whilst they were subject to a Commission's investigation.[7] All the Sarbanes-Oxley requirements for audit committees were adopted by the Commission and applied to the stock exchanges to prohibit the listing of any security of a company that has not met these requirements. It seems that at that time, not only the Commission but many others involved in the capital markets believed that these new rules would mean that the news headlines would no longer be 'dominated by reports of financial fraud, lapses in audit and corporate governance responsibilities and intentional manipulation of accounting rules'.[8]

In assessing the extent to which the board and the senior management of Lehman Brothers can be held responsible, the Examiner turned to Delaware law, since Lehman was incorporated there. The Examiner's conclusions are set out in the next section.

Corporate accountability under Delaware's General Corporation Law

This statute states that, 'The business and affairs of every corporation . . . shall be managed by or under the direction of a board of directors.'[9] The corporation law of all other US states also assigns corporate managerial power to the board of directors. Its meaning is determined by case law. One of the key cases is *Caremark International* (1996), which held that the board of directors' duty of oversight includes a duty to ensure that 'appropriate information and reporting systems are in place so that the board has access to timely, accurate information to ensure corporate compliance and business performance, but the level of detail is a matter of business judgement'.[10]

The judgement in this case seems to suggest that when evaluating a company's management systems and controls, the board or audit committee should test and challenge these systems, rather than just relying on the auditors' and management's reports to identify any deficiencies. Previous case law accepted a presumption of business regularity and did not require affirmative obligations on directors where there were no reasons for suspicion. The judgement in the *Caremark* case nevertheless indicated that directors are able to fulfil their duty of monitoring by making a good faith, reasonable effort to implement an adequate reporting system. The SEC, however, concluded in another case that 'an officer or director may rely on the company's procedures for determining what disclosure is required only if he has a reasonable basis for believing that those procedures have resulted in full consideration of those issues'.[11] The latter is a more stringent requirement. Under Delaware law, the directors' civil liability is mitigated by the business judgement rule, due diligence defences, and by good faith reliance on the records of the corporation and upon such information, reports, statements or opinions provided by corporate officers, employees, board committees and professional advisors.

The implications of the 'business judgement rule' are set out by the Examiner. Valukas provides clear analyses of the interpretations of duties recognized under the law: due care, loyalty and good faith, as well as the 'business judgement rule.' This principle protects officers and directors from personal liability for business decisions that have resulted in financial losses to the corporation unless their actions have been proved to be grossly negligent. Noting that the 'Delaware courts will not substitute their own judgements for those of corporate directors', the Examiner details the presumptions and conclusions of a number of court cases relevant to the apportionment of blame arising from Lehman's bankruptcy.

The business judgement rule creates a 'presumption that in making a business decision the directors of a corporation acted on an informed basis, in good faith and in the honest belief that the action taken was in the best interests of the company'.[12] Again under this rule, directors'

> decisions will be respected by courts unless the directors are interested or lack independence relative to the decision, do not act in good faith, act in a manner that cannot be attributed to a rational business purpose or reach their decision

by a grossly negligent process that includes the failure to consider all material facts reasonably available.

In other cases cited, the court considered that it was not per se a breach of fiduciary duty that a board of directors did not read a merger agreement but relied instead on a summary of the terms, and again that a board of directors could rely on an expert in making a business judgement and to rely on that opinion without necessarily evaluating the facts and the judgement independently.[13]

> A member of the board or a member of any committee designated by the board of directors, shall ... be fully protected in relying in good faith upon the records of the corporation and upon such information, opinions, reports, statements presented to the corporation by any of the corporation's officers or employees or committees of the board of directors.

The report must be germane to the subject on which the board is called to act. A later judgement stated that the 'court will not substitute [its] judgement for that of the board if the latter's decision can be attributed to any rational purpose'.[14] The business judgement rule does not protect the board for decisions involving fraud or illegality. Finally the 'business judgement rule does not apply to director inaction. The appropriate standard for determining liability for director inaction is generally gross negligence'.[15] One is tempted to ask exactly what the point of being a member of a board is, when no independent judgement, knowledge or research seem to be required.

Valukas then turns to an analysis of the business judgement rule as applied to officers, but given there are only a few cases in which breaches of fiduciary duty are brought against officers, he assumes that the fiduciary duties of directors and officers are 'identical' so that officers are protected by the business judgement rule when they act under an express delegation of authority from the board.[16] But the rule *may* not apply when the officer fails to be informed about all of the facts relevant to the decision or without disclosing relevant information to the board or to the superior officer about the decision or when the decision is beyond the scope of the officer's authority. Then the officer's action may be thought to have been taken in bad faith and would then fall outside the protection of the business judgement rule. The rule does not provide any protection against fraud, or in the case of AIG, for materially misleading financial statements that overstated the value of the corporation by billions of dollars and made AIG appear more financially secure than it really was. The officers who participated in a sham transaction 'violated their fiduciary duties by causing AIG to engage in illegal conduct'.[17]

Interestingly enough, when responding to questions during a House Committee hearing, Valukas described the 'business judgement' rule in the following terms:

> The business judgement rule pretty much says that if you have process in place and you are acting – you are making a rational decision – you are permitted to do so. I would say that the issue wasn't necessarily just within Lehman as to what Lehman was doing so much as it might have been with regard to the regulators who need to be able to say to a business person, that might be a business judgement you are prepared to make, but we are not prepared to let you make that judgement.[18]

He also made it clear that the risk committee and its senior officers did not have a direct line to the board. It is interesting because the regulators, in this case the SEC, would presumably apply regulations derived from federal securities law or from other laws such as the Sarbanes-Oxley Act, and, if they were held to account under such regulations or laws, pleading the business judgement rule would not help. The board's failure, in his eyes, was due to the behaviour of Lehman's senior management in withholding information from the board and the regulators. In his testimony before a Senate committee, Valukas stated that: 'If Lehman had earlier presented a fair and accurate picture of its financial condition, regulators and Lehman's board might have had a fighting chance to make a much-needed correction or arrange for a smoother landing.'[19]

Apart from the business rule, the Examiner considered the place given to the duty of care in Delaware company law. The duty of care required by directors is a duty of informed decision-making. Exercising 'due care in the decision-making context is process only'. Delaware 'protects directors from personal liability to the extent their decisions are based on information provided to them by management.'[20] Like many other Delaware companies, Lehman's certificate of incorporation provides:

> A director shall not be personally liable to the Corporation or its stockholders for monetary damages for breach of fiduciary duty as a director; provided that this sentence shall not eliminate or limit the liability of a director (i) for any breach of his duty of loyalty to the Corporation or its stockholders, (ii) for acts or omissions not in good faith or which involve intentional misconduct or a knowing violation of law, (iii) under Section 174 of the (Delaware Corporation Law,) or (iv) any transaction from which the director derives an improper personal benefit.[21]

There have been very few cases testing the meaning of a duty of care, but in some cases the courts have held that failing to consider a proposed transaction with sufficient information, consideration or deliberation might constitute a breach of the duty. A director's duty of loyalty 'essentially ... mandates that the best interests of the corporation and its shareholders takes precedence over any interest possessed by a director, officer or controlling shareholder and not shared by the stockholders generally'.[22] The duty to act in good faith is regarded as subsidiary to the duty of loyalty and apart from self-interested dealing, this duty imposes personal liability only on directors 'who have handled their responsibility in a reckless or irrational manner'.

The Delaware courts also seem to establish a 'duty to monitor', which can be breached, following the *Caremark* decision, if (a) the directors utterly failed to implement any reporting or information system or controls; or (b) having implemented such a system or controls consciously failed to monitor or oversee the operations thus disabling themselves from being informed of risks or problems requiring their attention. The Supreme Court ruled that the emphasis should be on the word, 'conscious', or to put it in another way, 'directors will be potentially liable for breach of their oversight duty only if they ignore red flags that actually come to their attention, warning of compliance problems'. Directors' liability for the failure to monitor is strictly limited.[23]

The Delaware courts redefined the duty of care as a duty of loyalty, arguing that

> where directors fail to act in the face of a known duty to act, thereby demonstrating a conscious disregard for their responsibilities, they breach their duty of loyalty by failing to discharge that fiduciary obligation in good faith ... To be able to hold a director liable for failure to monitor, the director's indolence [must be] so persistent that it [can]not be ascribed to anything other than a knowing decision not to even try to make sure the corporation's officers had developed and were implementing a prudent approach to ensuring law compliance.[24]

It also means that duty of loyalty claims do not fall under the protection of the law, as duty of care claims do. The bar for claims under the duty of loyalty with regard to monitoring what the company does are set too high, given that the picture of such an indolent director attending board meetings regularly seems improbable. He would have to face his colleagues at every meeting, and the 'indolence' would be clear to all. Both he and the rest of the board might fail with regard to a duty of loyalty because of a lack of understanding of the key issues and the presence of a strong and overbearing chairman who was also the CEO.

Indeed, analyses of the impact of failures and weaknesses in corporate governance do not suggest indolence as the main or even a contributory cause. What the Examiner's analysis of corporate governance shows is that, for a company incorporated in Delaware, it is very difficult to find colourable claims against Lehman Brothers. The Examiner therefore concludes that 'the conduct of Lehman's officers, while subject to question in retrospect, falls within the business judgement rule and does not give rise to colourable claims'.[25] Lehman's directors did not breach their duty to monitor the company's risks.

The answer to the first question is that, given the mishmash of laws and regulations, it would not be too far off the mark to say that the duties and responsibilities of the board were not entirely clear for a company headquartered in Delaware. Furthermore, laws and regulations changed during the time some of Lehman's board members were on the board. It is good practice for companies to ensure that their board members are aware of changes in the requirements placed on boards, and to ensure that the structure and practices of the board are altered accordingly. There is no sign that Lehman ever considered educating the board about changes in corporate governance or about matters such as their use of derivatives.

Was Lehman's board able to carry out its duties?

In his testimony to the House Committee on Financial Services, Thomas Cruikshank, former chairman of the Audit Committee and member of the board since 1996, stressed that the Examiner found no 'colorable claims against the independent directors', and also that their duties were confined to 'thoughtfully appointing officers, establishing or approving goals and plans and monitoring (a company's) performance'.[26] He also refers to the large number of meetings between the beginning of 2007 to September 2008, over 80 meetings in all. He describes the range of management presentations to the board during that period, but says nothing about the frequency of meetings before 2007. Management presentations to a board require careful consideration and should be subject to rigorous questioning.

> As directors, we took great comfort from management's reports regarding Lehman's risk management system, which was widely regarded as being among the best in the business ... how the firm's CEO, President and entire Executive Committee took an active and leadership role in key risk decisions and oversight

... how Lehman made decisions on large risk exposures by committee ... The Board was further reassured by the size, structure and expertise of Lehman's Global Risk Management Group.

The board, however, rather than being reassured by the structure of risk management, should have asked what exactly were the views of the Risk Committee and the Risk Management Group on at least the major decisions Lehman took at that time, and what the differences of opinion were between the two.

Events such as the removal of Madelyn Antoncic, Chief Risk Officer and Michael Gelband, head of Lehman's Fixed Income Division, are the kind of events a board should question, because of their possible significance. In fact, they were removed from their positions 'because of their opposition to management's growing accumulation of risky and illiquid assets'. Antoncic's public speeches as early as December 2006 had warned of 'a seemingly overwhelming sense of complacency', 'with volatility low, corporate spreads growing ever tighter, and markets all but ignoring bad news', although she was careful to defend her own company.[27]

It is true that Lehman had an impressive risk management structure, and an array of stress tests to determine the potential financial consequences of an economic shock to its portfolio of assets and investments. These, as the Examiner points out, were more for show, to impress investors, regulators and the rating agencies. They were not meant to influence Lehman's strategy or its decisions. He notes that the risk limits and stress tests, 'did not impose legal requirements on management or prevent management and the board from exceeding those limits if they chose to do so ... Lehman's management chose to disregard or overrule the firm's risk controls on a regular basis'.[28] Once again, Lehman's actions did not give rise to any colourable claims.

It would have taken determined questioning by the board to discover what happened to the risk limits. Lehman's management exceeded risk limits, that is, concentration limits, on their leveraged loan and commercial real estate limits, including single transaction limits, designed to ensure diversification, on their leveraged loans. As a result they exceeded the limits by 70 per cent on commercial real estate and by 100 per cent on leveraged loans. They left out their commercial real estate investments, private equity investments and its leveraged loan commitments for a time. The Examiner comments that Lehman 'did not have a regular and systematic means of analysing the amount of catastrophic loss that the firm could suffer from these increasingly large and illiquid investments'.[29]

Nor did they strictly apply balance sheet limits, designed to contain the overall risk of the firm and maintain its leverage ratio. No one asked any questions about the stress tests, such as which investments were covered by the stress tests. Lehman informed the SEC in their regular meetings that the firm-wide risk appetite limit was a real constraint of Lehman's risk-taking, although it was treated as a 'soft' target within the firm. It was clearly not enforced, since between December 2006 and December 2007, it was raised from $2.3 to $4.0bn in January 2008 and then backdated to 3 December 2007. It was not, however, unlawful for Lehman to secretly violate its increased limits and backdate its documents to disguise the breaches of its risk limits. They were self-imposed risk limits, exclusively intended to allow Lehman's management to make their own estimates about the future of the company. Its commercial real estate investments, such as their bridge equity position in Archstone of $2.3bn, were excluded from Lehman's risk appetite limit and from its stress testing. When Archstone was eventually included, Lehman continued to exceed the limit for a few months and raised its firm-wide risk limit again.

The Examiner did not find that there were colourable claims against Lehman's senior management on the grounds that they failed to inform the board about the level of risk that they were taking, nor that the board had failed in its duty to monitor Lehman's risk-taking activities. On the one hand, Lehman's management did inform the board that it was taking 'increased business risk in order to grow the firm more aggressively; that the increased business risk resulted in higher risk usage metrics, and ultimately firm-wide risk limit overages, and that market conditions after July 2007 were hampering the firm's liquidity'. The Examiner added, 'Lehman's risk limits and controls were designed primarily for management's internal use in making business decisions.'[30] Lehman's board 'fully embraced' the growth strategy, and was informed about the large increase in the risk appetite for fiscal 2007. All of the directors told the Examiner that they agreed with the strategy 'at the time it was undertaken'. They were not told about the exclusion of real estate owned and private equity from stress testing until January 2008, but none of the directors remembered the disclosure. They were also not informed about the decision not to apply single transaction limits to its leveraged loans.[31]

With regard to the board, in the context of Delaware law at that time, the Examiner does not find a breach of fiduciary duty. He notes that the board received reports about Lehman's business and its risk-taking at every meeting; that, although the level of risk was incomplete, management assured directors that it was taking prudent steps to address these risks in the context of the developments in the subprime markets and the credit markets. Management informed the board that they saw the unfolding crisis as 'an opportunity to pursue a countercyclical growth strategy', and their reports did not raise any "'red flags" imposing on the directors a duty to inquire further'.[32] Delaware law allows directors to rely on management reports and exempts them from personal liability when they do.[33]

The final question is more difficult to answer, partly because the board was not provided with *all* the relevant information by senior management. Lehman's senior management provided the board with just enough information to support the conclusion that the board was not actually deceived or misled, and that the frequent and full management reports gave the board the opportunity to raise questions, had they so wished. The Examiner's report does, however, indicate that significant information (such as what was actually covered in the stress tests) at perhaps sensitive times was not given to the board then, but management advised the board at another time. The board may have fulfilled their duties under Delaware General Corporation Law, but probably did not meet the standards expected at that time under Sarbanes-Oxley and the New York Stock Exchange Listing Rules, which envisaged an audit committee able to review and challenge financial statements and also to 'discuss policies with respect to risk assessment and risk management', but noting that 'it is the job of the CEO and senior management to assess and manage the company's exposure to risk'.[34] Most members of the board had senior positions in industry, but in 2007 only four had been on the board for five years or less. All the others had been independent directors for between 12 and 23 years. Only one, Jerry Grundhofer had recent experience of leading a large US bank, as a former director of Bancorp. The relationship can become very cosy between the board and the management after so many years. The legal requirements under Delaware law were fulfilled, but the board itself was hardly effective.

The fundamental issue for corporate governance is why boards were not effective before the crisis, especially since so much emphasis has been placed on internal controls although this was often restricted to financial accounts. The Institute of International Finance reported in July 2008 that 'events have raised questions about the ability of certain boards properly to oversee senior managements and to understand and monitor the business itself'.[35] Other analyses of banks' boards suggest that boards need further training on risk issues, and the ability to measure the company's risk appetite and measuring the firm's performance against it. But just enabling a bank to tick a box saying that there is a risk committee is not enough. Fuld usually made sure that the bank conformed to formal requirements.

Weak corporate governance and the financial crisis

In general, the quality of board members is a matter of particular concern, even where the 'fit and proper' test is applied. For the UK, that test is extended to 'fit and proper, honest and competent', which is an attempt to deal with the issue of independent board members being able to handle the technical knowledge required and the detail involved in monitoring the risks and activities of large, complex, global banks. Writing in the *Financial Times*, Guerrera and Thai-Larsen examined the boards of the eight most important US financial institutions (Citi, JP Morgan Chase, Bank of America, Goldman Sachs, Merrill Lynch, Morgan Stanley, Lehman Brothers and pre-rescue Bear Stearns), and noted that two-thirds of the board members had no significant recent banking experience and less than half had no financial services industry experience at all. Many of the directors without any financial background were also members of the highly technical board committees.

For example, Roger Berlind, director of Lehman, a theatre impresario and private investor, was a member of both the board's audit committee and finance and risk committee. At Citi, John Deutsch, a former head of the CIA and a Professor of Physical Chemistry at MIT, was a member of the audit and finance committee. Tommy Franks, a retired US Army general, was a member of the audit committee of the Bank of America.[36]

However difficult it may be to judge the quality of board members from the outside, the fact remains that boards at many of the major financial institutions failed to alert the CEO and management to the coming storm. In 2008 and 2009, opinions differed as to the causes of the failure, with some regarding this as being due to the attitude and lack of effort on the part of board members. Some described them as being asleep on the job, and others claimed that they did not want to disturb a quiet and lucrative position. Even when boards had knowledgeable and experienced individuals working on them, it appears that they did not ask the tough questions and work with the CEO to reinvent the business.

Strengthening corporate governance

Since the financial crisis, regulators in the USA, the UK and elsewhere, have set out new requirements for board membership and its conduct in overseeing senior management. The first steps in the USA were taken in the Dodd-Frank Act, which was signed into law by President Obama on 21 July 2010. NYSE and

NASDAQ listing rules require a majority of members of the board to be independent, as well as disclosure of the experience, qualifications or skills of each director nominee that led the board to nominate that person to serve as a director. They must also show whether and how its nominating committee considers diversity in identifying director nominees. The Dodd-Frank Act requires companies to disclose in their annual meeting proxy statements whether the same person serves as chair and CEO, and if so to explain why. The gradual governance trend is towards separating the functions of chairman and chief executive.

The Securities and Exchange Commission introduced new reporting rules on 16 December 2009, which took effect on 28 February 2010.[37] The rules apply to those regulated by the SEC and require new disclosures about compensation policies; director and nominee qualifications and legal proceedings; board leadership structure and the board's role in risk oversight, amongst others. The amendments about the leadership structure of the board are designed to provide shareholders with the reasons for combining or separating the role of the chairman and chief executive of the board. The company is also required to explain why it considers the choice it has made to be the most appropriate structure at the time of filing. If the roles are combined and a lead independent director is designated to chair meetings of independent directors, then the company has to explain why, as well as the specific role the lead independent director plays in the leadership of the company. 'These amendments are to provide investors with more transparency about the company's corporate governance, but are not intended to influence a company's decision regarding its board leadership structure.'[38] However, the lead independent director is one of the independent directors of the board, who takes over the position of chair for a limited period of time. It is only an informally instituted designation, without the responsibilities, it seems, of the role of chairman. The SEC agreed (with commentators on its proposals) that risk oversight is a 'key competence' of the board and that additional disclosures would benefit investor and shareholder understanding of the company. Disclosures about the board's involvement of the risk management process should provide information about how the company sees the role of the board and senior management in managing the risks the company faces, whether through a separate committee or the whole board and to whom individuals supervising the day-to-day risk management responsibilities report.[39] As it stands, this would seem to be a rather weak requirement. The chief risk officer should have a mandated role to report to the board or perhaps to one of its committees.

The SEC's new rule reflects a trend in corporate governance in the USA. At least a quarter of the major US companies have separated the roles of chairman and chief executive and over 70 per cent of the National Association of Corporate Directors have voted for separation. The logic is clear. 'The CEO should not be chairing the independent board which is supposed to be monitoring his or her activities.'[40] The matter is still being debated in the USA even after the financial crisis, and especially after the collapse of Lehman. The current expectation in the USA is that companies will increasingly and voluntarily accept the need for a separate chairman, followed by the banking regulators.

In various speeches, Thomas Curry, appointed as Comptroller of the Currency in April 2012, explained what led to the 'heightened expectations' for risk management and corporate governance. 'As much as any other factor, the financial crisis can be traced back to failures of corporate governance and risk management systems. At some institutions, boards of directors and senior managers did not sufficiently comprehend aggregate risk within their firms and lacked a sufficiently robust risk framework – that is, the people, systems and processes for monitoring a complex set of risks'. Other problems included inadequate and fragmented technology infrastructures, hindering the assessment of risk.[41] He reiterated the same point in a later speech to a conference on Governance, Compliance and Operational Risk: 'One of the central lessons coming out of the financial crisis was that supervisory expectations for risk management, internal audit and corporate governance in our largest and most complex banks needs to be substantially higher, especially for the most systemically important institutions.'[42] He regards these expectations as 'an important milestone on the road to completing the rules implementing the Dodd-Frank Act'. The largest banks are indeed large, including JP Morgan Chase, the main subsidiary of JPM with total assets in excess of $1,990 trillion; Bank of America with total assets at $1.439 trillion; Citibank NA at $1.334 trillion and Wells Fargo, the main subsidiary of WFL at $1.328 trillion.

The Office of the Comptroller of the Currency issued its final rules and guidelines for large national banks, insured with the Federal Deposit Insurance Commission, and insured Federal branches of foreign banks with average consolidated assets of $50bn or more on 2 September 2014. The guidelines may apply to any other banks that the OCC considers to be appropriate, that is, if the bank's operations are highly complex or otherwise present a heightened risk, based on the bank's complexity of products and services, risk profile and scope of operations. The focus is on the risk governance framework and minimum standards for the board overseeing the framework's design and implementation.

The guidelines specifically state that these are 'enforceable by the terms of a Federal statute that authorizes the OCC to prescribe operational and managerial standards for national banks and Federal savings associations.' The guidelines themselves are consistent with the principles embedded in the Federal Reserve's expectations for large bank holding companies.

The OCC has established a mandatory base upon which banks are expected to build their risk governance frameworks, and banks may well consider it wise to go beyond these basic principles. The risk governance framework has to be a formal written document setting out the management of risk-taking activities. The document itself will be wide-ranging, covering clearly defined roles and responsibilities, the risk appetite statement, risk policies processes and procedures; risk limits, metrics and analytics as well as risk data aggregation, monitoring and reporting. All of these elements should be combined in the bank's strategic plan and its risk appetite should be integrated, which may not always be the case for very large banks. It may seem obvious that they should be combined, and that a bank should not pursue certain strategies or opportunities which suddenly arise without considering if they fall outside the risk appetite. This is precisely what Lehman ignored when it continually overshot its own risk limits in pursuit of investments in commercial real estate.

Other important considerations in the management of risk include the issues of performance management and financial incentives, again lessons to be learnt from the collapse of Lehman. That also applies to the establishment of a risk culture and the ability to communicate the importance of awareness of risk and the way in which it should be handled. The OCC focuses on the ability of the bank to evaluate and manage risk separately from the parent company in order to 'protect the national bank charter', by ensuring that the bank operates in a safe and sound manner rather than simply as an extension of its parent holding company and other group affiliates. From the point of view of the OCC, banks should be able to manage risk so that it is integrated with the bank's strategy, but as these may change, it means that the risk appetite has to be reviewed, as it should be before the bank embarks on any new or evolving strategy. This, for example, may be due to sudden changes in the market or in economic circumstances. A risk management framework therefore cannot be set in stone, but any changes should be supported by a clear statement of the risks and risk limits, which are acceptable to the bank and risk monitoring, analytics and metrics.

The expected risk governance structure should include three distinct units: frontline units, independent risk management and internal audit. The frontline unit is any part of the company which is responsible for one or other of the full range of risks from credit risk to liquidity risk to reputational risk. The OCC sets out three additional criteria for the frontline units which may either generate revenue or reduce expenses for the parent company; operational support or servicing for the delivery of products or services to customers and technology services.

These guidelines are quite specific in that each frontline unit has to be accountable to the CEO and the board for assessing and managing all of the risks they take on. They have to work together with the frontline unit to set out and keep to written policies and procedures to manage risk and to be consistent with the bank's risk appetite statement. Frontline units must also report to independent risk management at least quarterly on their risk limits.

Each bank will have a unit which is responsible for identifying, measuring, monitoring or controlling aggregate risks independently of the CEO and other frontline units. This unit, headed by a Chief Risk Officer (CRO), will design a comprehensive written risk governance framework, and will be accountable to the CEO and to the board. The CRO is then responsible for identifying and assessing risks, ensuring that the frontline units keep to the risk limits and all the procedures involved, informing the CEO and the board of any significant increases in risks or breaches of the framework. The CRO and his staff review and report to the board at least quarterly on the bank's risk profile in relation to its risk appetite and its compliance with concentration risks. The most difficult task is to inform the board of any significant cases in which his assessment of risk differs from that of the CEO or cases in which the CEO is not sticking to agreed risk limits or is not ensuring that the frontline units do so. For this reason, the CRO in heading up the risk management unit should be only one level below the CEO.

The guidelines also repeat the existing requirement for an internal audit unit, headed by a Chief Audit Executive (CAE), with perhaps the only additions being that of the detail of the investigations and reporting requirements. The internal audit unit reports to the audit committee of the board, including any instances of failure to adhere to the framework. The internal audit unit's programme makes sure that its policies, procedures and processes comply with current regulations and are updated to take account of any changes in risk factors internal or external. This must of course be independent of all the operations of the bank, and again headed by a CAE at one level below the CEO.

The OCC requires a much more comprehensive risk appetite statement, setting out its risk appetite, that is, the aggregate level and types of risk that its board and management are willing to assume to achieve the bank's strategic objectives and business plan, consistent with the capital, liquidity and other regulatory requirements. It should also set out the safe and sound 'risk culture', quantitative limits, including stress tests, and deal with the bank's earnings, capital and liquidity. Both the risk limits and concentration of risk limits should be clearly defined and enforced. The board or its risk management committee should review and approve the framework at least annually, or any significant changes to it, as well as monitoring compliance with it. Banks are allowed to use the parent company's framework where appropriate, and may tailor it to their own requirements, but must document any material differences between the risk profiles of the parent company and the bank.

The guidelines make it clear that the board's responsibility is to actively oversee the bank's risk-taking activities and hold management accountable. This includes questioning, challenging and opposing recommendations and decisions made by the management when necessary. The board may rely on risk assessments and reports prepared by independent risk management and internal audit to support it in its role. The board should be provided with training programmes tailored to their specific needs. The programme should cover complex products, services, lines of business and relevant risks, as well as the laws, regulations and supervisory requirements applicable to the bank. The directors should also be 'independent', which is defined solely in terms of links with the bank; that is, they are not a current officer or employee of the bank and have not been such for the past three years. A director cannot be regarded as 'independent' if he is a member of the 'immediate family' of a person who is or has been an 'executive officer' of the bank or its parent company. 'Independence' is defined in terms of relationships to the staff of the bank, which would be seen to create obvious conflicts of interest, without any reference to the length of service which, when it runs to twenty years or more, means that a director is no longer independent of the bank. Indeed he or she has become part of the company.

The Federal Reserve Bank has not yet set out such a detailed programme for the reform of corporate governance. The most recent supervisory and regulatory letter about corporate governance was issued on 17 December 2012, and briefly summarizes the role of the board. Each firm's board of directors and its committees, with the support of senior management should:

(a) Maintain a clearly articulated corporate strategy and institutional risk appetite. The board should set direction and oversight for revenue and profit generation, risk management and control functions and other areas essential to sustaining the consolidated organization.

(b) Ensure that the firm's senior management has the expertise and level of involvement required to manage the firm's business lines, critical operations, banking offices and other material entities. These areas should receive operational support to remain in a safe and sound condition under a broad range of stressed conditions. 'Material entities' are subsidiaries or foreign offices of the firm that are significant to the activities of a core business line or critical operation.

(c) Maintain a corporate culture that emphasizes the importance of compliance with laws and regulations and consumer protection, as well as the avoidance of conflicts of interest and the management of reputational and legal risks.

(d) Undertake recovery testing and training exercises that consider a broad range of internal and external risk scenarios and account for interconnectedness across operations and legal entities.

(e) Ensure that the recovery plan is updated as needed and reflects lessons learned from reviews of trigger events, testing and training exercises.

(f) Ensure that recovery planning is sufficiently integrated into corporate governance structures and processes, subject to independent validation, and effectively supported by related MIS reporting to the board and its committees.

All of this applies particularly to the eight largest banks – Bank of America, Bank of New York Mellon, Citigroup, Goldman Sachs, JP Morgan Chase, Morgan Stanley, State Street Corporation and Wells Fargo, and to other large banks supervised by the Federal Reserve Bank.

Other regulations regarding corporate governance have been issued by the Federal Reserve Bank since the financial crisis, but in a somewhat piecemeal fashion. They add to existing regulations or introduce new regulations. For example, state member banks and bank holding companies must give the Federal Reserve thirty days' prior notice before adding or replacing a board member if the bank is not in compliance with all minimum capital requirements.[43] The Federal Reserve Bank has the power to disapprove the notice. A new election of board directors may be ordered if the bank is not in compliance with all minimum capital requirements applicable to the institution as determined on the basis of the institution's most recent report of the condition of the bank or the report of an examination or inspection. Since the crisis, expectations of the board have increased either in terms of federal law or regulations and the ones identified here are simply some of the requirements set out by the Federal Reserve Bank.

The regulations or expectations set out by the Federal Reserve Bank are incomplete, as the Bank has yet to flesh out its requirements. This will be completed in 2015. Their requirements will in all probability be in line with the OCC's 'heightened expectations', and both will reflect the Basel Committee's Corporate Governance Principles for Banks, due to be finalized in 2015.

It is interesting to compare the range of corporate governance requirements and their gradual development in the USA with developments in the UK, where the first and only corporate governance code, the Combined Code, was set out in 1998 and has developed over the years since then, culminating in the UK Corporate Governance Code 2014. This sets out standards for good practice in relation to board leadership and effectiveness, remuneration, accountability and relations with shareholders.[44] Listed companies are required to report on how they have applied the main principles of the Code in their annual report and accounts, and either to confirm that they have complied with the Code's provisions, or where they have not, to provide an explanation. This is a more effective provision than might appear at first sight, so that companies which are not required to publish their compliance with the Code, do so in order to show that they comply with the standards.

There are two vital issues: the division of responsibilities and the length of time a member serves on the board. The Code is entirely clear: the roles of the chairman and chief executive should not be exercised by the same individual. The division of responsibilities between the chairman and the chief executive should be clearly established, set out in writing and agreed by the board. The Code then spells out the responsibilities of the chairman. He is responsible for setting the board's agenda and ensuring that adequate time is available for discussion of all the agenda items, in particular strategic issues. The chairman should also promote a culture of openness and debate by facilitating the effective contribution of non-executive directors in particular and ensuring constructive relations between executive and non-executive directors. He is also responsible for ensuring the directors receive accurate, timely and clear information, as well as effective communication with shareholders. The chairman must also be entirely independent and should not be the former chief executive of the company, unless there are very specific reasons, which have to be publicly explained, and only after consultation with the major shareholders.

The separation of these two roles is a key principle for corporate governance of UK listed companies, given the significance of the role; for example, ensuring that there is a flow of all the required information to the board so that the board can challenge the management, providing a fresh perspective, especially when management can fall into the trap of 'groupthink.' The chairman's role is crucial to the effectiveness of the board, since he sets the agenda, ensures that directors receive accurate, timely and clear information, ensures that time is allowed for matters of substance to be discussed by the board, providing the opportunity for independent directors to discuss issues without the presence of executives as part of the process of co-operatively agreeing a strategy for the company. The chairman will be particularly involved in developing the risk strategy and will also engage with the major shareholders. This will lead to a time commitment of two or three days a week. It is a pivotal role between the independent directors and the CEO and senior management, and an especially difficult role to fulfil. Anyone appointed as Chairman of Lehman Brothers with Dick Fuld as CEO would have had an extremely challenging role. Probably few would have applied for the role. A dominant chairman and CEO has destroyed more than one company. This is why the separation of roles is vital.

The UK Corporate Governance Code effectively limits board membership to nine years, but each three-year break provides an opportunity for a director who has not made a contribution to the board to step down or be advised to step down. The issue of term limits was first raised in the USA by the National Association of Corporate Directors in 1996, but has clearly made little headway since then. The California Public Employees Retirement System, CalPERS, has raised the issue more than once on the grounds which underlie the UK approach, namely that after ten years or so, the lengthy tenure compromises independence. Whilst the issue of tenure and independence is becoming more important, the overriding view is that this is a matter of evaluation of directors, rather than strict term limits. Changes are also taking place in terms of length of tenure, with the average in 2008 being 7.6 years, according to the National Association of Corporate Directors.

The board of Lehman Brothers was obviously not in a position to provide proper oversight of the company or to prevent the excessive risks being taken on from 2006 onwards in a falling market. The severe limitations of most of the board members in terms of their lack of knowledge and the lack of a counterbalance of a strong chairman meant that Dick Fuld's powers as a domineering CEO were unshackled. Andrew Gowers, who served as Director of Communications, described the corporate governance structure as 'almost pre-programmed to fail'.[45] The separation of the roles of the CEO and the chairman together with time limits on the length of service of the independent directors might have helped, provided a chairman could have been found of sufficient stature and authority to challenge Fuld, and if the board had been composed of directors with relevant experience and independence of mind to question the company's strategy and the risks it was taking.

A clear summary of the role of corporate governance in the crisis and in its possible prevention is given by Sir David Walker:

> Serious deficiencies in prudential oversight and financial regulation in the period before the crisis were accompanied by major governance failures within banks. These contributed materially to excessive risk-taking and to the breadth and depth of the crisis. The need is now to bring corporate governance issues closer to the central stage.

Structure and procedures may be necessary conditions but they will not work if the chairman is weak and if the board is inadequate. Nor can better corporate governance ensure there will not be another crisis, but 'it will make a rerun of these events materially less likely'.[46]

Chasing a Chimera?

The role of the efficient market hypothesis

In previous chapters, the focus was on the various methodologies for determining value, noting the disadvantages in some of the important and relevant methods used. They often involved complex mathematical models in an environment in which it was believed that it was possible to find certainty. The efficient market hypothesis (EMH) prevailed. Capital markets are efficient, because competition between profit-seeking market participants will ensure that the prices of securities are continuously adjusted to reflect all publicly available information. Many argued that the dominance of the theory created the context in which the financial crisis occurred.

The theory influenced market participants, central bankers and regulators alike. Central bankers believed that market prices could be trusted and that bubbles either did not exist or could not be identified before they occurred, or even that they were beneficial for growth. Regulators seemed to accept the need for 'light touch' regulation, in which the view was taken that 'bankers knew how to run their business' and were best left to carry on with that. If the market is indeed efficient in incorporating and acting immediately on information about prices, then transparency is vital. Ensuring adequate, fair and prompt disclosure about a company's financial situation was one of the most important aims of financial regulation, especially in the early part of the last decade. Mark-to-market accounting can be seen as part of that approach to regulation, but does not depend on the efficient market hypothesis for its validity.

The Turner Review, the Financial Services Authority's analysis of the global financial crisis, issued in 2009, places the efficient market theory at the centre.[1] The report's conclusions on market efficiency follow.

> At the core of these assumptions has been the theory of efficient and rational markets. Five propositions with implications for regulatory approach have followed:

(i) Market prices are a good indication of rationally evaluated economic value.

(ii) The development of securitised credit, based on the creation of new and more liquid markets, has improved both allocative efficiency and financial stability.

(iii) The risk characteristics of financial markets can be inferred from mathematical analyses, delivering robust quantitative measures of trading risk.

(iv) Market discipline can be used as an effective tool in constraining harmful risk taking.

(v) Financial innovation can be assumed to be beneficial since market competition would winnow out any innovations which did not deliver value-added.

Each of these assumptions is now subject to extensive challenge on both theoretical and empirical grounds, with potential implications for the appropriate design of regulation and for the role of regulatory authorities. Putting the blame on the efficient markets hypothesis (EMH) was a widely held popular approach during and immediately after the crisis. The view has also been attributed to Alan Greenspan, Chairman of the Board of Governors of the Federal Reserve Bank from 1987 to January 2006, but his view is rather more nuanced than that.

In his book, *The Age of Turbulence*, Greenspan recalls how, as the newly appointed Chairman, he watched the stock markets very closely and asked,

> How does one make sense of the unprecedented drop (involving the loss of more than a fifth of the total value of the Dow Jones Industrial Average) on October 19, 1987? What new piece of information surfaced between the market's close at the end of the previous trading day and its close on October 19th? I am aware of none.... No financial information was driving these prices.[2]

It was simply due to the 'fear of the continuing loss of wealth'.
He continued:

> When markets are behaving rationally, as they do almost all of the time, they appear to engage in a 'random walk': the past gives no better indication than a coin flip of the future direction of the price of a stock. But sometimes that walk gives rise to a stampede. When gripped by fear, people rush to disengage from commitments, and stocks will plunge.

In his testimony before the House Committee of Government Oversight and Reform, Greenspan presented his views on the sources of the crisis. He admitted that his views of the operations of the market had been shattered:

> Those of us who have looked to the self-interest of lending institutions to protect shareholder's equity (myself especially) are in a state of shocked disbelief. Such counterparty surveillance is a central pillar of our financial markets' state of balance. If it fails, as occurred this year, market stability is undermined.[3]

His further criticisms were much more pointed:

> It was the failure to properly price such risky assets [mortgage-backed securities and collateral debt obligations] that precipitated the crisis. In recent decades, a vast risk management and pricing system has evolved, combining the best insights of mathematicians and finance experts supported by major advances in computer and communications technology. A Nobel prize was awarded for the pricing model that underpins much of the advance in derivative markets. This modern risk management paradigm held sway for decades. The whole intellectual edifice collapsed in the summer of last year because the data inputted into the risk management models generally covered only the past two decades, a period of euphoria. Had the models been fitted more appropriately to historic periods of stress, capital requirements would have been much higher and the financial world would be in much better shape today, in my judgment.[4]

Earlier, in an article for the *Financial Times*, he spelt out the 'essential problem' which is that 'our models-both risk models and econometric models-as complex as they have become, are still too simple to capture the full array of governing variables that drive our global economic reality. A model is, of necessity, an abstraction from the full detail of the real world'.[5]

A glance at some of his earlier views shows the depths of his disillusionment with financial innovations, or perhaps the way in which they had been used. He valued the technological innovations; the 'development of paradigms for containing risk to those willing and presumably able to bear it; the ability of modern economics to absorb unanticipated shocks'; lenders becoming considerably more diversified; the growth of the secondary mortgage market and the growth of financial derivatives.

> Conceptual advances in pricing options and other complex financial products ... have significantly lowered the costs of and expanded the opportunities for hedging risks. If risk is properly dispersed, shocks to the overall economic

system will be better absorbed and less likely to create the cascading failures that could threaten financial stability.[6]

To be fair, the conversation was not without its warnings. Risk management capabilities had to be improved. The 'underlying human traits which lead to excess are scarcely likely to be reformed', and the role of central banks is in preventing major market disruptions through the 'development and enforcement of prudent regulatory standards.'[7] Hence Greenspan's position is not quite the simplistic view of capitalism and the capital markets sometimes ascribed to him, nor does he believe that the markets are quite as efficient as the EMH apparently portrays them as being.

Other voices were much more strident. Professor of Economics at the University of Columbia and Nobel Prize Winner in Economics Joseph Stiglitz concluded in an interview: 'The Chicago School bears the blame for providing a seeming intellectual foundation for the idea that markets are self-adjusting and the best role for governments is to do nothing.'[8] George Soros stated bluntly: 'On a deeper level, the demise of Lehman Brothers conclusively falsifies the efficient market hypothesis.'[9]

To consider its role in the financial crisis, the theory itself must be defined. It originated in the work of Paul Samuelson and Eugene Fama, first developed in 1965 in 'Random Walks in Stock Market Prices', which they expanded and defended in many subsequent articles.[10] However, the most useful definition of the theory is in Fama's 1970 article:

> An 'efficient' market is defined as a market where there are large numbers of rational, profit 'maximisers' actively competing with each other trying to predict future market values of individual securities, and where important current information is almost freely available to all participants. In an efficient market, competition among many intelligent participants leads to a situation where, at any point in time, actual prices of securities already reflect the effects of information based both on events that have already occurred and on events which, as of now, the market expects to take place in the future. In other words, in an efficient market at any point in time the actual price of a security will be a good estimate of its *intrinsic* value.[11]

He identified three distinct levels (or 'strengths') at which the market might actually be efficient:

(i) The weak form: current prices of securities already reflect past price and volume information.

(ii) The semi-strong version is similarly already incorporated into a security's current market price not only the past price, but also information about the company as well, such as company quarterly financial statements. No one should be able to outperform the market by using something that everyone else knows.

(iii) The strong form refers to all information, both public and private, where this information is also incorporated in the price. Monopolistic information does not enable the possessor of that information to profit from that knowledge in an efficient market. Such a view seems to be counter-intuitive, to say the least. Insider dealers would be disappointed, if they realized that their careful acquisition of inside information did not provide them with a profit, at least as long as they disposed of the securities quickly enough before others acquired the information.

However, in a recent article John Cochrane pointed out that the term 'efficient' has a precise meaning. 'An "efficient" market is "informationally efficient" if prices at each moment incorporate all available information about future values'.[12] Cochrane further argues that the principle of the efficiency of the markets, though a simple one, has led to the production of countless papers testing the principle, or rather, the principle can only be tested in the context of an asset-pricing model that specifies equilibrium in expected returns. Or, in other words, 'to fully test whether prices fully reflect available information, we must specify how the market is trying to compensate investors when it sets prices'. However, Cochrane considerably lowers the power of EMH. The efficiency is only informational, not operational. The hypothesis can only be tested by assuming that equilibrium exists at all times, that is, by assuming that the hypothesis is true.

Fama recognizes that there is a 'joint hypothesis' problem right from the start. This is because the hypothesis that markets are efficient, that is, the general statement that prices reflect all the available information, is not an empirical statement and is not itself testable. As he put it in an interview in the *New York Times*, 'you can't test the hypothesis without also setting out what we call a "model of market equilibrium"'. He explained that what the market was trying to do in setting prices is also 'telling me something about how to measure risk, and then tell me, what is the relationship between the expected return on an asset and its risks?' That is what Fama, right from the start, called the 'joint hypothesis problem' and both have to be tested together. Fama cheerfully added, 'Testing all of that is where it gets tricky'. Many academics would certainly agree with that since Fama's thesis had led to hundreds of articles seeking to analyse the ever-increasing and more extensive data on stock and bond market returns in attempts to prove or disprove the EMH.[13]

The efficient market theory and its critics

However, almost from the start, supporters have attempted to prove that the EMH holds good. There is still no consensus even amongst financial economists as to its validity. Extensive reviews of the empirical evidence conducted by Martin Sewell led him to the conclusion that, given that an

> efficient market will always 'fully reflect' available information, but in order to determine how the market should 'fully reflect' this information, we need to determine investors' risk preferences. Therefore, any test of the EMH is a test of both market efficiency and investors' risk preferences. For this reason, by itself, is not a well-defined and empirically refutable hypothesis.[14]

The point about risk preferences is an important one. One of the assumptions underlying the hypothesis is that investors invest for the highest immediate returns in the form of dividends, whereas they may seek capital growth, for example, over a long period of time. This may well be the case if the investors are fund managers acting on behalf of pension funds. The reference to fund managers is important. Both Fama and Shiller see the market as being dominated by individuals, each investing on their own account, and, in the nature of the case having less access to all kinds of information, such as detailed analysts' reports on individual companies, industrial sectors and analyses of country risk. Markets outside the USA are dominated by institutional investors, with very few individual traders. The USA still has individual day traders, but even so their stock markets are dominated by mutual funds and 401K investments.

One of the most thorough, but not uncritical exponents of Fama's hypothesis, Andrew Lo, concluded as far back as 1999, that

> the Efficient Markets Hypothesis, by itself, is not a well-defined and empirically refutable hypothesis. To make it operational, one must specify additional structure, e.g. investor preferences, information structure, or business conditions. But then a test of the Efficient Markets Hypothesis becomes a test of several auxiliary hypotheses as well, and a rejection of such a joint hypothesis tells us little about which aspect of the joint hypothesis is inconsistent with the data. Are stock prices too volatile because markets are inefficient, or is it due to risk aversion, or dividend smoothing? All three inferences are consistent with the data. Moreover, new

statistical tests designed to distinguish between them will no doubt require auxiliary hypotheses of their own which, in turn, may be questioned.[15]

Lo reiterated this view in his contribution to *The New Palgrave: A Dictionary of Economics* almost a decade later, but added that the EMH might be a way of gauging the efficiency of a particular market *relative* to other markets, such as futures vs. spot markets, or auction vs. dealer markets. He also pointed to 'several new strands of literature' based on 'more realistic assumptions' including 'psychological approaches to risk-taking behaviour'.[16] More of that later.

Although it would be many steps too far to suggest that the efficient market theory was in any way a major cause of the financial crisis, its neglect of the context in which markets operate and the varying roles of the range of market participants may have encouraged regulators and policymakers to pay little attention to what was actually happening in the world outside the markets. The financial crisis did, however, cause some leading members of the Chicago School to abandon its main tenets, and in the case of Judge Richard Posner that meant turning to Keynes and to Keynes' General Theory of Employment, Interest and Money, in particular. Posner pointed out that that the failure of the Chicago School to understand the magnitude of the crisis is because much of modern economics, by contrast with the work of Keynes, 'is very mathematical, and, on the other hand, very ... credulous about the self-regulating power of the markets. That combination is very dangerous.'[17]

Another Nobel prize winner, Professor Gary Becker, admitted that Chicago got it wrong, saying, 'You take derivatives and do not fully understand how the aggregate risk of derivatives operated. Systemic risk: I don't think we understand that, either – at Chicago or anywhere else.' Elsewhere, Becker admitted that 'group rationality is questionable. When you look at what happened in housing and related credit markets, you cannot call those rationally functioning markets.'[18] Fama was quite unrepentant:

> I think it worked quite well in this episode. Stock prices typically decline prior to a recession and in a state of recession. This was a particularly severe recession. Prices started to decline in advance of when people recognized that it was a recession and then continued to decline. That is what you would expect if markets were efficient.

It would make more sense to say that stock prices declined before people knew what was happening; for example, Lehman's stock prices declined because people did not know the value of the company's assets, not because they did. He went on to blame the Federal government and its instructions to Fannie Mae and Freddie

Mac to buy subprime loans, which is certainly where it all started.[19] Perhaps Warren Buffett has the best answer: 'I'd be a bum on the street with a tin cup if markets were always efficient.'[20] He is the third richest person in the world, whose net worth in August 2014 was $66.3bn.

Irrational exuberance: introducing behavioural finance

At times, Fama seemed to contradict his own thesis that stock market prices are entirely unpredictable, but later he admitted that some factors may help to predict longer-term stock prices. When 'the dividend stock-price ratio is high, expected stock returns tend to be high, and when it is low, expected returns tend to be low'. In a joint paper with Ken French, they argued that 'for both bonds and stocks, there are several variables that affect stocks, all of which are highly related to business conditions. We concluded that it tells us that it is likely that the variation in expected returns is rational, and presumably predictable.'[21] However, the variation in expected returns, if it is related to business conditions, can be rationally or irrationally related to such business conditions. Fama's view is that 'there is variation in the expected returns, which leads to some predictability . . . but there is nothing in the available evidence that allows one to settle (whether it is rational or irrational in a convincing way)'.[22]

Shiller's argument, in a paper written in 1981, is that stock prices move too much to be justified by the subsequent changes in dividends, on the basis of data from 1871 to 1979. If the stock market prices fully reflected all available information, variability in the prices would be less, or at least not significantly greater than the variability in underlying fundamentals. Shiller concluded that 'the failure of the efficient markets model is thus so dramatic that it would seem impossible to attribute the failure to such things as data errors, price index problems or changes in the tax laws'.[23] This work was pursued by Shiller and others throughout the 1980s, leading them to the view that since EMH could not explain most of the volatility in the market, it called into question the basic underpinnings of the entire theory. The evidence suggested that changes in prices occurred for no fundamental reason at all, or that the explanation should be sought elsewhere, perhaps in another test for expected volatility that modelled dividends and stock prices in a more general way. But as they were developed, according to Shiller, they simply showed that stock prices had more volatility than any version of the efficient market hypothesis could confirm, at least as far as that applies to the whole market.

The 1980s were not all bad news for the EMH, as some of the research conducted then suggested that, even though the whole stock market appears to be highly inefficient, based on the indices, 'individual stock prices do show some correspondence to efficient markets theory.'[24] Shiller quotes Paul Samuelson's dictum that the

> stock market is micro-efficient but macro-inefficient, That is, individual stock variations are dominated by actual, new information about subsequent dividends, but aggregate stock market variations are dominated by bubbles. Modern markets show considerable micro-efficiency (for the reason that the minority who spot aberrations from micro-efficiency can make money from those occurrences and, in doing so, tend to wipe out any persistent inefficiencies). In no contradiction to the previous sentence, I had hypothesised considerable *macro* inefficiency, in the sense of long waves in the time series of aggregate indexes of security prices below and above the various definitions of fundamental values.[25]

Shiller hastens to point out that

> this does not mean that there are not 'substantial bubbles' in individual stock prices, but that the predictable variation across firms in dividends has often been so large as to largely swamp out the effect of bubbles.... When it comes to individual stocks, such predictable variations, and their effects on price, are often far larger than the bubble component of stock prices.[26]

Perhaps because the work on EMH seemed to have reached an impasse, academic attention turned towards behavioural models and the financial markets. The foundation of that was laid in *The Econometrics of Financial Markets*, published in 1997.[27]

The behavioural theorists shift the emphasis away from examining trends in the market data and developing models to explain them, to the behaviour of investors in the market, or rather to the factors influencing their behaviour. The work is based on Shiller's own observations and the results of the surveys of high-income individuals regarding their opinions of the stock market conducted by the International Centre for Finance at Yale from 1996 onwards at Shiller's instigation. The survey material balances the impressionistic and anecdotal evidence, which he sometimes cites in support of his views. The key question was whether or not they agreed with the following statement: 'The stock market is the best investment for long-term holders, who can just buy and hold through the ups and downs of the market'. During the boom years of the 90s and in the peak year of 2000, 97 per cent of the respondents agreed at least somewhat with the statement, falling to 83 per cent in 2004, with those who strongly agreed falling from 67 per cent to 42 per cent over the same period. Investors' decisions are driven by emotional reactions to stock market developments, including resentment of those who have invested well, and loss of respect if one's own investments have failed.

His theory focuses on a bubble and the behaviours which contribute to its formation. A 'bubble' is defined as

> A situation in which news of price increases spurs investor enthusiasm which spreads by psychological contagion from person to person, in the process amplifying stories that might justify the price increase and bringing in a larger and larger class of investors, who, despite doubts about the real value of an investment, are drawn to it partly by envy of others' successes and partly through a gambler's excitement.

This is part of what he describes as the 'feedback loops' in which 'the changes in thought patterns infect the entire culture, and how they operate not only directly from past increases but also from auxiliary cultural changes that past price increases helped generate.'[28] These changes are brought about by the media reporting of the possibilities of wealth through the stock market, thus propagating speculative price movements.

In his later lecture following the award of the Nobel Prize, he added: 'Bubbles are not, in my mind, about the craziness of investors. They are rather about how investors are buffeted *en masse* from one superficially plausible theory about conventional valuation to another,'[29] apparently unable to think for themselves. Individual reactions to the rise and fall of the markets are accounted for by various psychological factors, such as 'reasoning that is characterised by an inability to think through elementary conclusions one would draw in the future if hypothetical events were to occur', called 'non-consequentialist reasoning'. That failure is not enough to explain the reactions to the stock market so Shiller turns to the social basis of thinking, tendencies to herd behaviour and the contagion of ideas as leading to bubbles. Such attitudes to the stock market are reinforced by some basic tenets which people have 'learned', such as that stocks always go up again after they go down, and that stocks always outperform bonds over time, but since neither of these statements is true, it is not a new enlightenment and society needs to address this issues, so this last chapter is a 'Call to Action'.

Following on from Shiller's approach, many behavioural theorists continue to reject the traditional approach to understanding financial markets using models in which the agents are rational. Rational behaviour in buying or selling stocks is described as considering conditional probabilities of which the simplest example is that the chances of winning the lottery if you have not purchased a ticket are zero. Applied to buying stocks, such decisions are clearly much more complex; for example, weighing up the likely gains or losses on the purchase of stocks and shares in a major oil company, if the oil price suddenly collapses and, if purchased, whether to sell or hold. Such considerations are linked with weighing up the options and selecting the one that has the highest possible value for those making decisions.[30]

Just as Shiller does, but with a wider range of examples of irrational behaviour demonstrated by examining long-term trends in stock market prices and the volatility of movements in prices. There are two building blocks of behavioural finance: one is that in an economy where rational and irrational traders interact, 'irrationality *can* have a substantial and long-term impact on prices'.[31] The second building block is psychology. For guidance on this, behavioural theorists turn to the experimental evidence on the way in which people form beliefs, and on their preferences, or how they make decisions given their beliefs. These insights from cognitive psychology depend on psychometric tests, multiple choice questionnaires in which one is asked to make a judgement or assign a probability to a certain event or judgement without a wider context. The conclusion is that people are over-confident in their judgements; poorly calibrated when estimating probabilities; and display unrealistically rosy views of their abilities and prospects.

There is also much evidence that once people have formed an opinion, they cling to it too tightly and for far too long. This is because they are reluctant to search for evidence that contradicts their belief, and even if they find such evidence, they are likely to treat it with excessive scepticism, or may even misinterpret it as evidence for their beliefs. When forming estimates, people often start with some initial, possibly arbitrary value and then adjust away from it, but the adjustment is often insignificant. This is the kind of empirical evidence concerning human behaviour which the behavioural theorists apply to understanding and assessing the behaviour of individual investors in the stock market. They were assumed to make similarly irrational decisions about their investments. The irrational behaviour on the part of individual investors is held to have long-term and apparently adverse effects on the markets. Certainly people do behave irrationally in these and other ways. The point, however, is that no research has been done to discover how investment decisions are actually made, which can only be discovered by discussing the whole process of decision-making, in particular by fund managers. Such research has not yet been undertaken by behavioural theorists.

However, more recently, the attention of behavioural finance theorists has been focused on the selection of stocks by individual investors and what actually influences them. This is a step forward from trying to apply the general theories of cognitive psychology to investors. Alok Kumar and Charles M. Lee produced a study of retail investor sentiment, based on the personal trading records of individual investors, using a database of over 1.85 million buy and sell transactions made by over 60,000 retail clients of a large discount brokerage firm between 1991 and 1996. Individual investors are described as 'noise traders' and institutional investors are 'rational arbitragers'. The evidence they say, is not surprisingly that individual investors spend less time on investment analysis and rely (inevitably) on a different set of information sources from their professional counterparties. (It should be noted that far more information is freely available to individuals than ever was available in the 1990s.) Their results show that when one group of stocks is being bought or sold by retail investors, other groups tend to be bought or sold. Retail investor sentiments have greater effects on small stocks, value stocks and those with low institutional ownership and stocks with lower prices. The prices of these shares are most sensitive to changes in retail investor sentiment. They accept that they 'need to better understand the processes by which individual investors formulate their trading decisions, including the identification of the information sources they use in decision-making'.[32]

What seems to underlie these theories is the notion that irrational choices of buying and selling stocks on the part of individual investors distort the price of stocks and shares, which would be different if the prices were governed by the decisions made by the rational (institutional investors).

Interviewing investors is the only way forward. It would also mean bringing their databases up to date. The start-date, 1991, is well over twenty years ago, and the study ends before the dot.com boom, itself an interesting study. Since then, markets have become global markets, information is more widely disseminated, and the proportion of individuals trading in the New York Stock Exchange may well have declined.

A second paper by Barber and Odean, covering the same data and the same time period, sets out a model of decision-making in which agents, such as individual investors consider only those alternatives which attract attention.[33] The set of alternatives is limited by those stocks which have caught their attention. For individual investors, this is not surprising, since the time and access are limited. Preferences come into play only after time has limited the choice set, and having tested for attention-driven buying by sorting stocks on events which were likely to have coincided with catching individual investors' attention, and checked these facts against abnormal trading volumes and extreme one-day returns. They were net buyers on high-volume days, when particular firms both large and small, were in the news, whereas institutional investors were not.

Much of the work of behavioural finance is directed at a rejection of the Efficient Market Hypothesis, which is 'predicated on the notion that the current price of a stock, closely reflects the present value of its future cash flows'.[34] What seems to underlie behavioural finance for some theorists at least is that the irrational choices of buying and selling shares on the part of individual investors distorts their price, which would be different if the prices were governed by the decisions made by the rational (institutional investors).

If that were indeed the case, it would be impossible to discern the true price, since that would require knowing the decision-making processes of market participants and the true price (fundamental or intrinsic price, as it is sometimes called) would depend on an assessment of that. Both the theories of behavioural finance and the Efficient Market Hypothesis involve the notion that there is an intrinsic, fundamental or true price lurking behind the inefficiencies of the market, to be discovered by understanding that the market is efficient and delivers the price, provided it is interpreted and defined in the right way. It is impossible to find the true price behind the price people pay. That is to chase a chimera.

The price is simply the price that people will pay for a share at any one time. This is the essence of the mark-to-market definition of fair value as 'the exchange price in an orderly transaction between market participants to sell the asset or transfer the liability in the market in which the reporting entity would transact for the asset or liability, that is, the principal or the most advantageous market for the asset or the liability'. (Summary of Statement No 157.)

What is a market?

The market itself is neither efficient nor inefficient. To ascribe such epithets to the market is to fail to see that such references are to an abstraction, since the market is composed of the various participants operating in the market and only operates within a particular regulatory, legal, cultural and macroeconomic environment. Markets are dominated by the political structure and local political decisions and policies, but global markets are increasingly influenced by geopolitical events. Such views ignore the context in which they operate. The market itself is neither rational nor irrational, but the actions of some of the market participants *may* be irrational at times. That assessment is also more complex than it appears to be in the literature.

First of all, the market participants are not all individuals deciding to buy stocks and bonds for their own investments. Prices are not set by an army of private investors or the 'representative household', investing directly in equities, bonds and even across the spectrum of the derivatives markets. Most stock exchanges are dominated by institutional investors, and that has been the case ever since governments started encouraging individuals to invest for pensions, savings in equities and for their long-term security, especially from the 1980s onwards. Most individuals delegate those investment decisions to mutual funds, or such decisions are delegated for them when they save through pension schemes or purchase financial products such as life insurance or other packaged financial savings products. The value of saving through these indirect means is often incentivized by the provision of tax relief.

The 'real world complication is that investors delegate virtually all their involvement in financial matters to professional intermediaries . . . who dominate the pricing process'.[35] Vayanos and Woolley add that 'delegation creates an agency problem. Agents have more and better information than the investors who appoint them, and the interests of the two are rarely aligned'. They argue, correctly, that principals (or perhaps more clearly, consumers) cannot be certain of the competence or diligence of their appointed agents, which is certainly true and explains the reason for regulation designed to protect the consumer, not all of which is simply reactive; that is, it is in place before some disasters occur.

> Introducing the agents certainly does bring greater realism to asset-pricing models and can be shown to transform the analysis and output. Importantly, this is achieved whilst maintaining the assumption of fully rational behaviour on the part of all concerned. Such models have more working parts and therefore a higher degree of complexity, but the effort is richly rewarded by the scope and relevance of the predictions.[36]

It may explain some behaviours as illustrated below, but fails to explain that the actions of fund managers depend on the mandates for particular funds. A fund may be designed to provide capital growth over a period of time, for example, while avoiding the risks and costs involved in constantly churning securities or engaging in high-risk investments.

In other words, the objectives of the fund in which individuals invest has to be taken into account, but Woolley and Vayanos identify only two:

> fundamental investing, which uses estimates of cash flows to determine the worth of assets, whereas momentum investing disregards valuation and simply rides the trends usually over the short-to-medium term . . . Bizarrely and

damagingly, the rise in momentum investing means that the bulk of equity investment is now conducted *without regard to the value of the assets being traded.*

Our new asset pricing model shows the *a priori* risk-adjusted returns from competing strategies and their variants, and demonstrates their suitability for different categories of investor. In particular, it shows momentum to be the strategy of choice only for investors with short horizons. Most large funds have long-term liabilities, and for them it pays to invest based predominantly on valuation.[37]

The significance of these articles lies simply in the fact that they point in the direction of the complexity of the market by noting the major participants and that they have different objectives in mind, but this is still a long way from recognizing the complexities of the market and its context. It is also interesting to see the limited notion of value, which is disregarded by momentum investors and the long-term investors depending on valuations.

Looking at the market and the decisions taken in the wider context by various market participants leads to a fuller understanding of the information required. That will, or should, include a thorough knowledge of the company, the market in which the company operates, and all the factors which may affect its performance. These may include particular events; for example, decisions made by the central bank, sanctions against Russia, unrest in the Middle East, or the assassination of a leading politician, to take a few recent examples at random, and the economic situation of the country, region, the Eurozone, emerging markets or the global economy. Weighing all of these factors, determining their relevance and relative weight means that investment decisions are not simply reactive, not just based on all the relevant information, but are a matter of judgement. Taking long sets of data, however important they may be, out of context, and basing models on such simplified approaches means that the models will always be inadequate. If regulators, policymakers and those assessing investment risks thought that such models were sufficient then that could be part, but only part, of the explanation of what went wrong.

Trust and the market

Part of the context in which the market operates is the degree of confidence which market participants must have in each other. Once that confidence collapses, the market ceases to function. Hank Paulson explained at the time that the fall of Lehman Brothers led to a 'system crisis. Credit markets froze and substantially reduced interbank lending. Confidence was severely compromised throughout our financial system. Our system was on the verge of collapse.'[38] Bernanke made his now famous statement, 'We may not have an economy on Monday.'[39] It was indeed trust that was destroyed by the fall of Lehman, because no one could be sure about the quality of the assets held by other banks, and therefore no one was willing to lend.

Some see in this approach echoes of Walter Bagehot's *Lombard Street,* when he commented that we should not be

> surprised at the sudden panics [in the banking system]. During the period of reaction and adversity, just even at the last instant of prosperity, the whole structure is delicate. The peculiar essence of our banking system is an unprecedented trust between man and man; and when that trust is much weakened by hidden cause, a small accident may greatly hurt it, and a great accident for a moment may almost destroy it.[40]

Swedberg, in his analysis of the collapse of Lehman Brothers and its effects on confidence, draws on Bagehot's emphasis on trust, but moves the view in a different direction in which actions depend on 'proxy signs' which are used by investors when direct information is not available to them and they want to invest in a firm or lend someone some money. They play the role of stand-ins for information about the actual situation.

> Ideally, a proxy sign can be assumed to be either aligned with the state of affairs or not ... Confidence is maintained when a positive proxy sign signifies a positive state of affairs and a negative sign correctly indicates a negative state of affairs. If they are not aligned, and the proxy sign misrepresents the situation, then confidence suffers. When the proxy sign is positive and the state of affairs in the banking community is negative, we are then in Bagehot's dangerous situation, in which it is not known who has losses and who has not, and in which an accident may set off a general panic.[41]

The proxy signs may refer to the state of the economic affairs, but the proxy does not refer to 'some object and "true" reality but is a "social construction".'[42] The obvious problem here is: how do market participants know that the proxy signs are not aligned with the state of affairs, especially when the sign is negative, but 'state of affairs' is in fact positive?

Swedberg refers to Professor Gorton's analysis of *The Panic of 2007,* in which his references to relevance of the ABX.HE indices could be seen as just the kind of 'proxy sign' giving rise to the loss of trust, perhaps rather than the loss of confidence which Swedberg describes. Professor Gorton argued that the problems with subprime mortgages resulted in a systemic crisis because of the 'loss of information about the location and size of risks of loss due to default on a number of interlinked securities, special purpose vehicles, and derivatives, all related to subprime mortgages.'[43] The residential mortgage-backed securities (RMBSs), consisting of subprime mortgages, were placed in CDOs, and commercial mortgage-backed securities (CMBSs), and ultimately into off-balance sheet vehicles, with additional risk being created through credit default swaps. The latter were incorporated into hybrid or synthetic CDOs. This dizzying interlinking of securities, structures and derivatives 'resulted in a loss of information and ultimately a loss of confidence'. The introduction, Gorton argues, of the ABX HE (ABX) indices, which trade over the counter, enabled information about subprime values and risks to be aggregated and revealed for the first time.[44]

> While the location of the risks was unknown, market participants could, for the first time, express views about the value of the subprime bonds, by buying or selling protection. In 2007 the ABX prices plummeted ... The ABX information together with a lack of information about the location of the risks led to a loss of confidence on the part of banks in the ability of their counterparties to honour contractual obligations.
>
> ...
>
> The ABX indices allowed investors to realize that the market was now lowering the price on securities based on subprime mortgages, but they did not allow investors to figure out which securities were of low quality and which were not.'[45]

In the context of the collapse of Lehman Brothers, it is better to refer to market participants, since the lack of trust stemmed from the demands of Lehman's counterparties for increased collateral, which led to what amounted to a run on the bank. In the days before the final weekend, Lehman's clearing and settlement banks demanded increased collateral: JP Morgan, $5bn (which Lehman managed to find); Citigroup, $2bn for the trades it was settling and $500m. with the Bank of America. Lehman also had $500m. with HSBC and a further account with JP Morgan. Lehman counted all of these in its liquidity pool, allegedly $42bn, despite the fact that the withdrawal of any of this capital would impact on Citigroup and JPMorgan's willingness to clear and settle their trades.

Close market participants such as JP Morgan, Citigroup and others did not have to rely on factors such as indices to assess the strength of Lehman. It was not just a question of acting as clearing banks for Lehman, but being engaged in joint ventures such as the purchase of Archstone. Other investors had already decided on their verdict since its shares fell by 95 per cent between January and September 2008, given both the general environment (the collapse of Bear Stearns, Fannie and Freddie into conservatorship, falling house prices) and Lehman's announcement of losses in its June financial report. What was undermined was trust.

Reference has already been made to David Einhorn's work, but it is worth drawing attention again to some of the comments he made and hence to Swedberg's use of that assessment in what he has to say about confidence:

> Lehman does not provide enough transparency for us even to hazard a guess as to how they have accounted for these items. Lehman responds to requests for improved transparency grudgingly. I suspect that greater transparency on these valuations would not inspire market confidence.[46]

The effect of Lehman's bankruptcy was also to be found in the

> indirect effects or effects without direct interaction. This type of effect includes actions that were caused by the fear that was unleashed by Lehman's collapse, by rumours that began to circulate, and the like. Following Bagehot, we would assume that the indirect effects are more dangerous than the direct effects.[47]

He goes on to distinguish between the collapse of confidence; the 'hidden losses' that may emerge and the 'withdrawal of confidence', as a result of calm and rational deliberation, such as occurred with the freezing up of the money market, the repo market and the interbank market. However, the decision not to engage in these markets is not just a matter of fear and the belief in rumours, but is a direct result of the revelations about the nature of the CDOs, which ultimately depended on the value of the underlying assets, the mortgages, in this case. It continued until corrective actions were taken by the Federal government.

Swedburgh's paper is important in that it points out that trust underlies the smooth, or one might say, efficient functioning of the market. For that, transparency is a necessary but not a sufficient condition. The requirement for transparency in financial accounts and the nature of the various complex derivatives, which are currently traded on the markets is essential, but it is equally essential to ensure that takes place through clear regulations, the ability and competence of the company boards and regulators to ensure that all the information made to the market is timely, comprehensible and also true and to take the necessary enforcement actions if not. That will all seem obvious and indeed those involved in the market in whatever capacity will undoubtedly agree, but the point is to ensure that trust is well-founded. If that does not happen, then the market will simply not function.

Markets, prices and value

The value of a security or a derivative is encapsulated at any one time in the price that investors or buyers are prepared to pay for it. The price is determined by a wide range of factors and might be described as being mispriced or over-priced, if as in the years described above, the price is dependant on information which subsequently is shown to be false or to have been misrepresented in some way. Then the price may rapidly change, and usually falls.

At one stage, Fama in the definition quoted above referred to the 'intrinsic value' of a security, stating that at any point in time the actual price of a security will be a good estimate of its intrinsic value, taking into account the equilibrium price, depending on its earnings potential of the security, including the quality of management, the outlook for the industry, the economy etc., that is, factors in relation to the real economy. This version allows for the possibility that the value is the price that people are prepared to pay on the basis of the knowledge they have and the judgements they are able to make about the security and general trends in the market at that particular point in time. The market operates efficiently in the ordinary sense of the term if dealers and fund managers can be reasonably confident of the reliability of the information provided, that the judicial system is free from corruption, that judges are experienced, knowledgeable and competent in cases involving stock markets and the financial services industry and that accountants and other professionals are honest and competent. As the development of capital markets has taken place in emerging markets and a banking system has been established, it has become increasingly clear to policy makers that markets and banks cannot flourish without such a framework.

Prices fluctuate over time. Where the securities traded in the stock markets are shares and bonds issued by companies producing a range of goods and services, the value of the asset lies in its utility in the view of those managing the funds as agents for others or by the ever-dwindling number of individuals investing in the markets on their own account. As long as its utility remains, and if it is not overtaken by other events, such as technological developments, people are willing to pay *something* for it, or at least some people will be willing to pay for it, even in the worst of times. Perceptions of utility will shift over time, and often quite quickly. Hence the price people will pay varies over time and in differing circumstance. Since the term 'utility' is often confused with dismissing an object as purely 'utilitarian', that is, not decorative or extravagant, it should be noted that the value as equivalent to the price of a security, may include companies selling designer handbags and other luxury goods. To return to Lehman, however, apart from the derivative contracts in which a price was agreed between Lehman Brothers and the counterparty, the recoveries process rescued at least part of the original value of the investments in commercial and residential real estate. This is perhaps the clearest illustration of what is meant by utility as the key element in value, but value is not an intrinsic to the physical object or the services offered. They retain value as long as they are useful and desirable in a context of markets in which complex factors all play their part, making it hard to predict future prices, not because they are random but because of interrelated internal and external factors, which make the construction of models difficult. That is, however, all that there is to value. It is represented by the price. The hunt for any intrinsic or enduring value is another instance of chasing a chimera.

This chapter has covered the leading theories of the markets. They are abstract theories; indeed, more so than they should be, since they lack a sound empirical base. The dominant theory of the Efficient Market Hypothesis distracted regulators, market participants and central bankers from paying attention to market prices as signals or from recognizing the existence of bubbles in the housing market, as Alan Greenspan admitted. The decline in house prices should have been a signal, and was indeed a real indicator of deeper troubles in the market. Instead of regarding the market as being efficient, attention should have been paid to the real world – not chasing chimeras.

The Lehman Brothers Board of Directors in 2007

Chairman and CEO

Dick Fuld

Compensation: $40m., of which $5m. was reserved stock in the company.

Directors

Michael Ainslie

Director since 1996.
Private Investor and Former President and Chief Executive; Officer of Sotheby's Holdings.
Age 64.
Compensation (2007): $95,000 cash, $245,038 stock awards.

John F. Akers

Director since 1996.
Retired Chairman of International Business Machines Corporation.
Age 73.
Compensation (2007): $115,000 cash, $245,038 stock awards.

Roger Berlind

Director since 1985.
Theatrical Producer. Also a private investor, a former theatrical producer and principal of Berlind Productions since 1981.
Age 77.
Compensation (2007): $107,000 cash, $245,038 stock awards.

Thomas Cruikshank

Director since 1996.
Retired Chairman and Chief Executive Office of Halliburton Company.
Age 76.
Compensation (2007): $140,000 cash, $245,038 stock awards.

Marsha Johnson Evans

Director since 2004.
Rear Admiral US Navy (retired). Former President and Chief Executive Officer of the American Red Cross, 2002–5.
Age 60.
Compensation: $128,000 cash, $245,038 stock awards.

Sir Christopher Gent

Director since 2003.
Former Chief Executive Officer of Vodafone and non-executive Chairman of GlaxoSmithKline plc.
Age 63.
Compensation: $120,500 cash, $245,038 stock awards.

Jerry A. Grundhofer

Director from April 2008 until March 2009.
Chairman Emeritus and former Chief Executive Officer of US Bancorp.
Age 63.
Compensation: n/a.

Roland Hernandez

Director since 2005.
Retired Chairman and Chief Executive Officer of the Telemundo Group, Inc.
Age 50.
Compensation: $80,000 cash, $245,038 stock awards.

Henry Kaufman

Director since 1995.
President of Henry Kaufman & Company, Inc. since 1988. Former Chief Economist at Salomon Brothers.

Age 80.
Compensation: $95,000 cash, options $245,388.

John D. Macomber

Director since 1994.
Principal of JDM Investment Group.
Age 80.
Compensation: $132,000 cash, $245,038 stock awards.

In addition, board members held the following amounts of reserved stock in numbers of shares:

Ainslie 21,215
Akers 12,749
Berlind 41,076
Cruikshank 48,013
Evans 17,130
Gent 17,130
Hernandez 6,872
Kaufman 18,286
Macomber 46,263

APPENDIX 2

The Lehman Brothers Corporate Structure

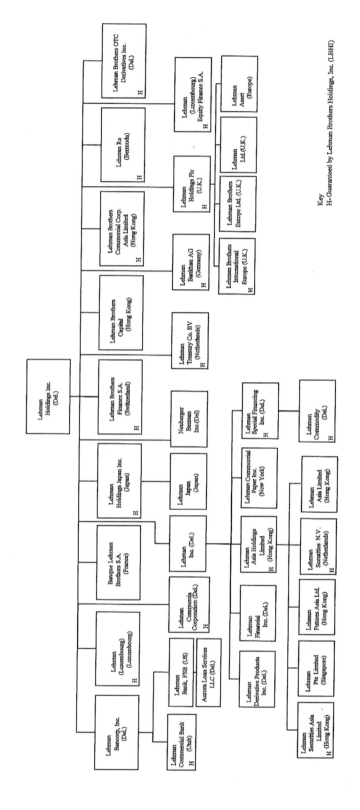

Report of the Examiner in the Chapter 11 proceedings of Lehman Brothers Holdings Inc.

Notes

Chapter 1: From Cotton Trader to Investment Banker: 1844–2008

1 History of Lehman Brothers – Lehman Brothers Collection – Baker Library, Maryland Business School, Contemporary Business Archives.

2 Peter Chapman, *Lehman Brothers, 1844–2008, The Last of the Imperious Rich*, pp. 198–9 (Portfolio, Penguin Group Ltd, 2012).

3 Ibid., p. 199.

4 Ken Auletta, *Greed and Glory on Wall Street* (Warner Books in conjunction with Random House, 1987), p. 17. Auletta provides a full and detailed account of the clashes between Peterson and Glucksman.

5 Scott Paltrow, 'American Express to Spin Off Lehman Brothers: The Investment Bank will Become an Independent Company', *Los Angeles Times*, 25 January 1994.

6 Chapman, n. 2, p. 222.

7 Ibid., p. 229.

8 'Lehman's New Street Smarts', *Business Week*, 18 January 2004.

9 'The Improbable Power Broker', *Fortune*, 23 April 2006.

10 Ibid.

11 *New York Times*, 23 July 2003.

12 'Lehman's New Street Smarts', n. 8.

13 Quoted in *The Director*, 'The King of Subprime', excerpts from J Oliver, *How They Blew It* (Kogan Page, 2010).

Chapter 2: From Hubris to Nemesis: January to September 2008

1 Annual report: Form 10-K submitted to the Securities and Exchange Commission for the fiscal year ending 30 November 2007.

2 Lehman Brothers 2007 Annual Report, p. 4.

3 Board of Governors of the Federal Reserve System, Bear Stearns, JP Morgan Chase, and Maiden Lane LLC, 17 March 2008.

4 'Lehman Weathers the Storm', *CNN Money*, 8 March 2008.

5 Partners Letter, 20 January 2009.

6 Pre-announcement of second quarter earnings Conference Call, LBHI_SEC07940_592160, p. 5: 'Lehman Brothers announce expected second quarter results. Expected to report a net loss of $2.8bn', 9 June 2008.

7 Lehman Brothers Holdings Inc., Q2 2008. Guidance Conference Call, 8 June 2008. LBHI_SEC0790_592160.

8 Citi's Corporate Bond Research Report (28/5/08) stated that Lehman followed a prudent funding practice and unlike Bear Stearns did not rely on customer balances in its prime brokerage operation to fund its balance sheet, and that it had reduced its leverage to 16X and that its exposure to subprime mortgages was $4bn, an amount that Lehman considered to be manageable, and planned to reduce its commercial mortgage exposure/CMBS to $5bn. Views amongst its analysts differed, however, with Ryan O'Connell commenting that 'another Bear-Stearns type funding squeeze is overblown for Lehman'.

9 Quoted by Zachery Kouwe, *New York Post*, 18 March 2008.

10 Examiner's Report, p. 1396. See also memorandum from Margaret Sear, Lehman et al. to Files, 11 April 2008 at p. 1 (accounting policy memorandum).

11 In reply to questions from Mr Bachus during the Committee on Financial Services, US House of Representatives, Washington DC, 17 March 2010.

12 Jan Voigt's email to Timothy Geithner, 9 April 2008. Reference: Meeting with Lehman's senior management team, 20 March 2008. Jan Voigt, Examining Officer Operational Risk Governance, Federal Reserve Bank, New York.

13 Email sent 15 April 2008. FCIC documents.

14 Willem Buiter, 'Three Hits and Three Misses for the Fed'. Maverecon, *Financial Times*, 17 March 2008.

15 Regulatory Reform. Primary Dealer Credit Facility, Board of Governors of the Federal Reserve System, 2 August 2013.

16 Under the provisions of the Dodd-Frank Wall Street Reform & Consumer Protection Act 2010, the Federal Reserve Bank is obliged to provide transaction data and detailed information about its loans to depository institutions and others. This information was published on 1 December 2010.

17 Quoted in 'Morgan Stanley used Credit Program 212 times', *Wall Street Journal*, 1 December 2010.

18 Ibid.

19 Final Transcript LEH-Q3, Preliminary Lehman Brothers Holdings Inc. Earnings Conference Call, 10 September 2008, Thomson Street Events, pp. 4ff.

20 Memorandum for the record, which is a paraphrase of the interview dialogue. Interview with Annette Nazareth, SEC Commissioner from August 2005 until January 2008, 1 April 2010.

21 Testimony Concerning Turmoil in the Credit Markets by Erik Sirri, Director of Trading and Markets, before the House Committee on Financial Services, 7 May 2008.

22 'Turmoil in the U.S. Credit Markets: Examining Recent Action Federal Financial Regulators before the U.S. Senate Committee on Banking, Housing and Urban Affairs'. Testimony of Christopher Cox, Chairman of the SEC, 3 April 2008, p. 13.

23 Robert Colby, Testimony Concerning the Consolidated Supervision at US Securities Firms and Affiliated Industrial Corporations, Before the House of Representatives Financial Services Committee, 25 April 2007, p. 1 (my italics).

24 Testimony Concerning the Turmoil in the Credit Markets; Examining the Regulation of Investment Banks by the SEC before the Senate Sub-Committee on Securities, Insurance and Investment, 7 May 2008.

25 Ibid.

26 Management's Comments, Appendix VII, pp. 83–5.

27 Office of Inspector General Response to Chairman Cox and Management Comments, Appendix VIII, pp. 116 and 117–18.

28 Memorandum for the record (not a transcript). Meeting with Members of the SEC Regarding the CSE Programme, 18 March 2010. Mike Maccahiaroli, Director of Trading and Markets; Sam Fortstein, Assistant General Council; Sarah Hancur, Office of the General Counsel.

29 Ibid., memorandum of the interview with Annette Nazareth.

30 OIG Report, above n. 6, pp. 29 and 30–1.

31 Ibid., pp. 40–1.

32 SEC Memoranda from April 2006 to March 2007.

33 Basel II International Convergence of Capital Measurement & Capital Standards, June 2004, Part 3, The Second Pillar-Supervisory Review Process.

34 Testimony Concerning the Lehman Brothers Examiner's Report, Chairman Mary L Shapiro, before the House Committee on Financial Services, 20 April 2010, pp. 1–2.

35 Footnote: Full details can be found in 'The SEC – Revitalised, Reformed and Protecting Investors', SEC government news, press release, 2012.

36 'Chairman Cox announces End of Consolidated Supervised Entities Programme', press release, 26 September 2008.

37 Christopher Cox, 'Sound Practices for Managing Liquidity in Banking Organisations', Letter to Dr Nout Wellick, Chairman of the Basel Committee on Banking Supervision, 20 March 2008.

38 Statement of Alan Schwartz, President and CEO of the Bear Stearns Companies Inc. before the US Senate Banking Committee, 3 April 2008.

39 SEC's Oversight of Bear Stearns and Related Entities: The CSE Programme, pp. 14–16.

40 Chairman Christopher Cox's Testimony concerning Recent Events in the Credit Markets, before the Senate Banking Committee, 3 April 2008.

41 Joint Economic Committee, Financial Meltdown and Policy Response, September 2008.

42 Chairman Ben Bernanke, Speech at the Federal Reserve Bank of Chicago's 43rd Annual Conference on Bank Structure and Competition, The Subprime Mortgage Market, 17 May 2007.

43 Speech by Chairman Ben Bernanke at the Kansas City's Economic Symposium, Housing, Housing Finance and Monetary Policy, 31 August 2007.

44 Joint Economic Committee of Congress, Financial Meltdown and Policy Response, September 2008.

45 Ibid., Testimony on 17 March 2010.

Chapter 3: The Fateful Weekend

1 Lehman Brothers Press Release, 10 September 2008.

2 Q3 2008 Preliminary Lehman Brothers Holdings Inc. Earnings Conference Call, 10 September 2008. LBHI_SEC07940_612771.

3 'Rating Action: Moody's places Lehman's A2 rating on review with direction uncertain', Moody's Investors Service, 10 September 2008.

4 James B Stewart, 'Eight Days. The Battle to Save the American Financial System', *The New Yorker*, 21 September 2009, p. 5; Henry M Paulson Jr, *On the Brink: Inside the Race to Stop the Collapse of the Global Financial System* (Business Plus, Hachette Book Group, 2011), pp. 123 and 155.

5 Timothy F. Geithner, 'Stress Test: Reflections on Financial Crises', *Deckle Edge*, May 2014, p. 177.

6 *On the Brink*, p. 92.

7 Ibid., p. 184. LTCM, Long Term Capital Management, had collapsed in 1998: 'Back then, a group of 14 Wall Street firms had banded together to craft a $3.6bn package, receiving 90% of the imperilled hedge fund, which they liquidated over time.' Ibid., p. 178. Paulson hoped that a similar consortium of banks would come to the rescue of Lehman Brothers.

8 Work had been carried out by staff of the New York Federal Bank on a liquidation consortium consisting of major bank and investment bank counterparties of Lehman – most notable in tri-party repo, credit default swaps and other OTC derivatives to discuss possibilities of joint funding mechanism that avert Lehman's insolvency. The Memorandum added:

   'FRBNY financial commitment (this section to be overhauled by Dudley, Schetzel)

– we should have in mind a maximum number of how much we are willing to finance before the meeting starts, but not divulge our willingness to do so to the consortium.

Term of any liquidity support should be long enough to guard against a fire sale but on a short enough fuse to encourage buyers of Lehman assets to come forward.

– Preferable to style FRBNY commitment as much as possible as a backstop rather than lending.'

Referenced in the Examiner's Report, FRBNY to Exam 003516, 10 Sept 2008.

9 The diary of events relies on Henry Paulson's record of events in his book, *On the Brink*, and also on Appendix 15, Narrative of 4 September to 15 September in Lehman Brothers Holdings Inc. Chapter 11 Proceedings, Examiner's Report. Both of these seemed to me to present the most careful accounts of the way in which the events of the weekend unfolded. My interpretation of events differs from the views expressed by some of those involved, however.

10 *On the Brink*, p. 187.

11 'Eight Days', p. 10.

12 *On the Brink*, p. xvii.

13 Those present included Wall Street's most prominent CEOs: Jamie Dimon from JP Morgan, John Mack from Morgan Stanley, Lloyd Blankfein from Goldman Sachs, Vikram Pandit from Citigroup, Brady Dougan from Credit Suisse and Robert Kelly from Bank of New York Mellon.

14 Examiner's Report, p. 45.

15 Appendix 15, p. 42.

16 *On the Brink*, p. 197.

17 Examiner's Report; Appendix 15, p. 49.

18 Geithner, 'Stress Test', p. 185.

19 Ibid., p. 178.

20 Statement of the Financial Services Authority (UK). In September 2009, the FSA received a request from the Examiner appointed by the US bankruptcy court to provide information about their involvement in the attempt by Barclays Bank plc to buy Lehman Brothers Holdings Inc during the period 12–15 September 2008. These sections draw on that report.

21 Alistair Darling, *Back from the Brink, 1,000 Days at Number 11*, p. 121.

22 Ibid., p. 123.

23 *On the Brink*, p. 220.

24 See Appendix 15, pp. 56–8.

25 Private information.

26 Opinion on Motions seeking modification of the Sale Order pursuant to Rule 60(b), the Trustee's motion for relief under the SIFA sale order, Barclays cross-motion to enforce sale orders and the adjudication of related adversarial proceedings, p. 11.

27 Statement by Thomas C Baxter Jr, Executive Vice President and General Counsel, Federal Reserve Bank of New York, to the Financial Crisis Inquiry Commission, 1 September 2010, pp. 3–5.

28 FOMC, 10 March 2008, p. 17.

29 Mr Angulo's report to the FOMC, 24–25 June, p. 144.

30 Email from Kirsten Harlow to Tim Geithner et al., 16 June 2008.

31 Federal Reserve Bank of New York, Primary Dealer Monitoring: Liquidity Stress Analysis, 25 June 2008.

32 Draft email to Shafran re Contingency planning re OTC Derivatives, 9 May 2008.

33 Email exchange between Chairman Bernanke, Donald Kohn, Tim Geithner and others, 17 June 2008.

34 Email exchanges and the proposal from Geithner, 11 July 2008.

35 William Brodows to Patrick Parkinson, 19 August 2008.

36 Financial Crisis Inquiry Commission Report, p. 329.

37 Geithner, 'Stress Test', p. 187.

38 Financial Crisis Inquiry Commission Report, January 2011, p. 340.

39 James Rickards, quoted in Robert Stowe England, pp. 201ff.

40 Senate Sub-Committee on Banking, Housing and Urban Affairs, Testimony on US Financial Markets, 23 September 2008.

41 Ibid.

42 Statement of Christopher Cox, Chairman, Securities and Exchange Commission, before the Senate Banking Committee, 3 April 2008.

43 Paulson, *On the Brink*, p. 178.

44 Quoted in the FCIC Report, p. 351.

45 'Revisiting the Lehman Brothers Bailout That Never Was', *New York Times*, 29 September 2014.

46 Paulson, *On the Brink*, p. 225.

47 Quoted in Bloomberg, 'Lehman Recovery Seen as Justifying $2bn Bankruptcy', 11 September 2013.

48 Quoted in 'Bear to Lehman: Documents reveal an Alternate History', 1 May 2012.

49 'Fed Fretted over the Demise of Lehman', *New York Times*, 21 February 2014.

50 *New York Times*, 23 October 2008.

51 Thomas Russo, Keynote speech, Hughes Howard Bankruptcy Roundtable, 'Too Big to Fail: Perspectives on Systemic Risk & The Evolving Regulatory Landscape', p. 1.

52 Ibid., p. 3.

53 Ibid., p. 3.

54 Ibid., p. 7.

55 Email from Rita Proctor to Chairman Bernanke, 11 September 2008 10.45 am.

56 Transcript of Federal Open Market Committee, 18 March 2008, p. 80.

57 Ibid., p. 3.

58 Ibid., p. 108.

59 Ibid., p. 10.

60 FOMC, 24–25 June, pp. 4–5.

61 Ibid., p. 50.

62 FOMC, 5 August 2008, p. 8.

63 FOMC, 16 September 2008, p. 48.

64 Ibid., p. 35.

65 Ibid., p. 51.

66 Ibid., p. 62.

67 Chairman B Bernanke, US Financial Markets, before the House Committee on Financial Services, 24 September 2008.

68 *New York Times*, 15 September 2008 and *Financial Times*, 16 September 2008.

69 M Kacperczyk and P Scnabl, *When Safe Proved Risky: Commercial Paper During the Financial Crisis of 2007–2009*, NYU Stern Business School, November 2009, pp. 18–19.

70 Figures released by the US Department of Commerce, Bureau of Economic Analysis, 28 July 2011.

Chapter 4: Regulating the 'Big Five'

1 Lawrence White, 'The Gramm-Leach-Bliley Act of 1999: A Bridge Too Far? Or Not Far Enough?', *Suffolk Law Review* (2010). White also points out that by February 2010, there were 543 FHCs in the USA, including 40 foreign banks.

2 The Glass-Steagall Act was passed in 1933, in the aftermath of the stock market crash of 1929, the collapse of thousands of commercial banks between 1929 and 1933, and the Great Depression. The securities activities of commercial banks were thought to have been the reason for bank failures. The Act separated commercial banks from investment banks, and the latter were not allowed to take deposits.

3 Section 16 as incorporated in 12 U.S.C. 24 (Seventh).

4 See 12 U.S.C. 377 and 378, repeal of Public Law 106-102 and Repeal of Public Law 106-012 Title I para. 101(a).

5 J Barth, D Brumbaugh and J Wilcox, *The Repeal of Glass-Steagall and the Advent of Broad Banking*, OCC Economics Working Paper 2000-5, April 2000, p. 2.

6 Fannie Mae (Federal National Mortgage Association) and Freddie Mac (Federal Home Loan Mortgage Corporation), also known as Government-Sponsored Enterprises, are unusual organizations in that they are shareholder-owned, profit-seeking corporations, but subject to government housing policy requirements as laid down by the Department of Housing and Urban Development. Fannie Mae was established in 1938 after the Great Depression in order to get the housing

market moving by purchasing mortgages from banks, thus freeing up capital for the banks to lend. Freddie Mac was established in 1970 to compete with Fannie Mae. Neither corporation provides mortgages, but purchases mortgages from lenders, pooling loans to create mortgage-backed securities, which are then sold with guarantees against defaults on the underlying mortgages, to investors. Their purpose is to provide a stable source of funding for residential mortgages, including loans for housing to low-to-moderate income families. Their mortgage-backed securities (MBSs) were not guaranteed by the US government.

7   Barth, Brumbaugh and Wilcox, *The Repeal of Glass-Steagall and the Advent of Broad Banking*, pp. 4–5.

8   Ibid.

9   Report to the Congress on Financial Holding Companies under the Gramm-Leach-Bliley Act, November 2003.

10 Framework for Financial Holding Company Supervision, 15 August 2000.

11 The Federal Reserve's Framework for Financial Holding Company Supervision, 15 August 2000, SR 00-13 (SUP), pp. 2–3.

12 Ibid.

13 Bloomberg, 20 April 2012.

14 Remarks made by Vincent Cable on the BBC's Radio 4 'Today' programme, as reported in the *Guardian* newspaper, 8 September 2010.

15 Opening Statement by Governor Daniel Tarullo, 10 Dec 2013.

16 Under the Office of the Comptroller of the Currency's regulations before and after the GLBA, banks could not underwrite or deal in MBSs or any other non-governmental securities, but they could do this before and after the GLBA. After GLBA, banks could be affiliated with a securities firm which undertook such activities. Reference is made to the OCC regulations. These apply to almost all the large banks, such as Bank of America and Citibank, which as national banks are regulated and supervised by the OCC.

17 For the full story, see Oonagh McDonald, *Fannie Mae and Freddie Mac: Turning the American Dream into a Nightmare* (Bloomsbury Academic, 2012).

18 Annette Nazareth, Testimony Regarding Certain Pending Proposals by the EU Commission, Before the House Committee on Financial Services, 22 May 2002.

19 Federal Register, Vol. 69, No. 118, 21 June 2004, Rules and Regulations.

20 Ibid., p. 34428.

21 Basel refers to the Basel Committee on Banking Supervision, promoting an international regulatory framework for banks. It does not have the power to impose regulatory or supervisory powers but in fact the regulatory framework results from discussions between central banks and banking supervisors; its proposals are subject to detailed consultation and most countries seek to incorporate Basel's regulatory

framework into their regulatory framework. The framework known as Basel II has been superseded by Basel III, which, following the financial crisis, is a comprehensive set of reform measures designed to strengthen the regulation/supervision and risk management of the banking sector and improve its ability to absorb shocks.

22 Testimony Concerning Certain Pending Proposals by the European Commission by Annette Nazareth, Director, Division of Market Regulation, SEC, before the Committee on Financial Services, 22 May 2002.

23 Testimony Concerning the Consolidated Supervision of US Securities Firms and Affiliated Industrial Loan Corporations by Robert Colby, Deputy Director, Division of Market Regulation, US Securities and Exchange Commission, 25 April 2007.

Chapter 5: The Largest Bankruptcy in American History

1 Harvey R Miller, 'Examining the Causes of the Current Financial and Economic Crisis of the United States and of the Collapse of Lehman Brothers', before the Financial Crisis Inquiry Commission, 1 September 2010, p. 12.

2 This chapter inevitably draws on the Report of Anton R. Valukas, Examiner on the Lehman Brothers Holdings Inc for the Bankruptcy Court, Southern District of New York, Chapter 11. It was published on 11 March 2010. The Report is over 2,000 pages long. The Examiner and his staff reviewed five million documents and conducted 250 interviews. The documents are readily available, but, although the Examiner quotes from the interviews, the full text is not available.

3 Examiner's Report Vol. I, Executive Summary, pp. 16–17. The Repo (repurchase) is a way for investment banks to borrow money from a large company and in return, the bank sells the company an asset, usually a bond, to protect the company, so that if the bank goes bankrupt, the company can sell the bond and retrieve the cash. The bank also agrees to buy back the bond at the end of the loan (usually after a very short term), less an agreed level of interest, which is paid to the company. Lehman took rather less cash than the bond was worth, so that the transaction was properly recorded in the accounts as a sale rather than a loan.

4 Examiner's Report, Introduction, p. 4.

5 Examiner's Report, p. 734.

6 Ibid., pp. 738–9.

7 Ibid., p. 748.

8 Ibid., Linklaters Letter, Appendix 17, Repo 105, 1 D, pp. 21 and 31.

9 Debt instruments whose face value is paid out only on the maturity date. They are issued by governments and municipalities and may be long-term or short-term.

10 Ibid., p. 790.

11 Lehman was able to argue, ultimately successfully, that since it over-collateralized the borrowings, the counterparties would not complain about a default by Lehman on the repurchase leg, since the counterparty/transferee would incur a gain of 5 per cent or 8 per cent if that occurred. In effect, Lehman netted liabilities and assets that had disparate counterparties, contrary to basic GAAP rules. Unless the counterparties are identical, a risk remains for the transferor, which means that it did not sell the assets, i.e. if the issuers of the bonds announced that they were defaulting, that would not excuse the Transferor's obligation to 'buy back' the now worthless bonds. The accounting procedures could have been greatly streamlined by reinforcing the rules: 'no offsetting of assets and liabilities already in place: unless both legs have the same counterparties, with a formal agreement in place to settle net, the transaction must be reported "broad", which means in the context of Lehman's accounting, as a secured borrowing. Accountancy rules have not been improved in this way.' Source: private comment from Dr Barry Epstein, lead author of Wiley GAAP, 1985–2010.

12 Examiner's Report, p. 742.

13 Ibid., p. 745.

14 Mary Shapiro, Evidence to the House Committee on Financial Services on 20 April 2010.

15 B J Epstein, 'When Window-Dressing Becomes Fraud: Repo 105 was Much More than Window Dressing', Russell, Novak & Co LLP.

16 FASB, Accounting Standards up-date 2014–11. Transfers, Servicing, Effective Controls for Forward Agreements to Repurchase Assets and Accounting for Repurchasing Finances.

17 Transcript of Lehman Brothers Holdings Inc for Second Quarter 2008 Earnings Call, 16 June 2008.

18 Quoted by the Examiner, op. cit., p. 205, from transcript of a speech by David Einhorn, Presentation to Grant's Spring Investment Conference, Private Profits and Socialised Risk, 8 April 2008, p. 9. At that same conference, Einhorn, manager of Greenlight Capital, announced that he was shorting Lehman stocks – an unusual announcement for a hedge fund manager, but also a way of ensuring that others would short the stocks as well, thereby increasing his profits. He had also been a board member of New Century Capital, a subprime mortgage company which had been forced to file for bankruptcy in 2007.

19 'The Confidence Man', New York Magazine, 15 June 2008.

20 Examiner's Report, p. 210.

21 Examiner's interview with Mark Walsh, 21 October 2009, p. 244.

22 'Mark Walsh, Lehman's Unluckiest Gambler', New York Observer, 10 January 2008.

23 'How Lehman Brothers got Its Real Estate Fix', New York Times, 5 March 2009.

24 Examiner's interview with Mark Walsh, 21 October 2009, pp. 225–6.

25 Mezzanine is debt capital that gives the lender the right to convert to an ownership or equity interest in the company if the loan is not paid back in time or in full. Mezannine debt capital is subordinated to debt provided by senior lenders such as banks and venture capital companies.

26 Lehman Global Real Estate Product Control, Global Real Estate Markdowns Presentation, January 2008, pp. 1–2, quoted by the Examiner, p. 229.

27 Remarks to the Economic Club, 9 June 2008.

28 Examiner's Report, p. 277.

29 Ibid., p. 285.

30 Ibid., pp. 291–2.

31 Ibid., p. 333 (emphasis added).

32 Ibid., p. 335.

33 Ibid., p. 354.

34 Comptroller's Handbook on Leveraged Lending, February 2008, p. 5.

35 At the Federal Reserve Bank of Chicago's 43rd Annual Conference on Bank Structure and Competition, 17 May 2007.

36 Board of Governors of the Federal Reserve System, Joint Press Release and Text, 6 December 2006.

37 'Mark Walsh, Lehman's Unluckiest Gambler', *New York Observer*, 10 January 2008.

38 Email from William Hughes to Alex Kirk, Lehman, 27 July 2007.

39 Examiner's Report, p. 373.

40 Ibid., p. 379.

41 Ibid., p. 386.

Chapter 6: The Destruction of Value

1 *Wall Street Journal*, 29 December 2008.

2 *NOLHGA* Journal, October 2013, interview entitled, 'Everyone was Caught Off-guard'.

3 Drawn from J Hughes, 'Winding up Lehman Brothers', *Financial Times*, 7 November 2008.

4 Ibid.

5 Quoted in *The New Yorker*: 'Eight Days. The Battle to Save the American Financial System', 21 September 2009.

6 As reported in *The New York Times*, 13 December 2008.

7 H Miller, Bloomberg, 28 April 2010. It should also be noted that no exact figure for the number of outstanding derivative contracts is available. Various estimates of the number and the amounts outstanding are provided by experts, including regulators.

It is not possible to find an exact figure from any reputable source, which explains why the numbers vary throughout this chapter.

8 Financial Crisis Inquiry Commission: Examining the Causes of the Current Financial and Economic Crisis of the United States and of the Collapse of Lehman, Testimony of Harvey Miller, 1 September 2010.

9 H Miller, 'Too Big to Fail: The Role for Bankruptcy and Antitrust Law in Financial Regulation Reform', before the Subcommittee on Commercial and Administrative Law of the House of Representatives Committee on the Judiciary, 22 October 2009, p. 8.

10 Ibid., p. 9.

11 Ibid., p. 10.

12 Financial Stability Board, 'Key Attributes of Effective Resolution Regimes for Financial Institutions', 2011 and 2014; Basel Committee, 'Report and Recommendations of the Cross-Border Bank Resolution Group', 2010. For 'living wills' for large banks in the USA Title I Dodd-Frank, New insolvency regime, Title II Orderly Liquidation Authority.'

13 Bank for International Settlements, Monetary and Economic Department, 'OTC Derivatives Market Activity', May 2009, pp. 1–2.

14 BIS Quarterly Review, December 2008, p. 4.

15 A derivatives contract is an ISDA Master Agreement, supplemented with a schedule. These together set out the fundamental contractual terms of all derivatives transactions which are executed between the parties. Each individual transaction is documented with a confirmation. There may be several confirmations, corresponding to individual derivatives transactions under a single Master Agreement and Schedule. There are typically multiple trades associated with each derivative contract.

16 Kimberly Summe, 'An Examination of Lehman Brothers Derivatives Portfolio Post-Bankruptcy and whether Dodd-Frank would have made any differences', *Harvard Business Law Online*, April 2011.

17 The exact size of Lehman Brothers Special Financing Inc (LBSF)'s derivatives portfolio pre-bankruptcy has not been published, but it was estimated to be $33 trillion in notional value. When the US estate filed for bankruptcy, it reported that it was counterparty to 930,000 derivative transactions documented under 6,100 ISDA Master Agreements. A figure of 1.3 million contracts is sometimes given, and at other times a lower figure of 960,000 is given.

18 K Ayotte and D A Skeel Jr, 'Bankruptcy or Bailouts?' *Journal of Corporate Law*, March 2009, Vol. 33, no. 3, p. 494.

19 Ibid., p. 494.

20 Ibid., p. 496.

21 Kimberly Summe, *Systemic Risk in Theory and Practice* (Board of Trustees of the Leland Junior University, 2010), p. 77.

22 Michael Fleming and Asani Sarkar, 'The Failure Resolution of Lehman Brothers', *Economic Policy Review*, Federal Reserve Bank of New York.

23 US Government Accountability Office, 2013.

24 'Policy Perspectives on OTC Derivatives and Market Infrastructure', Staff Report 424, Federal Reserve Bank, March 2010, p. 11.

25 Miller, 'Too Big to Fail', p. 10.

26 Summe, *Systemic Risk in Theory and Practice*, p. 2.

27 Ibid., p. 27.

28 Ibid., p. 28.

29 The Act in question is the Commodities Futures Modernization Act, signed into law by President Clinton in December 2000. The Act excluded a wide range of derivatives from the Commodities Exchange Act 1974.

30 Alan Greenspan before the Committee on Agriculture, Nutrition and Forestry and the Committee on Banking, Housing and Urban Affairs, US Senate, 21 June 2000.

31 Remarks by the Deputy Comptroller for Capital and Regulatory Policy, Charles Taylor, OCC, 3 March 2014, Institute of International Bankers, Washington DC.

32 Ibid., p. 6.

33 L Laeven, Lev Ratnovski and Hui Tong, 'Bank Size and Systemic Risk', May 2014, IMF.

34 Ibid., p. 18.

35 Taylor, OCC, p. 7.

Chapter 7: Lehman's Valuation of Its Assets

1 Conference call, 16 June 2008, p. 9.

2 Lehman Brothers-Quantitative Risk Management, p. 4. Internal document included in the Examiner's Report, it can be found as LBEX-DOCID 384020.

3 Examiner's Report, p. 288.

4 Ibid.

5 My emphasis.

6 Ibid., pp. 288–90.

7 Ibid., pp. 306 and 312.

8 The four agencies are: the Office of the Comptroller of the Currency (OCC), the Board of Governors of the Federal Reserve System (FRB), the Federal Deposit Insurance Corporation (FDIC) and the Office of Thrift Supervision (OTS).

9 Interagency Appraisal and Evaluation Guidelines, 27 October 1994, p. 2.

10 Concentrations in Commercial Real Estate Lending, Sound Risk Management Practices, 12 December 2006, Office of the Comptroller of the Currency, Board of Governors of the Federal Reserve System and Federal Deposit Insurance Corporation.

11 Ibid., p. 1.

12 K Friend, H Glenos and J Nichols, 'An Analysis of the Impact of Commercial Real Estate Concentration Guidance', April 2013.

13 Cap*105 calculated the current capitalization of the underlying property (i.e. the outstanding debt plus equity invested to date) and then multiplied this number by 105 per cent to estimate the value of the collateral as of a specific valuation date. The additional 5 per cent represented the presumed appreciation of the collateral. It was designed to limit valuations in the midst of rising real estate prices in order to keep the presumed appreciation of the property within limits. Its use was obvious if real estate prices were rising rapidly. The method did not seem to make use of inputs from the market. But as prices began to fall, the method led to an over-valuation of the property used as collateral.

14 However, the internal rate of return method (IRR) was supposed to be based on at least some inputs from the market. Under the discounted cash flow method, an IRR model assessed the value of the collateral by calculating the net present value (NPV) of all monthly discounted net cash flows (NCF). This was done by calculating the NCF produced by the asset by taking the monthly expected revenue and subtracting the monthly expected expenses. Then the IRR model applied a discount rate in order to reach the NPV of the NCF. To arrive at the fair value, the discount rate should reflect the yield an investor would require to purchase the property. But Lehman applied a discount rate based on their expected rate of return or an interest rate associated with the underlying loans at origination, not the yield the investor would want to buy the property.

15 Examiner's Report, Section IIIA(i), Lehman's issues with TriMont's Data, pp. 312 and 332.

16 Examiner's Report, Lehman's Syndication Efforts, p. 317.

17 SEC press release, 5 October 2007.

18 Examiner's Report, Examiner's Findings and Conclusions as to the Reasonableness of Lehman's Valuation of the PTG portfolio, Section 5 (i), p. 373.

19 FASB, Summary of Statement No. 157.

20 Christopher Cox, Chairman of the US Securities and Exchange Commission, Keynote Address to Investment Company Institute 4th Annual Mutual Leadership Dinner, 30 April 2008.

21 Report and Recommendations Pursuant to Section 133 of the Emergency Economic Stabilization Act of 2008: Study on Mark-to-Market Accounting, December 2008.

22 At an SEC panel on mark-to-market accounting, 'Fair Value Caused the Crisis', CFO. com. See also William M Isaac, *Senseless Panic: How Washington Failed America* (John Wiley & Sons, 2012).

23 Report and Recommendations Pursuant to Sec 133 of the Emergency Economic Stabilization Act 2008: Study on Mark-to-Market Accounting, Dec 2008, pp. 94–5.

24 Christian Laux and Christian Leuz, 'Did Fair-Value Accounting Contribute to the Financial Crisis?', *Journal of Economic Perspectives*, Vol. 24, Winter 2010, pp. 93–118.

25 FASB, 'Final Staff Positions to Improve Guidance and Disclosures on Fair Value Measurements and Impairments', News Release, 4 September 2009.

26 Examiner's Report, Vol. I, Section III, Examiner's Conclusions, Business and Risk Management, (a) Executive Summary, pp. 48–9.

27 She is now Treasurer and Vice President of the World Bank.

28 17 August 2007.

29 SEC Division of Market Regulation, Lehman Brothers, Consolidated Supervised Entity Market and Credit Risk Review (2005). Quoted in Examiner's Bankruptcy Report, Appendix 8, p. 7.

30 SEC's Division of Market Regulation: Consolidated Supervised Entities Market and Credit Risk Review (2005) quoted in the Examiner's Report, Appendix 8, p. 7.

31 Examiner's Report, Vol I, Examiner's Conclusions, Executive Summary, Business and Risk Management, p. 72.

32 Ibid., p. 77.

33 Basel Committee on Banking Supervision, Consultative Document: 'Fundamental Review of the Trading Book: A Revised Market Risk Framework', October 2013, p. 4. As part of its rapid response to the financial crisis, Basel initiated a requirement to hold capital against credit risk, which had not been considered previously. The VaR model is also likely to be abandoned in favour of 'expected shortfall'.

34 Office of Thrift Supervision, Report of Examination of Lehman Brothers Holdings Inc., New York, NY, Docket S2511, pp. 1–2. Examination Start Date, 8 July 2008. No completion date is given. The Report itself was probably designed to prove that OTS had taken appropriate action in relation to Lehman and the emerging problems in the markets.

35 Examiner's Report, Examiner's Conclusions, Business and Risk Management, Executive Summary, p. 50.

36 Examiner's Report, Section III, A. 1, Risk Section, (d) Lehman Increases Risk Appetite to Accommodate Additional Risk Attributable to Archstone Transaction, pp. 133, 141 and 153.

37 Ibid., Section III, A. 1, 52.

38 Ibid., pp. 55–6.

Chapter 8: Measuring Value

1 Press Release: 'International Valuation Standards Council and The Appraisal Foundation Agree to Bring Greater Consistency to Appraisal Standards', 24 October 2014. The Appraisal Foundation is authorized by Congress to set out appraisal

standards and qualifications, applying USPAP. The Appraisal Standards Board sets the rules for developing an appraisal and reporting the results. It provides the recognized standards for real estate, personal property and business appraisal. Since 1992, the Office of Management and Budget has required federal land acquisition and direct lending agencies to conform to USPAP.

2   The sources used to inform the brief descriptions of the methodology for commercial real estate properties and development land include the following: RICS Guidance Note, Discounted Cash Flow for Commercial Property Investment; RICS Valuation Information Paper, Valuation of Development Land no. 12; RICS Commercial Property Valuation Methods 1997; and RICS Valuation Professional Standards 2014. The methodologies used in the USA between 2005 and 2008 were similar. The Interagency FAQs on Residential Tract Development Lending in 2005 is the main source of guidance for valuation. In both countries, the methodology used and the standards set have been subject both to criticism and revision.

3   These sources are given in B J Curry, 'The Trouble with Rates in the Subdivision Development Method to Land Valuation', *The Appraisal Journal*, Spring 2013. The first is a resource for gross margins, net profit, financial ratios and profit margins. The second two are sources for residential development property yield rates.

4   Examiner's Report, p. 288.

5   Examiner's Report, Section III, A.2, Valuation, pp. 293–4.

6   Brian Curry, 'The Trouble with Rates in the Subdivision Development Method to Land Valuation', *The Appraisal Journal*, Spring 2013, p. 151.

7   Examiner's Report, p. 342.

8   Examiner's Report, p. 236.

9   Available at LBEX-WGM 000574-95.

10 See Chapter 7.

11 Examiner's Report, Vol. 2, p. 543.

12 Ibid., p. 550.

13 Ibid., p. 548.

14 The model was developed by David X Li in two papers: 'The Valuation of Basket Credit Derivatives', *CreditMetrics Monitor*, April 1999, pp. 34–50, and 'On Default Correlation: A Copula Function Approach', *Journal of Fixed Income*, 2000, 9/4 pp. 43–54.

15 Jon Gregory, 'Quant Congress: Gaussian Copula "Failing Dramatically" in Pricing CDOs', *Risk Magazine,* 8 July 2008.

16 D MacKenzie and Taylor Spears, 'The Formula that Killed Wall Street? The Gaussian Copula and the Material Cultures of Modelling', School of Social Science and Politics, University of Edinburgh, June 2012.

17 D Beltram, L Cordell and C Thomas, 'Asymmetric Information and the Death of ABS CDOs', Federal Reserve, International Finance Discussion Papers, March 2013, p. 5.

18 S Bergman, 'CDO Evaluator applies Correlation and Monte Carlo Simulation to the Art of Determining Portfolio Quality', Standard & Poor, Structured Finance, 12 November 2001. Full details of the model S&P used for CDOs composed of mortgage-backed securities are given in this article.

19 From a technical point of view, this meant that S&P added Monte Carlo statistical methodology to the Gaussian Copula.

20 'Quant Congress', *Risk Magazine*, pp. 4–5.

21 At least 44 SEC rules and forms incorporated agency ratings, as of June 2008. See JP Hunt, 'Credit Rating Agencies and the "Worldwide Credit Crisis". The Limits of Reputation, the Insufficiency of Reform and a Proposal for Improvement', *Columbia Business Law Review*, 2009, I, pp. 109–209 for a detailed review of the role of rating agencies in financial regulation in the USA.

22 Quoted in Beltram, Cordell and Thomas, 'Asymmetric Information and the Death of ABS CDOs', pp. 6–7.

23 Quoted by Cordell, Huang and Williams, Working Paper No 11, May 2012, Working Papers Research Department, Federal Reserve Bank of Philadelphia.

24 N Vause, 'Counterparty Risk and Contract Volumes in the Credit Default Swap Market', *BIS Quarterly Review*, December 2010.

25 Otis Casey, 'The CDS Big Bang', *Markit Magazine*, Spring 2009.

26 Ingo Fender and Martin Schneider, 'The ABX: How do the Markets Price Subprime Mortgage Risk', *BIS Quarterly Review*, September 2008.

27 Ibid., p. 80.

28 Richard Stanton and Nancy Wallace, 'The Bear's Lair: Index Credit Default Swaps and the Subprime Mortgage Crisis', University of California, Berkeley, Stanton Papers, 2011, pp. 3275–6.

29 Ibid., p. 3276.

30 Testimony before the Financial Inquiry Commission, 30 June 2010.

31 ISDA, 'The AIG and Credit Default Swaps', November 2009.

32 Quoted in 'On How AIG Got Deeply Involved with Credit Derivatives', *Washington Post*, 31 December 2008.

Chapter 9: Monitoring Value

1 A Emmerich, W Savitt, S Niles and S Ongun, *The Corporate Governance Review*, 3rd edn (ed W J L Calkoen) (Law Business Research Ltd, 2013), p. 401.

2 At the time of the collapse there were four federal banking regulatory authorities: the Federal Reserve Bank, the Office of the Comptroller of the Currency, the Federal Deposit Insurance Corporation and the Office of Thrift Supervision. The Dodd-Frank Act abolished the Office of Thrift Supervision and its role was transferred to

the Office of the Comptroller of the Currency. The Act also established the
Consumer Finance Protection Bureau.

3 NYSE CG Rules 303A.06-07 (2004).

4 NYSE CG Rules 303A.07(a) and 303A.03.

5 NYSE CG Rules 303A.04–07.

6 The full story may be found in her testimony to the Oversight and Investigations
Sub-committee of the House Energy and Commerce Committee on the Financial
Collapse of the Enron Corporation, 14 February 2002.

7 Testimony Concerning the Impact of the Sarbanes-Oxley Act, 21 April 2005, W.H.
Donaldson before the House Committee on Financial Services.

8 Ibid., p. 1.

9 Delaware General Corporation Law, section 141(a).

10 *Caremark International* A 2nd 959 (Del. Ch. 1996).

11 See R Strahota, 'The Effects of the Sarbanes-Oxley Act on Directors' Responsibilities
and Liabilities', 21–22 November 2002, slides 18 and 19.

12 A Valukas, Appendix 1, p. 22 (*Unocal Corp. v Mesa Petroleum Co.*, 493 A 2d 946, 954,
quoting *Aronson v Lewis* 473 A 2d 805, 812, Del. 1984).

13 Ibid., p. 23.

14 Ibid., p. 24.

15 Ibid., p. 26.

16 He depends on the Delaware Supreme Court's judgement concerning *Gantler* 965 A
2nd at 708–09.

17 A Valukas, Appendix 1, p. 30.

18 A Valukas, responding to questions after his testimony before the House Committee
on Financial Services, 10 April 2010.

19 Statement by Anton Valukas before the Senate Committee on Banking, Housing and
Urban Affairs, Sub-committee on Securities, Insurance and Investment, on The Role
of the Accounting Profession in Preventing Another Financial Crisis, 6 April 2011,
p. 3.

20 Ibid., pp. 30–1.

21 Quoted by Valukas, ibid., p. 32. Interestingly enough this was attached to Lehman's
Quarterly Report, 10-Q filed 10 October 2006, which is when Fuld decided to
move into the commercial and residential real estate market in a more aggressive
fashion.

22 Ibid., p. 33.

23 Ibid., p. 38.

24 Ibid., p. 40.

25 A Valukas, Appendix 1, p. 22 (*Unocal Corp v Mesa Petroleum Co* 493 A 2d, 946, 954,
quoting *Aronson v Lewis* A 2D 805, 812, Del 1984).

26 Here Cruikshank refers to F Balotti and A Finkelstein, *Delaware Law and Corporations and Business Organisation* (2009), a textbook on Delaware's General Corporation Law.

27 'Cinderalla Moment: Risk Management to the Fore', *The Economist*, 11 February 2010.

28 A Valukas, Appendix 1, p. 49.

29 Ibid., p. 50.

30 Ibid., p. 54.

31 Ibid., p. 77.

32 Ibid., pp. 55–6.

33 The Examiner's Report gives access to the minutes of some board meetings and the presentations made to the board. The minutes typically cover reports from the various sub-committees, which do not contain the views of the sub-committee, nor do they record any issues the board may have raised in response to those reports or to the management presentations. There were private sessions from which the CEO was excluded, but the minutes do not give any indication at all of the contents of those discussions.

34 NYSE Listed Company Manual, para. 303A(7)(c)(iii)(D) & Cmt (2010).

35 Final Report of the IIF Committee on Market Best Practices: Principles of Conduct and Best Practice Recommendations, p. 15.

36 F Guerrera and P Thai-Larsen, 'Gone by the Board? Why Bank Directors did Not Spot Credit Risks', *Financial Times*, 25 June 2008. The observation concerning the last two may not be entirely fair. It depends on the way in which they were able to reapply their skills and experience.

37 Proxy Disclosure Enhancements, SEC Release NOS 33-9089; 34-61175; IC-29092; File No S7-13-09.

38 Ibid., p. 43.

39 Ibid., p. 44.

40 Ira Millstein, 'The Great Divide, Board Leadership', *Directors and Boards* First Quarter, 2010, p. 21.

41 Remarks by Thomas Curry before the ABA Risk Management Forum, 10 April 2014.

42 Remarks before RMA's Conference, 8 May 2014.

43 12 CFR 225.72 2012.

44 First known as the Combined Code on Corporate Governance, it was first devised in 1992 and has been revised several times since then in the light of changing circumstances and requirements.

45 Quoted in 'King of the Subprime', *The Director*, 10 November 2010.

46 Sir David Walker, 'A Review of Corporate Governance in UK Banks and Other Financial Industry Entities – Final Recommendations', pp. 9–10.

Chapter 10: Chasing a Chimera?

1 The Financial Services Authority, 'The Turner Review: A Regulatory Response to the Global Banking Crisis', March 2009, p. 39.

2 Alan Greenspan, *The Age of Turbulence* (2007; with an epilogue, 2008), p. 465.

3 Alan Greenspan's Testimony before the House Oversight and Reform Committee, 23 Oct 2008.

4 Ibid.

5 Alan Greenspan, 'We will Never have a Perfect Model of Risk', *Financial Times*, 16 March 2008.

6 'A Conversation with Alan Greenspan', *Council on Foreign Relations*, 19 November 2002.

7 Ibid., p. 7.

8 Quoted in John Lippert's article, 'Friedman would be Roiled as Chicago Disciples Rue Repudiation', Bloomsberg, 23 December 2008.

9 George Soros, 'The Crash of 2008 and What it Means', in *The New Paradigm for Financial Markets* (Public Affairs, 2009), p. 165.

10 E Fama, 'The Behaviour of Stock Market Prices', *Journal of Business*, 38 (1965a) and E Fama, *Financial Analysts Journal*, 21 (1965b); E Fama, 'Efficient Capital Markets II', *Journal of Finance*, Vol. 46, Issue 5, December 1991 (a defence against a vast array of criticisms).

11 E Fama, 'Efficient Capital Markets: A Review of Theory and Empirical Work', *Journal of Finance*, Vol. 25, Issue 2, May 1970.

12 John H Cochrane, 'Eugene F. Fama, Efficient Markets and the Nobel Prize', *Magazine*, 25 November 2013. Not only is Professor Cochrane a long-standing colleague of Fama's, but also his son-in-law.

13 'Eugene Fama, King of Predictable Markets', Interview with Jeff Sommer, *New York Times*, 23 October 2013.

14 M Sewell, 'The Efficient Market Hypothesis: Empirical Evidence', *International Journal of Statistics and Probability*, Vol. 1, No. 2, 2012, p. 165.

15 A Lo and C MacKinlay, *A Non-Random Walk Down Wall Street* (Princeton University Press, 1999), pp. 6–7.

16 A Lo, *The New Palgrave: A Dictionary of Economics*, 2nd edn (New York, Palgrave Macmillan, 2008): 'Efficient Market Hypothesis'.

17 R Posner, 'A Failure of Capitalism', January 2010, cited by J Cassidy in 'After the Blowup', *New Yorker*, 11 January 2010.

18 Quoted in the *Wall Street Journal and Markets*, 28 April 2009.

19 Posner, quoted in the *New Yorker*, 11 January 2010.

20 *Fortune*, 3 April 1995.

21 Quoted in *The New York Times*, 26 October 2013: EF Fama and KR French, 'Dividend Yields and Expected Stock Returns', *Journal of Financial Economics*, Vol. 22, 1988.

22 Ibid.

23 R Shiller, 'Do Stock Prices Move too Much to be Justified by Subsequent Changes to Dividends?', *American Economic Review*, June 1981, p. 424.

24 R Shiller, 'From Efficient Markets to Behavioural Finance', *Journal of Economic Perspectives*, Vol. 17, 1, Winter 2003, p. 89.

25 This 'dictum' is from a private letter from Paul Samuelson to John Campbell and Robert Shiller and is quoted with approval by Shiller both in articles and in his book, *Irrational Exuberance*. The letter no doubt followed from Professor Samuelson's Opening Address to the Federal Reserve Bank of Boston's conference on 'Summing Up on Business Cycles', in which he stated that, 'We have come a long way, by moving, in two hundred years towards the *micro* efficiency of markets: Black-Scholes option pricing, indexing of portfolio diversification, and so forth ... But there is no persuasive evidence ... that macro-market inefficiency is trending towards extinction.'

26 Ibid., p. 90.

27 Authors JY Campbell, A Lo and A MacAuley, *The Econometrics of Financial Markets* (Princeton University Press, 1997).

28 Shiller, *Irrational Exuberance*, 2nd edn, p. 81.

29 'Speculative Asset Prices', Prize Lecture, 8 December 2013, p. 461.

30 The first is Bayes' Law, developed by the Reverend Thomas Bayes, published posthumously in 1763. It was the first expression of 'inverse possibility', or 'conditional probability' whose value depends on the value of another probability. These also come into play when we wish to decide how much confidence we wish to assign to a given belief. Like most of the early probability theories, Bayes' Law is derived from gambling, and the Reverend Bayes was a gambler. It is not known whether or not he was successful. The theory was rejected until it was used by Alan Turing in decoding the Nazi Enigma machine. Later, the development of the Markov chain Monte Carlo algorithm was crucial in the revival of the Bayesian inference. The second refers to the Subjective Expected Utility model (SEU) developed by L.T. Savage's Foundations of Statistics. This described the way in which people should decide, not the way in which they actually make decisions: to maximize their 'selective expected utility' – a subjective judgement of probability and value. A person has well-defined preferences and will select the option that is likely to provide the maximum satisfaction. The subjectivity lies in the estimation of the probability of the anticipated events or conditions. It has since been argued extensively that the empirical evidence contradicts his theory.

31 N Barberis and R Thaler, 'A Survey of Behavioural Finance', *Social Science Research Network*, September 2002, ch. 18, p. 1053.

32 A Kumar and CM Lee, 'Retail Investor Sentiment and Return Comovements', *Journal of Finance*, Vol. 61, Issue 5, October 2006, p. 2485.

33 Brad B Barber and Terrance Odean, 'All That Glitters: The Effect of Attention and News of the Buying Behaviour of Individual and Institutional Investors', *The Review of Financial Studies*, Vol. 211, No. 2, 2008, pp. 812–14.

34 Kumar and Lee, p. 4.

35 D Vayanos and Paul Woolley, 'Capital Theory after the Efficient Market Hypothesis', 5 October 2009, Vox EPR's Policy Portal.

36 Ibid., p. 2.

37 P Woolley and Dimitri Vayanos, 'Taming the Finance Monster', *Central Banking Journal*, December 2012. (My emphasis.)

38 Remarks by Secretary Henry Paulson Jr at the Ronald Reagan Presidential Library, HP-1285 Press Room of the US Department of the Treasury.

39 E Thomas and M Hirsh, 'Paulson's Complaint', *Newsweek*, 25 May 2008.

40 W Bagehot, *Lombard Street: A Description of the Money Markets* (Reprint Project Gutenberg), p. 104.

41 R Swedberg, 'The Structure of Confidence and the Collapse of Lehman Brothers', *Markets on Trial: The Economic Sociology of the U.S. Financial Crisis, Research into the Sociology of Organizations*, 2010, Vol. 30 A, pp. 76–7.

42 Ibid., pp. 71–114.

43 Gary Gorton, *The Panic of 2007*, Prepared for the Federal Reserve Bank of Kansas City, Jackson Hole Conference, August 2008, Abstract.

44 The ABX.HE indices were based on credit default swaps, tracking the price of credit default insurance on a basket of such deals. The Index referenced 20 subprime mortgage MBSs. Doubts have been raised about the validity of currently available models for the pricing of credit risk, especially for portfolio instruments, such as MBSs.

45 Gorton, *The Panic of 2007*, pp. 3, 11. In addition, Gorton points out the reasons for believing that house prices will always go up. The USA had not experienced a large, nationwide decline in house prices since the Great Depression. Between 2001 and 2005, homeowners experienced an increase of 54.4 per cent in the value of their homes. The S&P/Shiller quarterly home price index declined by 4.5 per cent in Q3 2007 versus Q3 2006, the largest drop since the index started recording data in 1988.

46 D Einhorn, 'Private Pofits and Socialised Risks', Grant's Spring Investment Conference, 8 April 2008.

47 Ibid., p. 91.

Bibliography

Adams, Stephen D., 'Derivative Safe Harbours in Bankruptcy and Dodd-Frank: A Structural Analysis', DASH Home, *Harvard Law Review*, 2013.

Adrian, Tobias and Shin, Hyun Sang, 'Liquidity and Leverage', Federal Reserve Bank of New York, *Staff Reports*, No. 328, May 2008.

Adrian, T., Burke, C.R. and McAndrews, J.J., 'The Federal Reserve's Primary Dealer Credit Facility', Federal Reserve Bank of New York, *Current Issues in Economics and Finance*, Vol. 15, No. 4, August 2009.

Adrian, T., Begalle, B., Copeland, A. and Martin, A., 'Repo and Securities Lending', Federal Reserve Bank of New York, *Staff Reports*, No. 529, February 2013.

Anderson, R. and Gascon, C., 'The Commercial Paper Market, the Fed and the 2007–2009 Financial Crisis', *Federal Reserve Bank of St Louis Review*, Nov./Dec. 2009.

Antoncic, M., Lehman Brothers Risk Management, 'Where Vision Gets Built', 17 August 2007.

Appraisal Standards Board, 'Uniform Standards of Professional Appraisal Practice', 2008–2009 Editions.

Avraham, D., Selvaggi, P. and Vickery, J., 'A Structural View of Bank Holding Companies', *FRBNY Economic Policy Review*, July 2012.

Ayotte, K. and Skeel, D., 'Bankruptcy or Bailouts', *Journal of Corporation Law*, Vol. 35.3, 2010.

Bagehot, W., *Lombard Street, A Description of the Money Markets*, Reprint Project Gutenberg.

Ball, Ray, 'The Global Financial Crisis and the Efficient Market Hypothesis: What have We Learned?' *Journal of Applied Corporate Finance*, Vol. 21, 4, Fall 2009.

Balla, E., Carpenter, R.E. and Robinson, B., 'Assessing the Effectiveness of the Paulson "Teaser Freezer" Plan: Evidence from the ABX Index'. Federal Reserve Bank of Richmond, April 2010, Working Paper, 10–06.

Bank for International Settlements, 'OTC Derivatives Market Activity in the Second Half of 2008', May 2009.

Barr, M., 'The Financial Crisis and the Path of Reform', *Yale Journal of Regulation*, Vol. 29, No. 1, 2012.

Bary, Andrew, 'Apartment House Blues', January 2008, LBEX-UBS 00886713.

Basel II, 'International Convergence of Capital Measurement and Capital Standards', June 2004.

Basel II, 'The Second Pillar-Supervisory Review Process', 2004.

Basel Committee, 'Report and Recommendations of the Cross Border Bank Resolution Group', 2010.

Basel Committee on Banking Supervision, Consultative Document. 'A Fundamental Review of the Trading Book: A Revised Market Risk Framework', October 2013.

Basel Committee on Banking Supervision, Consultative Document, 'Guidelines, Corporate Governance Principles for Banks', October 2014.

Basset, W. and Marsh, B., 'Assessing Targeted Macroprudential Financial Regulation: The Case of the 2006 Commercial Real Estate Guidance for Banks', 12 June 2014, Federal Reserve Board, Finance and Economics Discussion Series.

Baxter, Thomas, 'Testimony before the Financial Crisis Inquiry Commission. Too Big to Fail. Expectations and Impact of Extraordinary Government Intervention and the Role of Systemic Risk in the Financial Crisis', 1 September 2010.

Baxter, Thomas, 'Letter to the Financial Crisis Inquiry Commission', 15 October 2010.

Benmelech, E. and Dlugosz, J., 'The Alchemy of CDO Credit Ratings', *Journal of Monetary Economics*, 56 (2009), pp. 617–34.

Bernanke, Ben, 'The Recent Financial Turmoil and Its Economic and Policy Consequences', At the Economic Club of New York, 15 October 2007.

Bernanke, Ben, 'Developments in Financial Markets', Before the Senate Committee on Banking, Housing and Urban Affairs, 3 April 2008.

Bernanke, Ben, Before the Senate Committee on Banking, Housing and Urban Affairs, Turmoil in the U.S. Credit Markets, 'Recent Actions regarding the Government Sponsored Entities, Investment Banks and other Credit Institutions', 15 July and 23 September 2008.

Bernanke, Ben, Before the House Committee on Financial Services, 'Systemic Risks and the Financial Markets', 16 July 2008.

Bernanke, Ben, Before the Senate Committee on Banking, Housing and Urban Affairs, 'U.S. Financial Markets', 23 September 2008.

Bernanke, Ben, Before the House Committee on Financial Services, 'The Future of Financial Services: Exploring Solutions for the Market Crisis', 24 September 2008.

Bernanke, Ben, Chairman of the Federal Reserve, Before the House Committee on Financial Services, 'Regulating Reform', 1 October 2009.

Bernanke, Ben, Before the House Committee on Financial Services, 'The Federal Reserve's Role in Banking Supervision', 17 March 2010.

Bernanke, Ben, Before the House Committee on Financial Services, 'Lessons from the Failure of Lehman Brothers', 20 April 2010.

Bernanke, Ben, Testimony before the FCIC, Hearing on 'Too Big to Fail: Expectations and Impact of Extraordinary Government Intervention and the Role of Systemic Risk in the Financial Crisis', 1–2 September 2010.

Bernanke, Ben, Chairman of the Federal Reserve, 'Causes of the Recent Financial and Economic Crisis', 2 September 2010.

Bhatia, A., 'Consolidated Regulation and Supervision in the United States', IMF Working Paper, January 2011.

Blumen, Robert, 'Are Bubbles Efficient?', *Mises Daily*, 3 February 2004.

Board of Governors of the Federal Reserve System, 'Report to the Congress on Financial Holding Companies under the Gramm-Leach-Bliley Act', November 2003.

Board of Governors of the Federal Reserve System, 'Frequently Asked Questions on Residential Tract Development Lending', 8 September 2005.

Board of Governors of the Federal Reserve System. 'Consolidated Supervision Framework for Large Financial Institutions', 17 December 2012.

Brunnermeirer, M. 'Deciphering the Liquidity and Credit Crunch, 2007–2008', *Journal of Economic Perspectives*, Vol. 23, No. 1, Winter 2009.

Buccino, Gerald and Shannon, John, 'The Changing Role of the Board of Directors. Sarbanes-Oxley Reflects Demand for Increased Scrutiny', 1 December 2003, Turnaround Management Association.

Buiter, W., 'Three Hits and Three Misses for the Fed', *Financial Times*, 17 March 2008.

Business Week, 'Lehman's New Street Starts', 18 July 2004.

Casey Research, 'Nobel Prize Winner, "Bubbles Don't Exist"', 28 October 2013 from an interview with Eugene Fama, in *The New Yorker*, 13 June 2010.

Cassidy, John, 'After the Blowup', *New Yorker*, 10 January 2010.

Cecchetti, Stephen, 'Crisis and Responses: The Federal Reserve in the Early Stages of the Financial Crisis', *Journal of Economic Perspectives*, Vol. 23, Winter 2009.

Clarke, Robert C., 'Corporate Governance Changes in the Wake of the Sarbanes-Oxley Act: A Morality Tale for Policymakers Too', Discussion Paper No. 525, September 2005, Harvard Law School.

CNN Money, 'Lehman Weathers the Storm', 8 March 2008.

Cochrane, J., Introduction for Gene Fama, at Fama's lecture on 'The History of the Theory and Evidence on the Efficient Markets Hypothesis' and the University of Chicago, 10 October 2008.

Cochrane, J., 'Eugene F. Fama, Efficient Markets, and the Nobel Prize', *Magazine*, 25 November 2013.

Colby, Robert, Before the House Committee on Financial Services, 'Testimony concerning the Consolidated Supervision of U.S. Securities Firms and Affiliated Industrial Loan Corporations', 25 April 2007.

Combined Code of Corporate Governance, UK Financial Reporting Council, 2003.

Cordell, L., Huang. Y. and Williams, M., 'Collateral Damage, Sizing and Assessing the Subprime CDO Crisis', Federal Reserve Bank of Philadelphia, Working paper, 11–30, 2012.

Cornett, M., McNutt, J.J. and Tehranian, H., 'The Financial Crisis: Did Corporate Governance Affect the Performance of Publicly-Traded-US Bank Holding Companies?' September 2009.

Council of Foreign Relations, 'A Conversation with Alan Greenspan', 19 November 2002.

Covitz, D., Liang, N. and Suarez, G.A., Finance and Economics Discussion Series, Federal Reserve Board, 2009–36.

Cox, Christopher, 'Sound Practices for Managing Liquidity in Banking Organisations', Letter to Dr N. Wellick, 20 March 2008.

Cox, Christopher, U.S. Securities and Exchange Commission, Testimony before the U.S. Senate Committee on Banking, Housing and Urban Affairs, 'Turmoil in the U.S. Credit Markets: Examining the Recent Actions of the Federal Financial Regulators', 3 April 2008.

Cox, Christopher, Testimony before the Senate Banking, Housing and Urban Affairs Committee, 'Turmoil in the U.S Credit Markets: The Role of the Credit Rating Agencies', 22 April 2008.

Cox, Christopher, Testimony before the Senate Banking, Housing and Urban Affairs Committee, 'Turmoil in the U.S. Credit Markets, Recent Actions Regarding the Government Sponsored Entities, Investment Banks and other Credit Institutions', 15 July and 23 September 2008.

Cox, Christopher, Testimony on 'Market Regulatory Restructuring', before the House Committee on Financial Services, 24 July 2008.

Cox, Christopher, Securities and Exchange Commission, 'Chairman Cox Announces End of Consolidated Supervised Entities Programme', 26 September 2008.

Cox, Christopher, Statement of Christopher Cox, Former Chairman, SEC before the House Committee on Financial Services, 20 April 2010.

Cruikshank, Thomas, Statement to the House Committee on Financial Services, 20 April 2010.

Darling, Alistair, *Back from the Brink*, Atlantic Books, 2012.

Deloitte, Banking and Securities Issue Briefing, 'The SEC's Consolidated Supervision Program and Bank-owned Securities Firms', December 2007.

Denbeaux, M., Dabek, E., Gregorek, J., Kennedy, S.A. and Miller, E., 'Lehman Brothers: A License to Fail with Other People's Money', Seton Hall University School of Law, Research paper, 8 December 2011, No. 2003618.

Director, The, 'The King of the Subprime', Excerpts from J. Oliver, *How they Blew It*, Kogan Page, 2010.

Donaldson, W., 'Testimony Concerning the Impact of the Sarbanes-Oxley Act', 21 April 2005, Before the House Committee on Financial Services.

Duwel, C., 'Repo Funding and Internal Capital Markets in the Financial Crisis', Deutsche Bundesbank, No. 16/2013.

The Economist, 'Fuld of Experience', 24 April 2008.

The Economist, 'Efficiency and Beyond', 10 March 2009.

Einhorn, D., Greenlight Capital, 'Accounting Ingenuity', 21 May 2008.

Einhorn, D., 'Private Profits and Socialised Risks', 2008.

Elson, Charles, 'Director Term Limits Come Up for Review', *Directors and Boards*, Board Practices, 22 March 2008.

Elson, Charles, 'The Great Divide, Board Leadership', First Quarter, 2010.

England, Robert Stowe, 'Black Box Casino: How Wall Street's Risky Shadow Banking Crashed Global Finance', Praeger, 2011.

Euromoney, 'Richard Fuld Interview: Can Lehman Grow and Still Succeed?', July 2005.

Fama, E., 'Efficient Capital Markets, A Review of Theory and Empirical Work', *The Journal of Finance*, Vol. 25, No. 2. Papers and Proceedings of the 25th Annual Meeting of the American Finance Association, 1970.

Fama, E., 'My Life in Finance', *Annual Review of Financial Economics*, 2010, Feb. Vol. 15, No. 3, pp. 1–15.

Fama, E. and French, K., 'The Capital Asset Pricing Model: Theory and Evidence', *Journal of Economic Perspectives*, 2004, Vol. 18, No. 3.

Fama, E. and French K., 'Dissecting Anomalies', *The Journal of Finance*, 63, 4, 2008.

Federal Open Market Committee Meetings, Transcripts of 2007 (released in June 2013 and for 2008), released in March 2014.

Federal Register, 'Interagency Appraisal and Evaluation Guidelines', Vol. 75, No. 237, 10 December 2010.

Federal Register, 'Heightened Standards for Certain Large Insured National Banks, Insured Federal Savings Associations and Insured Federal Banks, Regarding Safety and Soundness Standards and Risk Governance', Vol. 79, No. 176, 11 September 2014.

Federal Reserve Bank, 'Interagency Appraisal and Evaluation Guidelines', Supervisory and Regulatory Letter, SR 10–16, 27 October 1994.

Federal Reserve Bank, 'Supervisory Letter SR 00-13, Framework for Financial Holding Companies Supervision', August 2000.

Federal Reserve Bank, 'Report to Congress on Financial Holding Companies under the Gramm-Leach-Bliley Act', November 2003.

Federal Reserve Bank, 'Interagency Guidance; Concentrations in Commercial Real Estate Lending. Sound Risk Management Practices', FR 74580, 12 December 2006.

Federal Reserve Bank of New York, 'Primary Dealer Monitoring: Liquidity Stress Test Analysis', 25 June 2008.

Federal Reserve Bank of New York, 'Primary Dealer Credit Facility: Frequently Asked Questions', 25 June 2009.

Fender, I. and Gyntelberg, J., 'Three Market Implications of the Lehman Bankruptcy', 8 December 2008, Bank for International Settlements.

Fender, I. and Scheicher, M., 'The Pricing of Subprime Mortgage Risk in Good Times and Bad', Evidence from the ABX Indices, ECB Working Paper, No. 1056, May 2009.

Fernando, C., May, A.D. and Megginsm, W., 'The Value of Investment Banking Relationships: Evidence from the Collapse of Lehman Brothers', *Journal of Finance*, Vol. 67, 2012.

Financial Accounting Standards No. 157, September 2006, Financial Accounting Standards Board.

Financial Accounting Standards Board, Summary of Statement, No. 157, September 2006.

Financial Accounting Standards Board, 'Final Staff Position to Improve Guidance and Disclosures on Fair Value Measurement and Impairments', 4 September 2009.

Financial Crisis Inquiry Commission Report, Ch. 8, 'The CDO Machine'.

Financial Services Authority, 'Statement regarding Lehman Brothers and Barclays'.

Financial Stability Board, 'Key Attributes of Effective Resolution Regimes for Financial Institutions', 2014.

Financial Times, 'Lehman to sell Archstone for $6.5bn', 26 November 2012.

Fitzpatrick, G., 'The Corporate Governance Lessons from the Financial Crisis', *Financial Market Trends*, OECD, 2009.

Fitzpatrick, T. and Thompson, J., 'How well does Bankruptcy Work when Large Financial Firms Fail, Some lessons from Lehman Brothers?' Cleveland Federal Reserve, 26 October 2011.

Fleming, Michael and Sarker, Asani, 'Large and Complex Banks, The Failure Resolution of Lehman Brothers', Federal Reserve Bank of New York, *Economic Policy Review*, March 2014.

Fleming, M., Keane, F.M. and Hrung, W.B., 'The Term Securities Lending Facility: Origin, Design and Effects', Federal Reserve Bank of New York, *Current Issues in Economics and Finance*, Vol. 15, No. 2, February 2009.

Forslund, E. and Johansson, D., 'Gaussian Copula, "What happens when models fail?"', 23 November 2012.

Friend, K., Glenos, H. and Nichols, J., 'An Analysis of the Impact of Commercial Real Estate Concentration Guidance', Federal Reserve Bank, April 2013.

Fuld, D., 'Written Statement of Richard S Fuld before the Financial Crisis Inquiry Commission', 1 September 2010.

Geithner, Timothy, Before the U.S. Senate Committee on Banking, Housing and Urban Affairs, 'Actions Taken by the New York Fed in Response to Liquidity Pressures in the Financial Markets', 3 April 2008.

Geithner, Timothy, 'Statement before the House Committee on Financial Services on Systemic Risk and the Financial Markets', 24 July 2008.

Geithner, Timothy, Before the House Committee on Financial Services, 'Testimony on Public Policy Issues Raised by the Report of the Lehman Bankruptcy Examiner', 20 April 2010.

Geithner, Timothy, *Stress Tests: Reflections on the Financial Crisis,* Crown Publishing Group, 2014.

Government Accounting Office, 'Financial Regulation: Industry Changes Prompt Need to Reconsider U.S. Regulatory Structure', GAO-05-61, 6 October 2004.

Greenspan, Alan, 'Remarks by Alan Greenspan', Before a Conference sponsored by the Office of the Comptroller of the Currency, Washington D.C., 14 October 1999.

Greenspan, Alan, Before the Senate Committee on Agriculture, Nutrition and Forestry and the Senate Committee on Banking, Housing and Urban Affairs, 'The Commodity Futures Modernisation Act of 2000', 21 June 2000.

Greenspan, Alan, 'Measuring Risk in the Twenty-First Century', Testimony before the Joint Economic Committee, Monetary Policy and the Economic Outlook, 17 April 2002.

Greenspan, A., *The Age of Turbulence*, Penguin Books, 2007.

Greenspan, A., 'We will Never have a Perfect Model of Risk', *Financial Times*, 16 March 2008.

Greenspan, A., 'The Sources of the Financial Crisis', Testimony before the House Committee of Government Oversight and Reform, 23 October 2008.

Guardian, The, 'Vincent Cable', 8 September 2010.

Guerrera, F. and Thai Larsen, P., 'Gone by the Board. Why Bank Directors did Not Spot Credit Risks?', *Financial Times*, 25 June 2008.

Harbus Online, The, 'Lehman Brothers CEO Shares his Qualities of Leadership at Distinguished Speaker Series', 16 October 2006.

Haubrich, J. and Meyer, B., 'Subprime Derivatives', Federal Reserve Bank of Cleveland, *Features*, March 2007.

Hrung, W. and Seligman, J., 'Responses to the Financial Crisis, Treasury Debt and the Impact on Short-Term Money Markets', Federal Reserve Bank of New York, *Staff Reports*, No. 481, January 2011.

Hunt, J. B., 'Credit Rating Agencies and the Worldwide Credit Crisis', *Columbia Business Law Review*, 2009, Vol. 1, No. 1, pp. 109–209.

Institute of International Finance, 'Final Report on Market Best Practices: Principles of Conduct and Best Practice Recommendations', 17 July 2008.

International Monetary Fund, 'Financial Sector Assessment Program, Consolidated Regulation and Supervision', Technical Note, July 2010.

Isaac, W., *Senseless Panic: How Washington Failed America*, J. Wiley and Sons, 2012.

Issa, Darrell, 'The SEC: Designed for Failure', Minority Staff Report for Committee on Oversight and Government Reform, May 2010.

Jung, J. and Shiller, R., 'One Simple Test of Samuelson's Dictum for the U.S. Stock Market', NBER Working Paper No. 9348.

Kotz, David H., Office of the Inspector General, 'SEC's Oversight of Bear Stearns and Related Entities: The Consolidated Supervised Entity Program', Report No. 446-A, 25 September 2008, including management responses..

Laeven, L., Ratnouski, L. and Tong, H., 'Bank Size and Systemic Risk', IMF, Staff Discussion Note, IMF, May 2014.

Larcker, D. and Tayan, B., 'Lehman Brothers: Peeking under the Façade', Stanford Graduate School of Business, 4 June 2010.

Laux, C. and Leuz, C., 'Did Fair Value Accounting Contribute to the Financial Crisis?' *Journal of Economic Perspectives*, Vol. 24, Winter 2010.

'Lehman Brothers Announces Preliminary Third Quarter Results and Strategic Restructuring', 10 September 2008, Press release.

Lehman Brothers Holdings Inc, 'Earnings Conference Call', 16 June 2008.

Levine, Ross, 'An Autopsy of the US Financial System: Accident, Suicide, or Negligent Homicide', *Journal of Financial Economic Policy*, Vol. 2, No. 3, 2010.

Li, David, 'The Valuation of Basket Credit Derivatives', *CreditMetrics Monitor*, April 1999, pp. 34–50.

Li, David, 'On Default Correlation. A Copula Function Approach', *Journal of Fixed Income*, 2000, 9, 4, pp. 43–54.

Lin, J. and Treicher, V., 'The Unexpected Global Financial Crisis: Researching its Root Cause', World Bank, Policy Research paper, January 2012.

Lo, Andrew, 'Efficient Markets Hypothesis', *The New Palgrave: A Dictionary of Economics*, Palgrave Macmillan, 2007.

Loomis, C., 'Derivatives: The risk that still won't go away', *Fortune Classic*, Reprinted, 20 May 2012.

Luzod, A. and Mann, G., 'Real Estate Lending', *The RMA Journal*, February 2006.

Mackenzie, D. and Spears, T., 'The Formula that Killed Wall Street: The Gaussian Copula and the Material Cultures of Modelling', June 2012, University of Edinburgh.

Madigan, Peter, Quant Congress: 'Gaussian Copula "Failing Dramatically" in Pricing CDOs', *Risk Magazine*, 8 June 2008.

Mann, Geoff, 'Value after Lehman', *Historical Materialism* 18, 2010.

Marsal, B., 'Everyone was Caught Off Guard', Interview with B. Marsal, *NOLHGA Journal*, October 2013.

Maux, J. and Morin, D., 'Black, White and Red All Over: Lehman Brothers' Inevitable Bankruptcy Splashed Across its Financial Statements', *International Journal of Business and Social Science*, Vol. 2, No. 20, November 2011.

Mehran, H. and Molineux, L., 'Corporate Governance of Financial Institutions', Federal Reserve Bank of New York, *Staff Reports*, 539, 2012.

Miller, Harvey, 'Too Big to Fail: The Role for Bankruptcy and Antitrust Law in Financial Regulation Reform', Before the Subcommittee on Commercial and Administrative Law of the House Committee on the Judiciary, 22 October 2009.

Miller, Harvey, Before the Financial Crisis Inquiry Commission, 'Examining the Causes of the Current Financial and Economic Crisis of the United States and the Collapse of Lehman Brothers', 1 September 2010.

Millstein, Ira, 'The Great Divide, Board Leadership' *Directors and Boards*' 1st qtr, 2010.

Mishkin, F., 'Over the Cliff: From the Subprime to the Global Financial Crisis', National Bureau of Economic Research, December 2010.

Nazareth, Annette, 'Testimony Concerning Certain Pending Proposals by the European Commission', Before the House Committee on Financial Services, 22 May 2002.

Nazareth, Annette, 'Memorandum for the Record regarding the CSE Programme', Telephone call with Annette Nazareth, 1 April 2010 (for the Financial Crisis Inquiry Commission).

New York Stock Exchange Corporate Governance Rules, paras 303A. 06–07, 2004 effective.

Office of the Comptroller of the Currency, 12 CFR Parts 30 and 170.

Office of the Comptroller of the Currency, 'Guidelines Establishing Heightened Standards for Certain Large Insured National Banks, Insured Federal Savings Associations and Insured Federal Branches'.

Office of the Comptroller of the Currency, 'Frequently Asked Questions on the Appraisal Regulations and the Interagency Statement on Independent Appraisal and Evaluation Functions', 22 March 2005.

Office of the Comptroller of the Currency, Federal Reserve Bank, Federal Deposit Insurance Corporation, 'Concentrations in Commercial Real Estate Lending, Sound Risk Management Practices', 12 December 2006.

Office of the Comptroller of the Currency, *Handbook on Leveraged Lending*, 2008.

Office of the Comptroller of the Currency, 'Commercial Real Estate Lending', August 2013.

Office of the Inspector General, 'The Federal Reserve's Section 13(3) Lending Facilities to Support Overall Market Liquidity', November 2010.

Office of Thrift Supervision, 'Report of Examination, Lehman Brothers', July 2008.

Paulson, Henry M. Jr., *On the Brink*, Business Plus, 2011.

Paulson, H., 'On the Competitiveness of the U.S. Capital Markets', Remarks at the Economic Club of New York, 20 November 2006.

Paulson, H., 'Systemic Risk and the Financial Markets', Before the House Committee on Financial Services, 10, 16 and 24 July 2008.

Paulson, H., 'Recent Developments in the Financial Markets and the Regulatory Response to Them', Before the Senate Banking, Housing and Urban Affairs Committee, 15 July 2008.

Paulson, H., 'Turmoil in the U.S. Credit Markets and Recent actions regarding the Government Sponsored Enterprises, Investment Banks and other Credit Institutions', Before the Senate Banking, Housing and Urban Affairs Committee, 23 September 2008.

Paulson, H., 'The Future of Financial Services: Exploring Solutions for the Market Crisis', House Committee on Financial Services, 24 September 2008.

Pollack, L., 'The Formula that Wall Street Never Believed in', *FT Alphaville*, 15 June 2012.

Prudential Regulatory Authority, 'Strengthening Accountability in Banking: A New Regulatory Framework for Individuals', CP/14. Consultation ends 31 October 2014.

Pyburn, Allison, 'CDO Machine? Managers, Mortgage Companies, Happy to Keep Fuel Coming', Asset Securitisation Report, ProQuest, 23 May 2005.

Reuters, 'Timeline: A Dozen Key Dates in the Demise of Bear Stearns', 17 March 2008.

Reuters, 'Lehman Emerges from 3.5 year Bankruptcy', 6 March 2011.

Rosato, J., 'Down the Road to Perdition: How the Flaws of Basel II Led to the Collapse of Bear Stearns and Lehman Brothers', *Connecticut Insurance Law Journal*, Vol. 17, No. 2, 2011.

Samuelson, Paul, 'Summing up on Business Cycles', Opening Address, June 1998.

Schapiro, Mary, 'Testimony concerning the Lehman Brothers Examiner's Report', Before the House Committee on Financial Services, 20 April 2010.

Scheicher, M., 'How has CDO Market Pricing Changed during the Turmoil?', Evidence from the CDS Index Tranches, European Central Bank, 2008.

Securities and Exchange Commission, 'Final Rule: Disclosure regarding Nominating Committee Functions and Communications between Security Holders and Boards of Directors', effective 1 January 2004.

Securities and Exchange Commission, 'Alternative Net Capital Requirements for Broker-Dealers That Are Part of the Consolidated Supervised Entities', February 2004.

Securities and Exchange Commission, 'Clarifications on Fair Value Accounting', 30 September 2008.

Securities and Exchange Commission, 'Report and Recommendations Pursuant to Section 133 of the Emergency Economic Stabilization Act of 2008: Study on Mark-to-Market Accounting'.

Securities and Exchange Commission, 'Meeting with Members of the SEC regarding the CSE programme', Memorandum for the Record, Financial Crisis Inquiry Commission, 18 March 2010.

Securities and Exchange Commission, 'Enforcement Actions Addressing Misconduct That Led To or Arose from the Financial Crisis', Key Statistics through December 2013.

Shefrin, H. and Statman, Meir, 'Behavioural Finance in the Financial Crisis: Market Efficiency, Minsky and Keynes, in Rethinking the Financial Crisis', Russell Sage Foundation, 2012.

Shiller, R., *Irrational Exuberance*, Princeton University Press, 2000.

Shiller, R., 'From Efficient Markets Theory to Behavioural Finance', *Journal of Economic Perspectives*, Vol. 17, Number 1, Winter 2003.

Shiller, R., 'Speculative Asset Prices', Prize Lecture, Yale University, 8 December 2013.

Shiller, R., 'Speculative Asset Prices', February 2014, Nobel Prize Lecture.

Siegel, J., 'Efficient Market Theory and the Crisis', *Wall Street Journal*, 27 October 2009.

Sirri, E., 'Testimony concerning the Turmoil in the Credit Markets: Examining the Regulation of Investment Banks by the SEC', Before the Subcommittee on Securities, Insurance and Investment, U.S. Senate, 7 May 2008.

Smithson, C., 'Valuing "Hard-to-Value" Assets and Liabilities: Notes on Valuing Structured Credit Products', *Journal of Applied Finance*, Issues 1 and 2, 2009.

Standard and Poor, 'Structured Finance, CDO Evaluation Applies Correlation and Monte Carlo Simulation to the Art of Determining Portfolio Quality', S. Bergman, 12 November 2001.

Stanton, R. and Wallace, N., 'The Bear's Lair: Index Credit Default Swaps and the Subprime Mortgage Crisis', February 2011, Haas School of Business, U.C. Berkeley.

Statement of Alan Schwartz, President and CEO of the Bear Stearns Companies, Inc before the U.S. Senate Banking Committee, 3 April 2008.

Strahota, Robert, 'The Effects of the Sarbanes-Oxley Act on Directors' Responsibilities and Liabilities', Prepared for the Third OECD South-Eastern Europe Corporate Governance Roundtable, 21–22 November 2002.

Stulz, R., 'Credit Default Swaps and the Credit Crisis', *Journal of Economic Perpsectives*, Vol. 24, No. 1, Winter 2010.

Summe, Kimberly Anne, 'Lessons Learned from the Bankruptcy of Lehman Brothers, Systemic Risk in Theory and Practice', Board of Trustees of Leland Stanford Junior University, 2010.

Summe, Kimberly Anne, 'An Examination of Lehman Brothers' Portfolio Post Bankruptcy and Whether Dodd-Frank Would Have Made Any Difference', Hoover Institute Working Group on Economics, Policy and the Resolution Project, 24 April 2011.

Summe, Kimberly Anne, 'Misconceptions about Lehman Brothers' Bankruptcy and the Role Derivatives Played', *Stanford Law Review*, 28 November 2011.

Swagel, Philip, 'The Financial Crisis: An Inside View', Brookings Papers on Economic Activity, Spring 2009.

Swedberg, Richard, 'The Structure of Confidence and the Collapse of Lehman Brothers', in *Markets on Trial: The Economic Sociology of the U.S. Financial Crisis. Research in the Sociology of Organisations*, Vol. 30 A, pp. 70–114.

Tarullo, D., 'Regulating Systemic Risk', Remarks before the Credit Markets Symposium, Charlotte, 31 March 2011.

Tarullo, Daniel, 'Opening Statement on the Volcker Rule', 10 December 2013.

Tarullo, D., 'Corporate Governance and Prudential Regulation', 9 June 2014, at the Association of American Law Schools.

Thornton, Daniel, 'The Federal Reserve's Response to the Financial Crisis: What it did and What it Should Have Done', Working Paper 2012-050A, Federal Reserve Bank of St Louis, October 2012.

Tuckman, Bruce, 'Systemic Risk and the Tri-Party Repo Clearing Banks', Centre for Financial Stability, February 2010.

Turner Review, The, 'A Regulatory Response to the Global Banking Crisis', Financial Services Authority, March 2009.

Turner, A. et al., 'The Future of Finance and the Theory that Underpins it', The LSE Report, The Centre for Economic Performance, July 2010.

Valukas, A., 'Statement before House Committee on Financial Services. Public Policy Issues raised by Lehman Bankruptcy Examiner's Report', 20 April 2009.

Valukas, A., 'Statement before the Senate Committee on Banking, Housing and Urban Affairs, Subcommittee on Securities, Insurance and Investment. The Role of the Accounting Profession in Preventing another Financial Crisis', 6 April 2011.

Vause, N., 'Counterparty Risk and Contract Volumes in the Credit Default Swap Market', BIS *Quarterly Review*, December 2010.

Walker, Sir David, 'A Review of Corporate Governance in UK Banks and Other Financial Industry Entities, Final Recommendations', 26 November 2009.

Woolley, Paul, 'The Future of Finance and the Theory that Underpins It', The LSE Report, The LSE Centre for Economic Performance, July 2010.

Yandle, Bruce, 'Lost Trust, The Real Cause of the Financial Meltdown', *The Independent Review*, Vol. 14, No. 3, Winter 2010.

Zaretsky, A., 'A New Universe in Banking: After Financial Modernisation', Federal Bank of St Louis, Staff paper, No. 494, April 2000.

Index

Li, Ada 124–5
Li, David X 167
LIBOR 125, 174
limited company, Lehman Brothers
    becomes 4
Lincoln Capital Fixed Income 8–9
Linklaters 93
liquidity
    in 2008 16, 19–21, 25, 41, 44, 50, 55
    and Bear Stearns 34, 36–7
    and consolidated supervision 28–9
    and the destruction of value 116
    and Lehman's risk management
        154, 190
    liquidity crisis 16, 36–7
    liquidity stress period 21, 36–7
    temporary liquidity 117
    and trust 220
'living wills' 128, 130–2
Lo, Andrew 208–9
loan losses provision 145
Lomas, Tony 114
Lombard St (Bagehot, 1873) 218
London Stock Exchange 114
Lowitt, Ian 20, 25, 89, 97–8, 100, 112
LTCM (Long Term Capital Management)
    5, 43, 62
Lubke, Theo 124–5

MacKenzie, Donald 168
Maiden Lane LLC 17, 62
market efficiency assumption 203–8
market-based yield 106, 139
markets, definition of 215–17
Markit 171
mark-to-credit 138–9
mark-to-market accounting
    and commercial real estate 26, 42
    and consolidated supervision 86
    and the efficient market hypothesis 203,
        215
    and Lehman bankruptcy 65
    and Lehman's asset valuation 97, 98, 99,
        100, 106–7, 144–9
    as valuation methodology 138–42
mark-to-yield 138–9
Marsal, Bryan 113
Master Agreements (ISMA) 120–30
Masters, Blythe 168

McCarthy, Callum 48, 49–50
McConnell, Meg 57
McDade, Bart 20, 94, 100
McGee, Hugh 'Skip' 6
Merrill Lynch
    asset valuation 146
    as bank holding company 27
    board 192
    and bridge equity 108
    and consolidated supervision 47
    credit ratings 20
    and the Gramm-Leach-Bliley Act 81–3
    and Lehman 6, 7, 9, 10, 46
    leverage ratios 38
    losses on CDOs 170–1
    and the OTC derivatives market 125
    rescue of 39, 46, 47, 65
Metavante 125
MetLife 102
Miller, Harvey 64, 115–18, 126
Min Euoo-Sung 42
money market mutual funds (MMMFs) 58
money markets 69, 72, 119
monolines 56
Monte Carlo approach 169
Moody's 6, 9, 20, 42, 55, 66, 177
moral hazard 59, 63, 64, 65, 69
Morgan Stanley
    in 2008 64
    as bank holding company 27, 120
    board 192
    and bridge equity 108
    and consolidated supervision 31
    credit ratings 20
    and Federal Reserve corporate
        governance guidance 198
    and Lehman 7
    leverage ratios 38
    and the OTC derivatives market 125
    and the PDCF 24
mortgage origination business 5, 10, 11,
    31, 33–4, 58, 105–6
mortgage-backed securities (MBS), *see
    also* subprime loans
    in 2000s 57–8, 81
    in 2008 46
    and CDOs 166
    and CDSs 173, 176
    classified as Level 2 or 3 assets 147